CRAB ANTICS

CRAB ANTICS

A Caribbean Case Study of the Conflict Between Reputation and Respectability

Peter J. Wilson

University of Otago

WAVELAND

PRESS, INC.

Prospect Heights, Illinois

For information about this book, write or call:

Waveland Press, Inc.
P.O. Box 400
Prospect Heights, Illinois 60070
(847) 634-0081

Copyright © 1973 by Peter J. Wilson
1995 reissued with changes by Waveland Press, Inc.

ISBN 0-88133-849-4

Printed in the United States of America

7   6   5   4   3   2

ALLISON

Contents

Foreword

The book you are about to read speaks very much for itself. Professor Wilson honors me by his invitation to introduce it to his readers; I shall try to be appropriately brief. *Crab Antics* grew out of its author's first anthropological field experience, on the Colombian island of Providencia, in the western Caribbean Sea. It began as an excellent doctoral dissertation, within which one may find some of the germinal ideas that led eventually to this ultimate rendering.

But *Crab Antics* is no thesis, not only because it has been happily divested of the trappings that conventionally adorn theses, but also because it has benefited from an exercise in which too few scholars indulge sufficiently: reflection. This is not an anthropological monograph in the conventional sense, so much as a test of some of the author's basic hunches about the organization of social life in Caribbean societies, with special reference to the anglophone islands. I use the colloquial term "hunch" in the hope that the author will take to it kindly. Hunches, of course, are supposed to be predictive as well as intuitive, and the author is not so much predicting here as inferring. But his inferences aim at making sense of a wide variety of data that do not seem to him otherwise to lend themselves to elegant summation.

He also calls into some question the whole direction that anthropological inquiry has traditionally taken in the Caribbean region, arguing—with reason, it seems to me—that a number of preconceptions have dominated the consciousness of its students. That Caribbean communities exhibit neither the elaborate linealities of African kinship on the one hand, nor the town meeting atmosphere of New England on the other, appears to have unmanned a whole generation of anthropologists; Professor Wilson dares to suggest that the motes have been in the eyes of the beholders. Because of the way he synthesizes his insights, and because his book implicitly or explicitly criticizes a good deal of scholarship that has preceded it, Professor Wilson can probably count on exciting a certain amount of controversy.

I suspect that such controversy will proceed on two rather different levels. There will be, first, the arguments among scholars or anthropological technicians: are the concepts convincing when put against the data from which they flow and which they are intended to explain? Are the theoretical assertions generalizable to a class of social phenomena, shedding light not only upon the original society from which the data come, but upon other societies as well? Are the ideas testable by additional operations? Second, however, there may be another level of dialogue or dispute, having to do with the character of a class or type of society (of which Providencia is one example), in terms of the basic ways in which people organize their values and act them out. On this level, the disputants may as well be playwrights and poets as anthropologists and other social scientists, for this book is a humanistic assessment of one kind of society as much as it is a scientific assessment. In order to be clear, I must say a little more about Professor Wilson's contentions and about the societies to which he expects them to apply.

The author suggests that we may look at Providencia according to two significant and opposed themes, or beliefs, or value systems, which he calls "reputation" and "respectability." Such counterposed themes inhere in the structure of Providencia society and also transcend it: that is, they express the way people are divided up in terms of their productive relations, yet they overarch the attitudes defined by such relations. Respectability, for Professor Wilson, is the summation of colonial dependence: the axis of social assortment in a world originally designed for others by the European holders of power. A stratified system of classes embraces the colonial population; they differ in their access to respectability, since its availability depends in the last instance upon their access to other kinds of validation in the class system. They may embrace its significance, live with the need of attaining it, seek it actively; but when all is said and done, it is their socioeconomic position that ultimately declares their having—or lacking—respectability.

Reputation is a response to colonial dependence and to the accompanying elusiveness of respectability. It serves, in Professor Wilson's view, as a leveling device of some kind to com-

pensate for the scarcity of respectability, and it operates in the interest of equality in systems where socioeconomic equality for
more than the very few is in fact unattainable. Not surprisingly,
then, reputation depends upon individual achievement measured
by, and against, the performance of one's peers. Because reputation is a solution to the scarcity of respectability, its realization
may sometimes involve acts which, in the view of "the respectable," are anti-social, illegal, or characteristic of those who are
poor and illiterate—that is, the acts of those who are cut off
from access to socioeconomic mobility. Thus, respectability and
reputation are counterposed and interlocked principles of social
behavior: "The principle of stratification that subsumes all others
is, I suggest, the principle of *respectability* . . . [while] the
philosophical principle by which equality is guided, which men
'have in mind,' is what I have designated *reputation.*"

The author demonstrates for us how these principles are at
once abstracted from the data on a single case, yet sufficiently
penetrating to describe other societies besides Providencia. In
essence, he argues that the parallel historical experiences of
Caribbean lands have repeatedly given rise to a social dialectic
in which all of the values and behaviors distilled into the concepts of respectability and reputation are regularly pitted against
each other. The resulting struggle takes place as between whole
groups, and in the minds of single individuals. To this bipolar
perspective, Professor Wilson adds an additional dimension:
generally speaking, women are more concerned with respectability, men with reputation. Thus men and women, he implies,
participate in somewhat different, though overlapping, value
systems, and manifest this difference in their behaviors. Moreover, in their later years, men incline more toward the principle
of respectability. Thus sex and age differences mesh with class
in determining how the contrasting principles of respectability
and reputation function. Finally, color plays a role as well, since
culturally conventionalized norms of physical appropriateness
affect everyone, whether one be young or old, rich or poor, male
or female.

To demonstrate how the basic thematic principles operate,
Professor Wilson describes for us Providencia society. This rocky
bit of land epitomizes the tangled historical web of Antillean

life: an insular colony of hispanophone Catholic Colombia, populated by anglophone Protestants of mixed (European and African) ancestry. From Providencia, Professor Wilson turns to various anglophone Antillean islands, filling out his hyphothesis with data drawn from many other societies in the region.

The lands stretching from Venezuela's coast to the Florida peninsula and scattered through the Caribbean Sea have attracted anthropological interest in recent decades, but much of that interest has been at best casual, at worst sensationalistic. For most anthropologists, the Caribbean region may be "worth a field trip," rather the way that a good dinner is worth an appetizer: a preface to more important things. Its relative lack of aborigines, handicrafts, complicated kinship systems, dangerous fauna, and remoteness has resulted so far in a good many anthropological workouts, but hardly any championship bouts. Moreover, as Professor Wilson points out, most anthropologists have come to the Caribbean with expectations of a certain kind, and their lack of fulfillment has rarely produced novelty in the way of insight, so much as the impression of a deadly sameness.

Yet the societies of this region, ranging in size from Cuba, Haiti, and Santo Domingo down to tiny islets with populations of hundreds, and as various culturally as any area of comparable size in the entire world, are alike mainly in terms of what they lack. The oldest colonial sphere in the modern world, almost wholly populated from afar, the Antilles point a significant moral for Africa, Asia, and the rest of the so-called Third World: to be colonial is a matter of spirit as well as of power and politics. What Professor Wilson suggests at the conclusion of his book is that liberation, too, is at least in part a spiritual concern. It is not reputation (as opposed to respectability) that represents such liberation, but the value of equality it stands for, that could constitute a freedom of the spirit equal to political freedom, in Professor Wilson's view.

There is a good deal to quarrel with in *Crab Antics*. If there were not, it would certainly be a much less important book. But no one familiar with Caribbean societies, or interested in understanding what makes them tick, will be able to ignore what Professor Wilson has done here. Like many readers-to-be, I have begun to test his hypotheses against Caribbean realities as

I think I understand them. I expect to find that any exceptions I discover will neither prove nor disprove his rule, so much as enhance my present understanding. I think that the considered opinions of other readers will confirm this expectation. But like the author, I leave it to you to judge.

SIDNEY W. MINTZ

Acknowledgments

I come to say thanks after I have finished the writing of this book. In this writing, memories of times, of pleasures, and of pains have been revived and relived. Friends that I have not seen for ten years, real people whom I loved and respected, have come back to life. But some I shall never see again, for now they are dead. And the others? Perhaps we shall meet again. But if nothing else, the writing of *Crab Antics* is one way I can say that I have not forgotten them.

But as I try to say thank you I am led once again to wonder why I write such a book; and I must confess I am not clear about the answer. Lamely one says that one is an anthropologist, and anthropologists are expected to write such a book—expected, that is, by other anthropologists. Then I must admit that I have used the people of Providencia for my own purposes, and thence for anthropology, and what is anthropology to them? All I can hope is that when they read it, as they surely will, they may find some measure of truth in it, some meager measure of assurance that an outsider, and the outside, has some glimmering of understanding of what life means to them. Or perhaps they will find in it something worthwhile that I cannot here anticipate.

All the names used are fictitious, though they are names found on the island. I have tried as hard as I can to make sure no one can be identified in such a way as to lead to his embarrassment. I have attributed actions performed by one person to several. I have switched venues and times of specific events and sometimes associated people with actions they did not perform, and so on. Still, there is no doubt that some will be able to recognize themselves and others, and I hope I do not cause them offense or embarrassment. Futhermore, ten years and more have gone by since all that is reported here happened, so that whatever problems might have been raised by an earlier publication will long since have been resolved.

There are some people who cannot remain anonymous, for I owe them too much. During the three visits I made to the island, from May to September 1958, May to September 1959, and December to March 1960–61, I was extended gracious hospitality and willing assistance by Mr. and Mrs. Ronald Taylor, Mr. and Mrs. Victor Howard, Mr. and Mrs. R. T. Newball, Mr. and Mrs. Lynn Newball, Mr. and Mrs. Bert Archbold, Mr. Alvarro Howard, Mr. Irmo Howard, Mr. Alpheus Archbold, and Mr. Oscar Bryan. I also wish to offer particular thanks to Mr. Vance Lever, my special friend in San Andrés, and I am especially grateful to Dr. Luis Duque Gomez, then director of the Instituto Nacional de Antropologia, for granting me permission, and encouragement, to work on the island.

No one who does anthropological work in Colombia can do so without paying homage to Dr. Gerardo Reichel-Dolmatoff and his wife Alicia. As friends and scholars they have earned the gratitude of all who work in Latin America. My sincere regret is that my own particular debt has been so ill and tardily repaid.

Dr. and Mrs. Tom Price first initiated me into the wonder and excitement of the islands, and nothing gives me greater pleasure than to acknowledge this and the pleasures of a great friendship that resulted. Professor Sidney Mintz has taught me more than even he suspects about the Caribbean and about anthropology. He supervised my Ph.D. thesis, which was about Providencia, and I have discussed problems with him for many years. His writings about the Caribbean hit so many nails on the head that I feel my claims in the present work must appear pretentious by comparison. He has read and criticized the present manuscript and through his friendship has given me a certain confidence for which mere thanks are inadequate. Thomas Standish of Bennington College read and criticized the final chapter but bears no responsibility for its errors and argument. Parts of the manuscript were typed by Jean Snow and Mai Furlong, and the maps and figures were drawn by Peter Duncan, all of the Department of Anthropology, Otago University. And many thanks to Cynthia Brodhead of the Yale Press for most helpful editing.

In earlier times only the wealthy could enjoy extended trips to beautiful tropical islands. Today, thanks to the benevolence of democracy and the reverence for science, impecunious graduate students and scholars are able to bore their way into such exotic worlds. My fieldwork was financed, at various times, by the Social Science Research Council, the Research Institute for the Study of Man, the Society for the the Study of Problems of Sex, and the Department of Anthropology, Yale University. Grants-in-aid from the Social Science Research Council and the Wenner-Gren Foundation for Anthropological Research enabled me to write this book. The responsibility for all that is said in it rests entirely with me and in no part with these foundations.

Finally, I wish to pay tribute to Lambros Comitas's work *Caribbeana 1900–1965: A Topical Bibliography* (1968). Anthropological research in a region has rarely been so well served.

P.J.W.

University of Otago
Dunedin, New Zealand

Introduction 1995

Waveland Press has done me the honor of republishing my two books about the Caribbean island of Providencia. First *Oscar,* and now *Crab Antics.* I would like to take this opportunity to explain the connection between the two books. *Oscar* is a book that literally presented its subject to me, but *Crab Antics* is a book that resulted from well-defined intentions — even if those intentions did not work out exactly as planned. Writing the two books as a total project, however, was quite deliberate. The link that I want to stress, especially now that they are available from the same publisher, is that *Oscar* tries to present the view from the inside. Not just from inside the individual, Oscar, but from within the feelings of his kin and neighbors. *Crab Antics* is cast in a more traditional mold, but tries to present Providencia from the outside — as I, the anthropologist-observer, saw it, interpreted it, and sought to relate it to the world at large. In neither book do I seek to withhold myself, but whereas Oscar is the major spokesman in his book, both about himself and about the island, I am the chief commentator in *Crab Antics.*

My fieldwork on Providencia was carried out between 1958 and 1961 — thirty years ago! This, in one sense, is not so much an ethnography but, rather, part of a history. Sometimes events change rapidly, but mostly the nature of everyday life changes slowly and imperceptibly. From the privileged vantage point of a reprint of this book, I would like to emphasize that all ethnography is, or rather becomes, history and in that sense slips out of the grasp of the ethnographer and into the hands of the people whose history it becomes. In this spirit I offer *Crab Antics* to the reader, and especially to the people of Providencia, as a small slice of their history.

January 1995
Dunedin, New Zealand

Introduction

The intention of this book is twofold. It is a detailed study of the social system of the Caribbean island of Providencia. And it is a critique of studies of other Caribbean societies made by social anthropologists.

My criticism of the work of others is not so much of what they have said and done as of what they have failed to do. For it is an extraordinary feature of Caribbean social anthropology that it has been preoccupied with the description and analysis of forms of the family and household, and to some extent of social class, while virtually excluding from its consideration other, no less vital, features of the social system. This preoccupation has tended to preclude any attempt to understand Caribbean social life as a totality. It has at best given rise to hypotheses of purely local or partial application, and it has resulted in the peculiar situation whereby writers have been unable to appreciate the significance of their own observations or, worse still, have failed to observe what was there in front of them. Further evidence of the narrowness and involution of Caribbean social anthropology can be inferred from the fact that it finds no place in the comparative and synthesizing work of scholars engaged outside the region or in general anthropological theory. Haitian *vodun* is about all that has drawn the interest of general scholarship—that and a quick glance at the "matrifocal" family.

I am not quite sure why social anthropological research in Caribbean societies has become so bogged down in the study of the family and the household.[1] Sidney Greenfield (1968) has recently suggested that social anthropologists have transferred to their Caribbean studies, more or less without question, the assumptions and emphases on family and kinship developed by their colleagues working among tribal peoples of Africa in particular. By and large I think this suggestion plausible. I also think that this concentration and the general approach may partly be a result of the fact that the first of these sociostructural studies, by Raymond Smith, of the *Negro Family in British Guiana* (1956), was so successful and revealing that it is

1

only now that we have exhausted the mine that he opened and are able to see that there are other, equally important matters to study and understand.

Doubtless there are other reasons, but I see no use in harping on the question. For a fuller retrospective of anthropological work in the Caribbean there are the surveys by R. T. Smith (1957 and 1963), M. G. Smith (1966), and N. Whitten and J. Szwed (1970). Once this involution is recognized it seems preferable to begin looking for a constructive alternative, which I hope the present work offers.

The best way I can set about proposing an alternative is to present a detailed analysis of a single society to serve as an example, pointing out whenever possible its relevance to other societies. Such comparisons will also demonstrate how factors that are merely hinted at in other studies might be understood in terms of a total system. This method also allows me to place on record the ethnology of a hitherto undescribed and rather remote Caribbean society. But a word of caution is in order. The comparisons woven in and out of the detailed analysis and achieving some degree of autonomy in chapter 8 are in no way complete and systematic. They are gleanings from the works of others which offer barely enough to suggest that the social systems of other Caribbean societies might closely resemble the one I describe for Providencia. They are clues pointing to a situation other than that proposed by the respective authors, and they are also hints confirming that my own analysis is on the right track.

This analysis revolves around two primary considerations. One, an empirical matter, concerns the attempt to "take account of the importance of informal grouping lacking any institutional articulation" (Mintz n.d.). The other is a theoretical matter and concerns the identification and interrelationship of the two primary principles of the social structure—*reputation* and *respectability*. Both matters are really just different sides of the same problem, and since this problem does have a bearing wider than the Caribbean, some further comment seems justified.

Previous social anthropological studies of the Caribbean have, as I have already noted, concentrated on the household and family. Of necessity, then, they have taken an institutional view of the social structure, for the family is perhaps the archetypical institution. This means a view of structure which emphasizes the parts and more or less takes the relations between the parts for granted. Thus the object of investigation is to identify and describe the parts of the social system. Traditionally these are formalized groupings: the institutions or their approximations. The groupings, which are both inclusive and exclusive, are measurable by their boundaries and identifiable by their composition—both of which are revealed through modes of recruitment and the definition of rights and duties, mostly with respect to property (which category also includes members). Relations between individuals are therefore secondary and are derived from the structure of the group and the place of the group in a larger structure.

With such a view of social structure it is easy to see why anthropologists working in the Caribbean have concentrated their attention on the family and household. These are the only visible social "facts" that come anywhere near to resembling the groupings contingent on this view of social structure. But, as is plain from every account, these groupings and this view of structure prove quite inadequate in accounting for or interpreting observed behavior. So much of Caribbean social life appears to fall outside the scope of such a formalized institutional structure of groupings that it has at best been reported incidentally and at worst been quite ignored. Nor is this a problem limited to the Caribbean. One can see evidence of it in the writings of those anthropologists studying populations that are no longer tribally organized—whether they be a rural or "civilized" peasantry or an urbanizing proletariat.

As the sort of thinking about social structure I have indicated here becomes more and more inadequate to handle the problems of conceptualizing observation, we find such anthropologists adopting a vocabulary that in some instances is better suited to weaving: social structures are networks, meshes, many-stranded, skeined, warped and woofed. Or, to vary the metaphor, they have become flabby; loose and informal are the key "concepts" here. This is going too far. Certainly metaphor has the power to open up new vistas and suggest new relationships, but "loose

structure"? This means, presumably, that the behavior observed and recorded is, in fact, evidence of something that is not
"really" structured or institutionalized but is something like it,
only the anthropologist cannot think of a good way to put
it! Sarcasm aside, one wonders what lies behind this rigid,
mechanistic way of thinking in anthropology. I think it stems
in part from the takeover and working out of one aspect of
Durkheim's thoughts on mechanical solidarity, with its emphasis
on corporateness and group cohesion. But what about Durkheim's other thoughts on the matter of social structure or
social system? And most crucially, what about Durkheim's own
view that segmentary society and mechanical solidarity are
indicative of less visible but deeper and more basic matters such
as collective conscience? It is at this level that the heart of the
"system" lies (cf. Dumont 1970 : 40–41, and 274, n.23b).

Another implication of the present tendency would seem to be
that anthropologists have ceased to listen to their own data,
which tells them that there may be a framework for living
alternative to the familiar formalized structures based on
institutions. Or it may be telling them that they must probe
toward a deeper and more comprehensive level of theory. Since
this book pretends to suggest a deeper and more comprehensive
theory of Caribbean social life and to recognize an alternative
framework, and since such pretensions may be applicable beyond
the Caribbean, it is important that the problem be stated more
extensively.

Let us take as a starting point a paper that recognizes the
problem of the inadequacy of present theory to cope with social systems such as those of the Caribbean and that offers suggestions for the modification of present theory. But even as the
author does this, we can see that he remains so bound to the
mechanical idea of social structure that his advice only becomes
more confusing. Eric Wolf writes that "the formal framework of
economic and political power exists alongside or intermingled
with various other kinds of informal structures which are interstitial, supplementary or parallel to it" (1966*a* : 2).

This brief quotation offers a view of the world as essentially
constructed of pigeonholes, perhaps becoming a little out of
line. Wolf goes on to say that "the system [i.e. the formal struc-

ture] is logically, if not temporally prior" to the informal structure. Even granting the distinction between informal and formal
structure, one may well ask if this is, in fact, so? Or is this
not yet another example of theoretical brainwashing?

We have studies of London families, both lower and middle
class (Bott 1957; Young and Willmott 1960), of Welsh
villagers (Frankenberg 1957), Spanish peasants (Pitt-Rivers
1961; Kenny 1962), Greek shepherds (Campbell 1964), Mexican townsmen (O. Lewis 1966) and Mexican rural Indians
(Reina 1966), Arab nomads (Bourdieu 1966), Italian peasants
(Davis 1969), Pitcairn Islanders (Frazer 1970), Malagasy
tribesmen (Wilson 1971b), New Guinea Highlands people
(Strathern 1968), and countless more, especially in New
Guinea where confusion over "structure" is chronic. And they
all insist on a pattern of ordered social behavior that springs
autochthonously from the daily cares, interactions, values, and
interrelations of people with each other and with their environment. But in spite of the affirmations of the anthropologists
that this behavior is what counts among the people themselves
and what best expresses their ideals—is in fact the very stuff
of their lives—the generalizers and even the ethnographers
seeking to achieve a respectable conclusion come up with the
idea that these patterns are only the "informal" structure—or
some other suitable synonym.

Yet if study after study tells us that real people, living in
communities representative of the way of life of the majority
of a given national, tribal, ethnic, or cultural population, fulfill their lives through each other in ways that the anthropologist
chooses to call informal, parallel, supplementary, interstitial,
secondary, subordinate, loose, flexible, or even quasi—then,
there is something cockeyed somewhere. The anthropologist and
the rest of the world seem to have different orders of priority,
or the anthropologist simply feels constrained to assimilate other
social systems to his own. In spite of his own findings to the
contrary, he appears to impose his own preference or priority for
the rationalized, objectified, legalistic framework of his own
institutionalized society, founded as it is in the bureaucracy of
the state, economic power, and the rationalizing justifications of
sociological theory (cf. Gellner 1964 : 34).

Perhaps nowhere else is this arthritic viewpoint more evident than in social anthropological writings about the Caribbean. And perhaps nowhere else is the primacy of the so-called informal structure more in need of recognition. For virtually every island society here is in a colonial or quasi-colonial status. This means that the supposedly "core" structure of institutions is, with its attendant ideology of norms and standards, no more than a graft, an imposition on the lives and society of the people. This formal structure in fact has its origin and validity elsewhere than in the Caribbean, specifically in Europe and the United States, and it commands only an uncertain allegiance of convenience within Caribbean society itself. This in turn is chiefly confined to an ambivalent minority led by the elite, the "mimic men" as V. S. Naipaul pointedly calls them. This formal structure may be taken over, but it is not taken in.

One may ask again why anthropologists, when confronted by their own findings about other peoples' lives, have refused to believe what they see. Why have they succumbed to finger-walking through the thesaurus looking for yet another synonym for loose structure? I have already suggested that modern anthropologists have mistaken Durkheim's basic position. They have come to assume that the visible "social fact" is the reality, the basis of a social structure, and they have forgotten that social facts are but the indexes of an invisible but universal phenomenon which is the structure—something of the order of "mind" or "states of mind" (cf. Scholte 1966). How is this position, that structure is the social fact, manifest in theories about Caribbean society? There are four major theoretical positions.

1. We observe that the peoples of the Caribbean belong to several different racial or ethnic groups, and that each of these displays differences of culture. The structure of the society is the particular way in which each race or ethnic group is assorted and related to the institutional frames of activity, economic and political activity in particular. The form of any single sociological grouping, such as the household or the family, is explained according to its place in the section(s) of the "plural" society.

2. We observe that the peoples of the Caribbean enjoy

differential access to the productive resources of the land and to wealth and the control of force. Accordingly we may group together those with comparable access and see the structure of the society as being founded on an arrangement of classes, each ranked, defined, and bounded. The particular form of identifiable sociological groupings, such as the household and the family, may be seen as a function of the particular social class to which their members belong.

3. We observe that the Caribbean society we study is not in fact a society but a part society, the dependent or marginal part of a society. Its members therefore enjoy little or no autonomy, having to service the dominant and independent sector. The particular form of any identifiable sociological groupings such as the household and family may therefore be explained as a function of the dependent or part status of the sector of the society to which they belong.

4. We observe that the major population sector of the particular Caribbean society is of a specific alien cultural origin: namely, African. The particular forms of identifiable sociological groupings such as the family and household are a result of the African origins of this part of the society.

These theories are all of the same type. They divide the whole into parts of differing orders and explain the form of the smaller parts by their position in the larger parts. There is no doubt that these theories have proved fruitful; but they have now exhausted themselves. They fail utterly to direct any attention to what the people being studied "have in mind" or "think they are doing" when they behave in a certain way and produce (incidentally?) or fail to produce certain identifiable sociological groupings. What is more, such failure has the added consequence of forcing the observer to omit consideration of the individual as a person except insofar as he is an instance within the group.[2]

In the following chapters I seek to develop an explanation based on a somewhat different kind of theory, one which is rather more emic in quality than those outlined above. It is one that attempts to isolate the principles of thought and sentiment that produce not only actual behavior but also the groupings and segments of the society.[3] My method of exposi-

tion is a rather crude dialectic—crude because I have neither
philosophical nor methodological intent or claim; dialectic because this seems to me an inherent feature of island social
behavior as well as a technique of analytical exposition.

Chapters 2 and 3 elaborate the proposition that social life
in general arises out of the continuing relations of people to
each other *in* space and time and *with* space and time. In the
first instance, men in their relations must adapt to the environment; in the second instance they appropriate it. Thus
the people living permanently in a particular place and nowhere else (e.g. Providencia) at a given time (i.e. now) share
this placement and contemporaneity as the lowest common
denominator of their specific and shared identity. In this
broad sense of space and time they can consider each other
as equals. To a great extent, in their perception of their relationship to a fixed and autonomous environment and in their
differentiation from those attached to another environment,
people are each others' moral equals. In turn, this common
environment, as experience, is called upon to justify this
claim to equality.

At the same time, though, islanders live with as well as in
their environment. In their development of relations with each
other they use and appropriate land and interpret time (history) and the external cultural environment as well as react
to these conditions. But they do so in an ordered rather than
a haphazard way, in a socially logical (sociological) manner. This manner centers on the means of expressing differences among people, which in turn leads to a reinterpretation
of the environment to back up the categorization of these
differences followed by a ranking of differences. In their relations to each other and to their environment people classify
themselves on the bases of their differences. The environment
is, in a sense, appropriated to signify these differences, and
at this level of conceptualization we can identify a social
structure of a mechanistic nature founded on social class. But
this stratification depends on and is the result of what people
think to be significant as difference. They have in mind a
philosophical principle or "policy," as Hume calls it, from
which they can instill, defend, and justify their actions. The

principle of stratification that subsumes all others in the Caribbean is, I suggest, the principle of *respectability*.

The equality discussed in chapters 2 and 3 and the stratification described in chapters 4 and 5 are not of the same order of generality; they represent quite different levels of social structure. There is, however, a particular level of structure which is the dialectical complement of stratification and respectability and which supports an ideal of sociological equality. At the empirical, mechanical level of structure this is to be found in the interpretation of kinship ties on the one hand and in the elaboration and specification of friendship ties on the other. These latter are centered in groups called *crews*. The philosophical principle by which equality is guided, which men "have in mind," is what I have designated *reputation*.

The structure of Caribbean social life is, then, the dialectical relation between the two principles, respectability and reputation. This is what is being expressed by the more observable features of social relations and social behavior; but in the end I would argue that all levels of the structure are explicable as products of reputation, respectability, and the dialectical relation between them. On Providencia this relationship is known as *the crab antics*, hence the title of this book.

The real situation is not, of course, as simple as the model I make of it, and there are factual complications. Thus reputation is largely specific to men, while respectability is most particular to women and concerns men only at certain times of their lives, or only certain men in the society. This, in turn, raises the point that there is, at a certain level, a clear distinction to be drawn between the structure of social life for men and for women, a distinction that is reflected in day-to-day life and activity. Respectability has its roots in the external colonizing (or quasi-colonizing) society, though in any given instance its reality depends on the integral role of the colonizing society in the social system of the colony. Reputation, on the other hand, is "indigenous" to the colony (or quasi-colony) and is *both* an authentic structural principle and a counterprinciple. This is made clear in the final chapter.

I have selected only societies of the English-speaking Caribbean for comparison. Originally I had intended to survey the entire region, but this was when I was contemplating a purely critical and synthetic study. To have attempted such a broad-scale comparison in the present study would have diffused (though not de-fused) my argument, would have made for far too cumbersome a book, and would have necessitated taking into account many diverse cultural features, thereby diverting me from my concern with structure. Nevertheless, I willingly admit that such a comparison is not only necessary but that it most certainly should lead to modification of the present argument.

The final chapter might, at first glance, appear rather out of tune with the rest of the book. But though it is a polemic and is concerned with change, it is meant to argue, if not to demonstrate, that the theory of Caribbean social structure offered in this book is in fact more realistic, even more practically (or politically) applicable than its apparently more empirical, mechanistic rivals. Like all polemics, however, it is meant as a challenge or, perhaps less ambitiously, as a provocation.

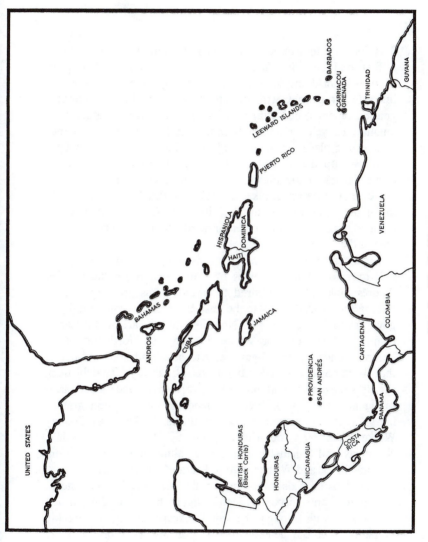

Fig. 1. The Caribbean.

1 Providencia: An Island in the Sun

The journey to Providencia begins in New York and makes a first real stop in Cartagena—perhaps the most European of New World cities. Mellow, so inconvenient to traffic, so intimate for people, with the stones of its buildings seemingly gnarled or smoothed with age, its lines are curved rather than angular, its yellows and reds muted and calm. Here a corner is a resting place for busy people who have sought and bought their way up the street—not a trap gate to spring you across a murderous road. Flowers and filth, coffee and tobacco—not cans and paper, smoke and rubble—these are what people make their impressions on the city with. City and people are blended, take each other for granted. Neither seeks to overwhelm the other.

From Cartagena to San Andrés is a flight of an hour and a half over four hundred miles of empty sea. From the air San Andrés looks like a hundred thousand palms growing straight out of the sea. It used to be just a coconut island until the government "developed" it. Now it is the "pearl of the Caribbean," a free port for weekend shoppers. North-end sands became concrete, palms gave way to steel and concrete pillars that became the Hotel Miami, or Broadway. Thatch bars, shanty shops, and boutiques sprang up where once stood jacaranda and frangipani. Electric blenders, radios, phonographs, lamps, typewriters, cameras, wristwatches, Parker pens, Johnny Walker, Vat 69, Coca-Cola, spaghetti, Del Monte, Nestlé's, Newports and Salems, plastic bowls, aluminum pans, Jantzen, Chanel No. 5, and Wrigley's gum. Flora of San Andrés.

Hundreds of taxis honk and smoke their way between stores and hotels and airport. Electric lights burn all day in the bright sun and through the night, except during the weekly breakdown of the generator. Water is always short, and the food comes from a box or can.

From San Andrés to Providencia is only forty-eight miles, but you have to wait for a boat that intends to go there. Not many boats do, because Providencia is not "developed" and

12

not much money is to be made by calling there. About every three weeks or so, a boat makes the trip before going back south to Cartagena or Colon for more supplies to feed San Andrés. I check every morning with the agent about the boats. I am lucky, having to wait no more than ten days. In the meantime, since San Andrés is the seat of government for the two islands, I introduce myself to various officials and, of course, the S.I.C. (police), hoping thereby to forestall any "inquiries" into my presence. More pleasurably, I play billiards with my friend Vance, drink beer, meet Vance's friends and one or two people from Providencia.

The first time I went from San Andrés to Providencia I sailed on the M.V. *Victoria,* skipper, Captain Jamesie Howard, red faced, blustery, no nonsense. He invited me to dine with him since we had set sail at about 7 P.M. We sat in the galley at sea level, and dinner was a lump of pork fat, some fried plantain, and boiled manioc. Out beyond the reef the sea rose and fell carrying the little boat with it. In the steadiest voice I could muster I told Captain Jamesie I had already eaten supper (which was true) and that since I was not too good a sailor I ought to get to my bunk. He didn't believe an Englishman could be a bad sailor. I apologized for any disillusionment I had brought him and left to spend the night in abject, pathetic, vomiting misery.

Much to my astonishment I was still alive at dawn when we dropped anchor. A mug of hot coffee encouraged the blood to go through my veins again and now I could walk around the boat and, much more to the point, take my first look at Providencia. At the moment, it was no more than a black hulk looming out of the sea waiting for the sunrise to bring it to life.

Quickly the rugged hills disengaged themselves from the sky, changing from black to violet to green and unveiling their features. As I watched the hills light up I saw out of the corner of my eye a delicate tangle of palms and trees begin to glint. Then as I shifted my gaze downward brown and white wooden houses took shape, spirals of blue smoke slithered through the trees, and small figures began to move about on the shore. When I looked northward, over the prow of the

boat I saw St. Isabel, the island's capital, red-roofed and
white-walled, looking for all the world like a Mediterranean
village.

By the time the sun was up above the horizon, canoes and
rowboats were swarming across the bay toward the *Victoria*.
For a moment I was Captain Cook discovering a new part
of the globe—but then I remembered the night before! As the
boats tied up at the *Victoria,* young men and old clambered
aboard and all was shouting and excitement. Families were
welcomed back, inquiries were yelled back and forth about the
cargo. Captain Jamesie just told the crowd that they had to
wait until the captain of the port came aboard. Everyone took
a quick look at the white stranger, and though they were all
too polite to stare or ask questions out loud, there was a lot
of nudging and whispering.

In spite of its rugged hills and massive bulk, the island is
small, measuring only five miles by three at its broadest points.
The even smaller island of Santa Catalina provides a third
side for the symmetrical bay where we were anchored. Two
thousand people live on Providencia. They dwell in fourteen
villages connected by a path that encircles the island keeping
as close as possible to the flat shoreline. At two places, however, one on the east and the other on the west coast, the path
has to traverse high and precipitous bluffs. During the rainy
season the path is washed out here and the island cut in two.
Canoe is the only way to get around. In 1960 the government
built a road around the island and the first vehicles made their
appearance. For a while the to-ing and fro-ing was quite
hectic; but the old cars were no match for the rocks and holes,
spare parts were hard to come by and expensive, gasoline was
scarce, and after one boat blew up with a cargo of gasoline,
no one was willing to ship it. In a very short while horses
and Shanks' Pony regained their eminence.

During my stays on the island I walked or rode around it
many times. I was always awed and overwhelmed by the idea
of imminent power suggested by the hills, thrown up eons ago
from a violent sea bottom. Against a limitless, flat sea they
struck me as more mighty than "real" mainland mountains.
Green—light and dark, dense and transparent, still and shim-

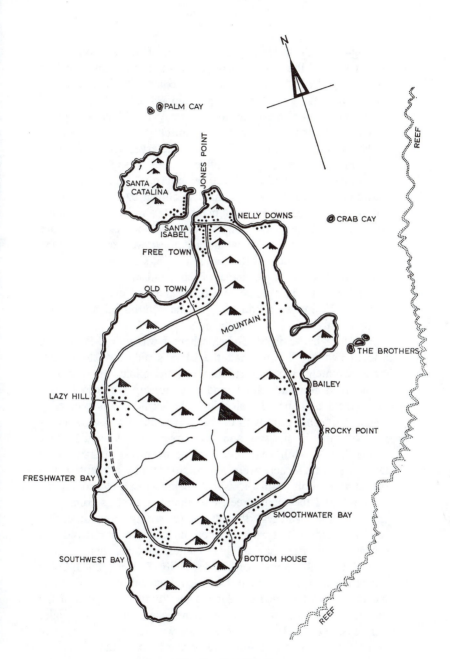

Fig. 2. Providencia.

mering—was the color of the island, set off by the cool transparent blue of the sea. I doubt there are many islands so true to literary "type," and as islanders constantly reminded me and themselves, it was "tranquil and reposeful."

The first time I was taken on a tour of the island, my guide was a man who had introduced himself to me as Professor Oscar Bryan de Newball. His story deserves its own telling (Wilson, forthcoming), but suffice it here to say that he was the island "madman," who yet gained from all a certain admiration for his knowledge and intelligence. In his sixties, strong and agile, he had no home but wandered the island, foraged and begged his living or did odd jobs and at various times regaled those who would listen as well as those who would rather not hear with stories, gossip, sermons, and jokes. All were told in a language of euphemism, aphorism, and biblical allusion in a voice that resonated and a style that declaimed. We made an odd pair, but he determined to "aid me in my researches"—so off we went.

The tour began in St. Isabel, where I was living. St. Isabel, also known as "Town," had the island's only stretch of concrete pavement, the four main stores, the clinic, three schools including a convent school, and the municipal offices housed in a single building, the alcaldia. The alcaldia was painted a dismal battleship gray with dark green trim, quite out of keeping with the island sun and the larger houses, which were painted white with red, blue, green, or brown trim. Poorer houses, of which there were many, stood sadly unpainted with rusted iron roofs. Still St. Isabel, being clustered around the "square" and the main street, had shape as well as color. The island's other villages, though, were strung out along the roadside and with certain exceptions gave no impression of communality. But they all had names, and the first one we passed through, going north, was Nelly Downs. Since Oscar did not like anyone in Nelly Downs, we passed quickly through. Nevertheless he singled out for me the "notable" houses of the village and did not fail to indicate the island prison and police barracks. Not visible from the road was the small village of Jones Point, where forty-one people live right on the shore.

At the barracks the road curves round, for this is the northern tip of the island. Turning to the southwest, we passed first through Mountain, then Bailey, with its Catholic church and government school, until at McBean Hill we looked out over the spectacular Maracaibo Bay and its mangrove swamp, across to the imposing Ironwood Hill. After a smoke, Oscar and I made our way round the bay to Rocky Point, which was really the next "major" village. Nelly Downs, Jones Point, Mountain, and Bailey were all within easy reach of St. Isabel and people living in these villages depended on St. Isabel for supplies, churches, and schools. Rocky Point has a couple of stores, smaller than those in St. Isabel, two schools—one government and one Adventist—and the main Adventist church. There were a few larger, painted houses similar to those in St. Isabel, so undoubtedly there were some better-off people living here. What is more important is that the people think of themselves as being beyond the orbit of St. Isabel. They don't pop around there; they don't talk about what goes on there but are concerned with their own business. Oscar was from Rocky Point, so we went in and out of houses meeting some of his kin and other inhabitants. I met Uncle Bug, ninety-eight years old and bedridden, noted for his storytelling; and Aunty Jane, tall and toothless with a loud man's voice. Black and ugly, she said she was, but for all that she could have married the fairest man in Panama if she had wanted to. But she didn't want to. We lunched with Miss Effy on boiled fish, beans, and rice, followed by pineapple stewed in cane syrup and washed down with fever grass tea.

Just south of Rocky Point was the bluff, but the weather being good we had no difficulty. A forty-minute walk brought us to Smoothwater Bay, sometimes called Luckton or Lupton. Here was a large Baptist church and school both tended by Mr. 'Pheus, and a number of large but decaying houses. This was where the descendants of Francis Archbold, the island's first settler, lived. It was an "all white," "high class" community, but the wealth, having come not from trade but from land and professions, was neither as evident nor as great as in St. Isabel. Oscar had some enemies in Smoothwater Bay, so we passed through hurriedly. However, I was to spend half my fieldwork time living here.

Almost before I realized we had left Smoothwater Bay we were in Bottom House. No big houses here—in fact, for the first time I saw palm-thatch huts. Most of the houses were small, two-room affairs built of unpainted wood, some with a separate kitchen and all with an old oil drum to catch the rainwater runoff from the roof. These were quite a contrast to the large concrete cisterns typical of Smoothwater Bay and St. Isabel. Bottom House was the island's largest village, with about 340 people, all "black" and most of them descendants of slaves who, on emancipation, had been given this southern section of the island to cultivate. We stopped at Minty's little store for a warm lemonade and visited Captain Hector, "King" of the community. Here, as elsewhere, Oscar told inquirers I was a scientist come to research on the island. There was a quaint Catholic church in Bottom House but only one Catholic—an old, demented spinster. Everyone else was Baptist, and every Sunday the churchgoers walked to Smoothwater Bay. A few small stores and a government school for infants completed the inventory of amenities for Bottom House.

The road veered away from the shore and cut across the southern tip of the island to Southwest Bay. In fact, since Southwest Bay was on the beach at the end of a turnoff from the main path, we did not on that occasion go there. Southwest Bay was notable for its fine beach, where the major horse races were held. Its people were closely related to those of Bottom House, and the two communities, in their own eyes and in those of the rest of the island, had a similar social standing. We passed without stopping in Freshwater Bay, a few houses lining the beach in which lived members of what is basically one family, and went on to Lazy Hill.

Lazy Hill regarded itself as the village most independent of St. Isabel. Here lived families who had come originally from the Cayman Islands, who had farmed successfully and done well sailing. In island terms many of them were fair-skinned and high class. Unlike any other village, most of the people here were Catholic—in fact the village was dominated by quite a large, squat, stone church. There was also a school and several stores.

Just north of Lazy Hill was the other bluff, and it was this as much as anything else that cut off Lazy Hill from St. Isabel. We managed it, though, and walked our longest stretch, to Old Town, the village I had seen first from the deck of the *Victoria*. By now it was dusk, and little kerosene lamps flickered inside the houses. We had a fish supper with Manfred, his wife, and their curious children, and afterward walked around the village. Old Town was like all the others, distin-

TABLE 1. Village Structure, 1960

Village	Pop.	No. of Houses Occupied	Schools	Stores	Religious Sympathy by % of Pop.[a]		
					Baptist	Catholic	7 Adv.
Old Town	284	61	1	2	70	30	–
Free Town	80	15	–	–	100	–	–
St. Isabel	184	44	3	7	34 [b]	63 [b]	3 [b]
St. Catalina	121	21	–	1	20	80	–
Jones Point	41	7	–	–	–	100	–
Nelly Downs	127	26	–	2	20	80	–
Mountain	93	17	–	1	30	70	–
Bailey	148	37	–	2	30	70 [b]	–
Rocky Point	175	40	2	2	40	35	25 [b]
Smoothwater Bay	105	28	1	2	30 [b]	20	50
Bottom House	341	83	1	6	100	– [b]	–
Southwest Bay	206	37	1	4	25	75 [b]	–
Freshwater Bay	45	9	–	–	–	100	–
Lazy Hill	245	56	1	5	15 [c]	80 [b]	5
Total	2,195	481	10	34	37	57	6

[a] Percentages approximate
[b] Church
[c] Meeting house

guished only by one or two large houses in good shape and some houses right on the beach. We were back within the domain of St. Isabel, so the stores were small, stocked only with daily necessities, and many of the children went to school in St. Isabel. Only the infants were schooled in the village.

Walking up the beach we went past an abandoned "park" with a stone wall, a toppled bust of former dictator Rojas Pinilla, and a sagging basketball net. We passed the small

village of Free Town and entered St. Isabel. The only village
we did not visit was Santa Catalina, which was over the narrow channel on the island of that name. I thanked Oscar for
the tour and went exhausted to bed. I was to see much of
him during my stay, and learn more of the villages we had
passed through.

The interior of the island is dominated by seven ranges
of hills spoking out from the central Peak (1,190 ft.). The
lower slopes and the narrow valleys have been cleared by
burning, and this is where islanders make their gardens. Farther up the hills are pastures for horses and cows. Much of
the interior, though not primeval vegetation, is a wild tangle
of brush and young trees with now and again a stand of an-

TABLE 2. Total Population According to Age and Sex

Age Group	1958				1959			
	Male	Female	M/F Ratio *	Total	Male	Female	M/F Ratio	Total
0–13	572	542	105.5	1,114	562	526	106.8	1,088
14–49	198	363	53.2	561	204	356	57.3	560
50 and over	266	254	104.7	520	251	241	104.1	492
Total	1,036	1,159	89.4	2,195	1,017	1,123	90.5	2,140

* The M/F ratio is the ratio of males to females.

cient mango, goatwood, or cedar trees. In the rainy season the
foliage is thick and lush, but in the dry season the hillsides
turn brown and the trees look tired. Through the "jungle"
and over the hills runs a network of footpaths, most of them
following the course of the various freshwater streams that
begin up in the hills. By means of these paths people get to
their gardens and cattle to their pastures, while an added but
by no means coincidental function results from the fact that
one can get to villages on the other side of the island more
quickly, though less conveniently, on these foothpaths than
by the peripheral path or road. Over these paths the news
travels faster than the police.

Besides gardening and herding, fishing is a major source of

subsistence. The island is encircled by a reef which lies from one-half to about three miles off shore. Within the reef small sailing canoes can operate without danger of heavy seas or sharks. Occasionally, looking for a little more sport, a crew may sail a larger boat out beyond the reef—but they always return the same day. Casting nets and traps, the latter for crayfish, are the equipment most commonly used, and while sailing out to the reef the men may drag a line. Fishing is very leisurely and done as much for the sport as for subsistence. As my friend Isaac put it once: "Out on the reef is no woman to vex you, is jus' a good sport an' a bottle of Jom's Toddy [rum]."

Most of the island's houses are built of wood, which has to be imported, usually from Nicaragua. Nowadays a small but increasing number of men are building houses of poured concrete or breeze blocks. Wooden houses vary in style from small single-room huts to two-storied, multiroomed dwellings with a veranda running half-way or completely around them. The same men who are building with concrete are also departing from the traditional style and adopting a "Spanish" style copied from Cartagena.

Size and condition of houses is a function of wealth. So too is the furniture. Some enjoy the comforts of upholstered armchairs and eat off china that says "Made in England" with silver that is "Made in Sheffield." The poorest have only a rickety table, a home-made bench, enamel plates, and an odd assortment of aluminum cutlery. The majority of houses are furnished somewhere between the extremes, but everyone tries at some time or other to acquire a glass-fronted cupboard where glasses, trinkets, plastic flowers, *memento mori,* and sepia photographs are displayed. And almost every house, much to its credit and comfort, boasts at least one large iron bedstead, well sprung and well covered.

Few houses have glass windows, though all are shuttered and during the day are open to the breezes. Since all but a few houses have corrugated zinc roofs to catch rainwater, it is fortunate that they are well aired, for when the noonday sun shines down on a tin roof one feels like a loaf of bread in the oven. Water can be a problem, for although there is said to be a natural underground lake beneath Peak, the government has not yet followed up its promise to explore it and construct a water supply system. People must still depend on rainwater run off the roofs into cisterns, or oil drums if they can't afford a cistern. Except for a few privately owned generators in St. Isabel there is no electricity. There used to be a public generator which served the northern side of the island, but it broke down years ago and is now quite beyond operation. Kerosene lamps are the usual illumination, the kerosene being imported. Poorer people make do with a rag soaked in kerosene and stuck in a bottle. Kerosene stoves are widely used, but nowhere do they supplant charcoal, which is burned locally and said by all to give the food a better taste.

Food is plentiful, though its availability varies according to season. People enjoy their food and are proud of such dishes as pumpkin pudding; curried crayfish; *ron-don,* which is fish cooked in coconut; *san cocho,* a thick soup with chicken and dumplings; and numerous cakes. Yet in spite of such a variety of fresh, exotic foods, raised organically because no one trusts chemical fertilizers, most peoples' idea of a gourmet dish is a can of Del Monte pilchards in tomato sauce or a can of Spam. Happily it was quickly apparent that I was not a weekend guest who had to be served "fancy" food, namely, canned meat and fish, and I ate as well as anyone else.

Providencia is indeed a green and pleasant island, and its people are certainly not insensitive to this, for most of them have experienced the outside world and have a good base for comparison. There are, however, certain unavoidable disadvantages to life there. Illness is one—not that Providencia is prone to more diseases than other Caribbean islands, but its isolation and limited medical facilities make treatment difficult. Malaria, tuberculosis, hepatitis, cancer, cirrhosis of the liver, high and low blood pressure, and anemia present constant threats to peoples' equanimity. Although there are two doctors and two nurses, they rarely have more than aspirin to treat their patients. Those who become really ill must go to San Andrés, and from there they may be transferred to Cartagena, Barranquilla, or Panama. Emergencies are beyond hope. In addition to the doctors there are a number of "bush doctors," each with his own specialty and reputation.

Government is also an unpleasant part of life. The history of the island's isolation from Colombia is described in chapter 2; here it is necessary only to note that this isolation and the difference in language and culture between Providencia and Colombia have created an antipathy toward government resembling that felt by colonized peoples toward their alien colonial governments. This sense of alienation has been aggravated by the religious difficulties that have beset Protestants in Colombia. Since the middle of the last century, both San Andrés and Providencia have been overwhelmingly Baptist. But as the Colombian government has become more aware of some of the possibilities of the islands, there has been a concerted attempt by both government and the officially recognized Catholic church to convert the islanders. Throughout Colombia there has been, from time to time, persecution of Protestants (Goff 1965), and the islands have had to face this. As a result, and in response to such blandishments as school scholarships and guaranteed jobs, an increasing number of islanders have converted to Catholicism. Many of these say they don't really "mean" their Catholicism but are simply exploiting the situation. Those who remain Protestant term the renegades "job" Catholics. By the time I arrived on the island, overt enmity between Protestants and Catholics had pretty well disappeared, though each enjoyed any opportunity to malign and sneer at the other.

The close ties between church and state in Colombia also have their reflections in official island politics. There is, however, a curious reversal of the national situation. On the island the Conservative party, which nationally is closely linked to the church, is led by Protestants, while the Liberal party is headed by Catholics. This is really to be explained by a local situation: the rivalry between two of the wealthiest islanders, one Adventist and the other Catholic, who use the party organization to enact their rivalry.

Administration officials are all islanders. The island being a *municipio*, these officials are subordinate to San Andrés, which is the seat of the *intendencia,* and the key intendencial posts are held by mainlanders. But for the past few years the islands have been increasingly successful in winning the assent of the central government in Bogotá to have islanders fill island administrative posts. The island administration, which is housed in the alcaldia in St. Isabel, includes the alcalde, the secretary, the personero (tax collector), the registrar, the municipal policeman, three secretarial assistants, a postmistress, a judge, who is not an islander, and a judge's clerk. There are also in each village keepers of the pound responsible for impounding trespassing animals. Eight policemen, commanded by a sergeant but directed by the alcalde and a captain of the port, complete the government apparatus. These functionaries are all career men, all from the mainland, and are posted to Providencia for only a short period, usually three months. The Marconi Company maintains a transmitting and receiving set which operates twice a day for half an hour at a time.

The administrators are all government employees who receive a salary. Their job is to maintain order and to execute the directives that originate from the *intendencia* in San Andrés and the central government. They also carry out the proposals made by the Island Council, which comprises seven elected members who deliberate on local matters including maintenance, disposal of the island budget, and collecting taxes to meet municipal assessments, and approve or disapprove the issue of licenses for stores, bars, and so forth. They keep an eye on the "morality" of the island, calling for the censure of individuals who they feel are out of line. By and large, so people told me, the council is a fairly somnolent body that now and again flares to life as a particular issue assumes importance. One such occasion was when the council president's son applied for a license to build a *kiosko* in St. Isabel. This was objected to on the grounds that it violated a bylaw that there should be no drinking-place nearer than 180 meters from a place of worship. The kiosko was planned for a spot about 100 meters from the Baptist church. Numerous personal rivalries centered on this issue, most of them quite irrelevant to licensing matters.

Schooling is not compulsory, but education is greatly respected by most people and every effort is made to give children at least a minimum of schooling. Island schools, however, can barely fulfill island hopes. The Baptist schools and the Adventist school are coeducational and go up to the fifth and sixth grades respectively. Though it is against government ruling, they carry out most of their instruction in English, using American textbooks. The government schools instruct in Spanish, at least officially, but teachers frequently revert to English. Possibly the highest standard is set by the convent school in St. Isabel, where instruction is given by two Spanish nuns, each with degrees in education. Education is free in the government schools, but the church schools charge a fee varying from 2.80 pesos to 5 pesos (Colombian) a month. The teaching is largely responsive, the learning largely rote—hardly a method to develop intelligence. Nevertheless the literacy rate on the island is high and a comparatively large percentage of students have managed to secure a higher education in Colombia, Panama, or the United States.

The schools have one day a year when they become the cynosure of all eyes: Colombian Independence Day. Each school has its own uniform color and design, and for weeks mothers work frantically sewing new uniforms for their sons and daughters. Unfortunately, parents have to pay for the uniform and many of them can hardly afford to do so. Meanwhile, the children practice drill routines and rehearse patriotic tableaux (each requiring costumes—more sewing for mothers). When July 21 arrives, the children converge on St. Isabel and, watched by their parents and teachers, assemble on the green opposite the alcaldia to perform their drill routines and tableaux, to listen to speeches, and finally to enjoy a party. In the evening there are games—the favorite is the greasy pole—with prizes given by the government. Adults are entertained to light refreshments in the alcaldia and, finally, very tired children are taken home.

Among the other, more informal occasions at which islanders enjoy themselves en masse are the horse and canoe races. The beaches at Old Town and Southwest Bay are the best suited for horse racing, the latter being especially fine because it is a little wider and, though it curves, it is possible to race

for over half a mile. When news of a race is broadcast, islanders converge on Southwest Bay. The inhabitants there rise to
the occasion by cooking huge tureens of san cocho, mountains
of pies and cakes, pots of coffee and lemonade. A good supply
of rum is gathered stealthily from the distillers, and everyone
brings his own as well. Only two horses at a time can race on
the narrow sands, but each race is a challenge backed by a
sizable wager. The jockeys, who are young boys, take their
instructions from the owner, and with everyone yelling and
waving encouragement, off they go. Before the first horse has
passed the post the crowd turns and races after, converging
on the horses and the frightened jockeys, then breaking up
into small groups to argue at the tops of their voices. No race
can possibly be run without an infringement, so no race can
be run without an argument following. This may last unabated
for one or two hours, then the next race will be run. But the
pros and cons of each race will be argued until the next meeting. There is always a champion horse, and for many years
the championship has changed hands between Richie's stallion
and Mr. Winston's bay mare. As darkness descends, dancing
and drinking begin, and while the former may come to an end
about midnight, the latter goes on for as long as the rum
lasts.

Sailing is probably the most respected and coveted skill on
the island, so a canoe race is more than just a race. The canoes
are specially built sailing craft, most of which were brought
to the island from the Cayman Islands, with one from Jamaica,
another from Florida, and two built on Providencia. As with
horses, there is a champion canoe that others challenge, but
much depends on the crew recruited by the owner. Everything
hangs on the final tack of the race, enabling the canoe to run
straight for the finishing post, which a crew member must touch
without leaving the boat. Canoe races lack the immediacy of
horse races, but because more skills are involved, there is
more to argue about—and as spectators watch from different
vantage points, the arguments get more intense as the result
gets closer. Betting is always heavy and, unlike the horse races,
the canoe races provide a sense of community involvement

since canoes, besides being identified with their owners, are identified with communities.

Events such as these have an air of spontaneity about them. They are extemporaneous, and even though there is some organization, it is achieved by individuals making their own decisions. This is an important characteristic of islanders, who display a positive dislike for being organized, for working or playing according to someone else's "plan." Nowhere was this better illustrated than in the fizzle of the island baseball league, brainchild of the newly formed Sports Council of Providencia. Five teams were organized, each from a community, their team colors were assigned and their pennants designed. They were to play on a specially cleared field each Sunday, using equipment purchased from the island budget. The first few games were a resounding success and several hundred people watched the proceedings. By about the fifth Sunday, teams were turning up at half strength, people of one community were accusing people in another community of cheating, of *obeah,* of trying to lure star players. In the end, after nine weeks or so, the whole thing tailed right out. Providence people, they said, don't like taking orders from no one. "Providence people can't pull together, man, so they pulls apart."

This antipathy to "structure" and "organization" and the preference for "communitas" are central to any understanding of island life and lie at the heart of the present inquiry.

2 The Presence of History

Ever since Radcliffe-Brown's admonitions against "conjectural history" or the speculative reconstruction of the past of the nonliterate world, social anthropologists have felt a little guilty and very apologetic about history. In a recent collection of essays devoted to the marriage of anthropology and history, the editor, I. M. Lewis, plaintively writes that the essays may strike the orthodox historian as "unhistorical in the extreme." "Yet," he apologizes, "our object is far from being anti-historical" (1968 : ix). But Radcliffe-Brown himself was not averse to speculatively interpreting the past by applying contemporary hypotheses from structural anthropology, as his famous introduction to *African Systems of Kinship and Marriage* bears out. Now that anthropologists have gone beyond traditional tribal studies and are passing out of the "ultimately stultifying mystique of *status quo* maintenance" (I. M. Lewis 1968 : xv), which has for long been their form of explanation, evidence from the past confronts them, forcing them to change interpretations and to interpret change.

The recognition of historical data does not only lengthen the perspective and lend credence to objectivity. It further complicates the problems of selection that already faced the "synchronic" anthropologist, and rather than improving objectivity, it could be argued that the use of history makes the anthropologist's work even more subjective. As E. H. Carr points out, though history comprises facts, these speak "only when the historian calls on them, it is he who decides to which facts to give the floor, in what order of context" (Carr 1962 : 9). The historian, furthermore, makes his selection according to his present interests, which in turn are a reflection of the interests of his time, beginning with what his colleagues consider important (cf. ibid., pp. 5, 26). One historian, Peter Laslett, goes so far as to argue that history, as knowledge about ourselves, is derived at least in part from an understanding by contrast with the past (Laslett 1965 : 231).

When an anthropologist uses history, he too is calling up

certain facts to speak on his behalf. He culls them to suit a certain pattern intrinsic to his anthropological concerns—the theory to which he presently subscribes—which reflect to some extent the concerns of his own society at present. What sort of "truth," then, is he telling about the people of whom he writes? Unlike the historian, the anthropologist has not been deputed by his own society as its spokesman for reconciliation of present with past. The anthropologist consciously views himself as an outsider and is so viewed. The society or people viewed by the anthropologist re-present the past to suit their own purposes, which we must regard as being at least as authentic for them as our own version of their history is for our intentions.

These ruminations are occasioned by the circumstances of my study of the "history" of Providencia. I can discern, and will present, two histories of the island: one I have gleaned from European written sources reporting outsiders' observations and such written island sources as wills, land deeds, and the like, which are documents drawn up without historical intent (though they may be true history). The other history is that told by any islander and held in common mind by all, but for which there is no documentary reference. The juxtaposition of the two seems to me to reveal first the possibility that history is what historians do, rather than that it is a thing-in-itself, a position taken by such historians as Collingwood (1956).[4] The historian doing history plays a role which is, to quote Giedion "to put in order in its historial setting, what we experience piecemeal from day to day" (1948 : 2), that is, to apply the constantly revising concepts of rationality. Second, this juxtaposition suggests that the historian performs as an interpreter of the past-as-environment, whereas the anonymous "oral" history is an adaptation of and to the environment. The one appears as time submitting to reason, the other as reason submitting to time.

A HISTORY OF PROVIDENCIA

Santa Catalina and Old Providence are two islands about seven leagues in circumference, situated 13 deg. 10′ W. longitude, 50 leagues to the S.E. of Cape Grace à Dios.

These islands are perhaps the best in the West Indies (in
proportion to their bigness) both as to their healthful air
and richness of soil, and capable of producing anything
the West Indies afford: the sea is well stored with plenty
of turtle and fish, and abundance of wild hogs are on
the largest island. The natural products of these islands
is fustick; cedar; and several sorts of West India woods;
they are surprisingly free from those insects which are
natural to the West Indies, neither are there any snakes
or poisonous animals to be found in them. [Jeffreys 1762]

Modern maps give the location as 13° 20′ N, and 81° 22′ W,
and the fustick and wild hogs have disappeared; but otherwise
Jeffreys's favorable notice of the island of Providencia applies
as well today as two hundred years ago.

The first mention of the island in European documents was
in the *carta universal,* published in 1527 (Parsons 1956). It
seems to have been used by Dutch pirates and smugglers in
the early part of the seventeenth century and was first settled
in 1629–30 by Puritans from England and Bermuda under the
auspices of the "Company of Adventurers of the City of West-
minster for the Plantation of the Islands of Providence or
Catalina, Henrietta or Andrea, and the adjacent Islands lying
upon the coast of America." With diligence the Puritans culti-
vated cotton and tobacco in addition to staple foodstuffs; but
they very quickly found that more profitable pickings were to
be had by raiding the Spanish treasure ships that constantly
passed within sight of the island.

The strategic position had been noted and reported before
the Puritans settled, so who knows that their piratical intentions were not uppermost from the beginning? Sir John Cooke
had written in 1630:

It [Providence] lieth in the highway of the Spanish
fleets that come from Cartagena, from which it lieth about
100 leagues and from Porto Bello 80 leagues and about
80 leagues also from the Bay of Nicoraga, at which place
of the *terra firma,* the Spaniards have great trade for their
treasure, and all ships that come from those places must
pass on one or other side of the island within 20 leagues

and may easily be discovered from thence. [Newton 1914 :
204]

As Sir John warmed to his subject he turned to the tactical
advantages of Providence:

> [The island] will yield provision sufficient for 1,000
> men besides women and children. . . . For strength the
> access is very difficult and a ship cannot get in without
> much danger of rocks and shoals. . . . The enemy can-
> not land otherwise than by shallops and therefore there
> should be boats to hinder their landing. The Spaniards
> also send treasure in shallops, which they can freight at
> places along the coast and by these shallops may be met
> with much advantage. . . . Many are very rich. [Ibid. :
> 205]

Taking full advantage of their strategic and tactical position, the Puritans raided passing Spanish vessels at will and
after a very short period received full backing for their adven-
tures from the Company. The effectiveness of their exploits
(conducted doubtless in the name of the Lord) is evident from
the following contemporary observation:

> The greatest fear, that, I perceived, possessed the Span-
> iard in this voyage was about the Island of Providence,
> called by them Sta Catalina or St Katherine from whence
> they feared lest some English ships should come out
> against them with great strength. They cursed the English
> in it and called the Island the den of Thieves and Pirates,
> wishing that the King of Spain would take some course
> with it. [Quoted in ibid. : 231]

The king of Spain did indeed take a course, and twice the
island withstood full-scale assaults by large Spanish fleets. But
at the third try, in 1641, the Spanish succeeded in defeating
the garrison and, having done so, removed the entire population, presumably to make doubly sure. Soon after the Spaniards
left the island empty, John Humphry of Massachusetts arrived
to assume his duties as governor of the island!

Over the next thirty years Providence changed hands on a

number of occasions, being taken over at one time by the buccaneer Edward Mansveldt and later, in 1670, by Henry Morgan, who used it as the springboard from which to launch his infamous attack on Panama.[5] Morgan took everybody off the island, destroyed eight of the nine forts, and threw the guns into the sea. Though he apparently expressed a desire to return to the island, there is no evidence that he ever did so.

When two Spanish vessels inspected the island in 1688 they found "no evidence of recent habitation. Curious soldiers who searched the ruins of the old Spanish fortress of Santa Theresa found a few rusted twelve pounders, about the only relics of former occupations which had survived" (Rowland 1935 : 312). No attempt to colonize or garrison the island seems to have been made for the next one hundred years. Rowland cautiously suggests that it may have served "as a haven for an occasional pirate vessel or as a refuge for escaped slaves" (ibid, p. 313). Another writer is of the firm opinion, however, that many persons now living on the island may be descendants of buccaneers or escaped slaves (Eder 1913).

The resettlement of Providence began in 1787 or 1788 when Francis Archbold, the Scottish captain of a slaving ship trading between West Africa and Jamaica, received permission of the Spanish government in Cartagena to settle there as a planter (Parsons 1956 : 18). In 1790 the population of the island was reported to consist of ten people of both sexes and twelve negroes, all living on the small adjunct island of Santa Catalina (Sanz : 1808). In 1793, Don José del Rio mentions that there were four families living there: Francis Archbold, the wealthiest and the only Catholic, Juan John, Andrés Brown, and José Hygges, who were Protestants. There were thirty-two people in these four families and they were served by twenty-one slaves of both sexes described as negro and mulatto (Peralta 1890 : 138). Peralta notes that boats from Jamaica called frequently to take off cotton and timber. Fish, turtle, and conch pearls "the size of chick peas" were also sold to these Jamaican traders—some of whom may well have settled on the island. Don José was impressed with the excellent timber that covered the hillsides and much regretted its export to Jamaica. He remarks on the fertility of the soil, expresses his pleasure and relief at the absence of poisonous animals and the presence of certain unique medicinal herbs, particularly "rata" and "Chinese root." His only recommendation was that a Spanish flag be sent to the island (Peralta 1890 : 138). By 1813 the population had reached three hundred, of whom many were planters from other Caribbean islands, principally Jamaica.

Suddenly in 1818 the placid pastoral tranquillity that so impressed Don José was shattered, and for a while it looked as if the good old days of swashbuckling mayhem had returned. Luis Aury, a French soldier of fortune, landed on the island with his private army of eight hundred men and a fleet of fourteen vessels. He had decided to give up piracy temporarily and give Simón Bolívar a hand liberating Spanish colonies. Bolívar disdained help from such riffraff, and Aury waited in vain for the call to an honorable place in history. While waiting he kept his men up to scratch by raiding the coast of Central America and plundering shipping in the western Caribbean. He rebuilt the island's former chief fortress on Santa Catalina and lived in some style in St. Isabel. What in great men appears as tragedy in little men seems farce—Luis Aury fell off his horse and died soon afterward, thus bringing to a close his three-year "reign" on Providence (Faye 1941). Though we cannot know for certain, it is reasonable to suppose that some of Aury's men settled down on Providence after the death of their leader and the disbanding of his force.

As the strategic importance of Providencia receded, historians consigned the island to obscurity. Only one informative account survives, dating from 1835, of life and events during the nineteenth century. Meanwhile, the nearby island of San Andrés assumed economic importance as a major supplier of coconuts to the United States, rising as a consequence from historical obscurity to prominence.

In 1835 the population of Providence was given as 342, "about half" of whom were slaves. These were used to cultivate cotton, of which about 30,000 pounds was exported annually along with 170 pounds of turtle shell. The cotton and turtle shell were exchanged with Jamaican traders for calicoes and other cloth, but "the exorbitant prices of these cause the

island purchasers to incur a debt which the next year's produce
serves to liquidate" (Collett 1837 : 206). Some other crops
mentioned in this account are sugar cane and coffee, which
were not exported; yams; cocos; plantain and pumpkin, which
sold for six shillings a hundredweight; fruits of various kinds
including mangoes, sapodilla, oranges, limes, tamarinds, and
plums. Bullocks weighing from four to five hundredweight
sold for three to four pounds sterling apiece; pork was four-
pence halfpenny per pound; fowls, in abundance, were twelve
shillings a dozen, and turkeys were four to six shillings apiece.
Wild pigeon, hicatee or land turtle, and iguanas were abun-
dant and good eating, while fish "peculiar to these latitudes
abound in profusion on the banks." [6] Collett makes note of
the fine horses which, though rather small, could be purchased
at three to four pounds a head. There were also a few donkeys
on the island. Wood for fuel and boat-building was plentiful
and included mangrove, calabash, grape, and goatwood; the
cedars were said to square twenty to twenty-four inches and
ironwood was seen on the promontory known today as Ironwood Hill. St. Isabel, so named by Aury when it was a "flour-
ishing and populous place" now comprised only eight or nine
huts. Several houses and plantations were scattered around
the island, being accessible by a "sort of road which passed
around the island." There was no church, so marriages were
contracted by a civil ceremony and by "bargain"—by which
Collett may mean consensual union. "However, though there
is no church the people cease labour on Sunday and pay es-
pecial attention to external appearance" (ibid.).

From this time until the present day there is only incidental
information such as can be gleaned from private documents.
The signatures on the proclamation of adherence to Colombia,
dated 1822, include some of the names found on the island
today (Parsons 1956 : 59). A bill of sale for two slaves, dated
1833, shows that the slaves were purchased from Jamaica, and
a second document dating from 1846 specifies that these same
two slaves are to be freed "as soon as my affairs on the island
are fairly settled, and that my executrix and executors will give
both of them a piece of land at Rock Ground, or anywhere

they may think proper to give them to work on, for their life time only." This same will directs that land be divided equally among the children and that what money is left over after all debts have been paid be also shared equally. Movable property, though, is not so divided:

> All my bed furniture I leave to my daughters, I leave all my wearing apparel to my male children. I give to Sarah Ann my diamond ring. I leave my son Andrew my young horse named Dandyprat and a young cow. I leave them all the rest of my animals equally to Mrs. Archbold and all my children. I leave my son James my writing desk, dressing case, blue coat and my large pair of pistols. I have a large silver cross studded with glass, the same I was given by my father, I now leave it to my son James to remember his grandfather and myself.[7]

Other possessions disposed of include a saddle, musket, pocket pistols, fowling piece, compass, large cedar chest, blue chest, a second smaller blue chest, a mahogany chest, three large iron pots, and brooches.

At least we learn from this will something of the inventory of a wealthy household at that time, and with some imagination we can picture some favorite pursuits—such as hunting and riding. An interesting codicil to this will orders that the deceased's illegitimate daughter Amelia be given a young heifer and that a small tract of land be bought for her. The equal inheritance of land by all siblings is the custom today, as is the differentiation between full and half siblings, implicit in the will's discrimination of the illegitimate daughter Amelia.

Another will, dating from 1852, indicates that slavery was still a part of island life and that by this time coconuts had been introduced to the island. The signatures on this particular will, both officials and witnesses, indicate that ancestors of today's prominent families were already settled. These names include Archbold, McKellar, Livingston, Britton, Newball, Howard, Robinson, Barker, and Bowden.

From these wills we can see that slaves could own land. Possibly this land was given to them as provision ground where they could raise their own produce. Another document, a deed of transfer dated 1842, describes a gift of land made to "our loving friend, Francis Archbold" by eight Livingstons who signed by their name with a mark and who indicate that the land was given to them originally by their master and mistress Philip and Mary Livingston of Scots Hull, Jamaica. This same document also indicates that land was measured for allotment from shore to summit, as it is today.

All of these documents are in English, even though Providencia was a part of Spanish-speaking Colombia. A number of official documents have a note in the margin to the effect that legal stamped paper was not available, but that the stamp duty had been paid. The currency most frequently mentioned is New Granada dollars, but sterling was also kept, perhaps because it was the more easily negotiable in the trade with Jamaica. Many local transactions appear to have been made by barter, and bartering is recalled by a number of older contemporary islanders as being typical of their youth: "a bag o' plantain for a bag of yam."

Slavery was abolished officially in 1853, although, as is evident from the documents quoted above, slaves were freed by individual masters before then. Abolition coincides more or less with the establishment of the first organized church. The Baptist church was established in 1847 on San Andrés and it is likely that the one on Providencia was not far behind. Church officials on the island, however, claim that William J. Davidson was the first to set up a church on Providence, and that he came direct to the island from Scotland. The Catholic church does not seem to have been formally established on the island until the turn of the present century, though by 1911 there were reported to be 360 Catholics. In 1905 a Seventh-day Adventist missionary boat called and the missionaries succeeded in converting a few islanders who, in turn, converted others. The island's first convert is still alive—and zealous as ever.

The political status of the island has changed a number of times since 1822, when it fell, more or less by default, under the jurisdiction of the liberated Republic of New Granada, which later became Colombia. Under the Constitution of Cu-

cutá, the islands of Providencia, San Andrés, and Corn became the sixth canton of the province of Cartagena. From 1822 to 1869 the islands enjoyed the benefits of total neglect. In 1869 a delegation from the islands protested their position and convinced the central government in Bogotá to administer them directly. The islands were now known as the Territory of San Andrés y San Luis de Providencia, the Corn Islands having been passed over to Nicaragua. In 1888 the islands again came under the administration of Cartagena, which again chose to forget they ever existed; and once more, complaints made to the central government resulted in a change of status. In 1912 the islands were designated the Intendencia of San Andrés y Providencia, led by an *intendente* appointed by the president of the republic and responsible to the Ministry of Territories. San Andrés and Providencia still enjoy the status of an *intendencia,* and Providencia is a *municipio* within this, headed by an *alcalde.* The position of alcalde has never been one enthusiastically sought after: Providencia is too "foreign" for mainlanders, and islanders are a little too aware of the ambiguity of the office. For many years the post was rotated annually among the few qualified islanders, and it is only recently, in fact with the present alcalde, that the island has produced a civil servant willing to serve. Day-to-day affairs are conducted in English, although proclamations and other official communications are in Spanish. The municipal budget provides for an interpreter, though today most officials coming from the island are fluent in Spanish.

The vagaries of Providencia's political standing are indicative of the more than physical isolation and neglect imposed by the mainland. Politically, socially, culturally, and even economically it has been left to find its own way. Consequently it has staunchly, one might almost say defiantly, upheld its Jamaican English language and culture while asserting disdain for Spaniards (*panyas* or *pays*) and matters Spanish. Only since the early 1960s, when Colombia's own political situation seemed at last to be settling in an upright position, has there been any sign of mutual recognition between island and mainland —accompanied by promises to Hispanicize in return for promises to allot funds to modernize.

In the earlier part of this century the Anglo-American ori-
entation of islanders was strengthened by the construction of
the Panama Canal, for, living quite close and speaking English,
islanders could easily get jobs. The availability of these jobs
began the era of cash economy on Providence, and they have
been continuously available until the present time. Close ties
still exist between Panama and the islands (there is a Pan-
amanian consulate on San Andrés) and many islanders have
made their homes in the "Zone" but keep in touch by returning to the island for visits. The beginning of the canal seems
to have coincided with the attainment of what might be considered an optimum population size of two thousand on
Providencia, thus siphoning off a surplus and preventing over-
crowding.

Such, then, is what might be called the "observer's history"
of Providencia. In general terms it echoes, albeit on a smaller
scale, the pattern of settlement and vicissitudes of growth of
other Caribbean islands. True, there was no plantation economy serving a rapacious metropolis; but the disdain of the
mainland for the island, accompanied by neglect, in the full
knowledge that all power was in its hands, led to the sort of
frustration and reaction that characterized the experience of
other Caribbean colonies. Without the economic exploitation
suffered by these societies, the only difference between them
and Providencia was the degree of outrage felt against the
mighty motherland.

There are other parallels, less political and more social.
The original population was ethnically heterogeneous and hier-
archically structured: white "British" planters, mulattoes, and
Negro slaves. On Providencia, relations between master and
slaves seem always to have been fairly amicable, unlike San
Andrés, where there was a slave revolt in 1799. On emancipation, slaves were given the entire, very fertile southwest-
ern portion of the island, an area that had comprised the estates of the Livingston, Archbold, and Davidson families. This
is the part of the island where the villages of Bottom House
and Southwest Bay, with their predominantly "black" population, are located, thus preserving in gross form that original

hierarchy. When the estates were divided, each slave received a given amount of land which was parceled in strips running from shore to summit. This striped pattern is evident today in aerial photographs.[8]

Racial, religious, and social differentiation has been a characteristic of social organization ever since Providencia was settled. We can infer from the will of James Archbold, quoted above, that his life style was probably quite different from that of his slaves; and although we have no basis for speculating further about such matters as values and mores, the picture of a basic social pattern to island life is sufficiently clear to suggest, when compared with our account of present social patterns, that the past is indeed encapsulated in the present.

OLD PROVIDENCE ISLAND: AN ETHNOHISTORY

Our second history of Providence is told by no one in particular, but one can hear it, in part or in toto, from virtually any islander. There are one or two men, highly educated and professional people, who will recount a history closer to our first history. But as they readily admit, their chief source is James Parsons's book. In any case, these men live in Bogotá. The second history is a composite put together from accounts offered at different times by different people, though usually in public on such occasions as wakes or rum shop expatiations. I have not included "private" accounts, although these tallied, simply because they could not be spontaneously confirmed. The second version covers all the themes that concern people in their history. As may be seen, it is very much an ideological history, showing a concern for what islanders perceive to be their major problems in relation to their past as an environment: their origin, their racial heterogeneity and its social implications, and their isolated and anomalous political position, from which stems their ambiguous cultural status. I see it as a positive history, as all ideological histories are, affirming the present with validation from the past.

Providence people are descended from Henry Morgan and his sailors. Henry Morgan was an Englishman and a famous sailor and a pirate. Everyone was afraid of him and he was not afraid of anyone. Henry Morgan's chief mate was a man called Berelski, a Pole. When Morgan left the island to attack Panama, this Berelski jumped overboard and swam back to the island. He changed his name to Robinson, and the Robinsons are now an important family on the island. Hawkins was also one of Morgan's captains and the Hawkins family is also descended from this Hawkins.

Morgan used the island as his headquarters for raiding ships and for attacking Panama. After he attacked Panama he returned to the island and buried some of the treasure that he had taken so that he would not have to give it to the king. He buried it at Morgan Fort, which he built to defend the island against the Spaniards. After burying the treasure he sailed for England. He always intended to come back to Providence because he loved it so much and because he wanted to collect the treasure he left buried. He left behind some sailors to guard the gold and he also buried a slave with it so that the gold became enchanted. Morgan also had a mistress, who was very beautiful with red hair, and she stayed behind as well with Morgan's son. That's another reason why he wanted to come back.

The people are descended from Morgan and his crew. There is still treasure buried on the island but it is guarded by spirits, it is "enchanted" and so no one has dared to look for it, and for sure no one has found it. These spirits are too strong even for the government soldiers that came to look for it.

These people who were Morgan's crew and who lived on the island had slaves to work for them, and the slaves were black. The slaves took the names of their masters and that is how it is you find people with different skin have the same name. Also, naturally, these white men had babies with the black women and that is how you come to get the mixture, the mulatto.

All the people here on this island are Englishmen. They speak English, except it is not correct English, but they are not Spanish, and they do not act the same way as the pays [Spaniards]. We are English because we are descended from Henry Morgan. All the people here are good sailors—the best sailors in Colombia. That is why the government wants only people from Providencia in their navy. We are good sailors because Henry Morgan was the best sailor that ever lived.

Of course, there are some families not descended from Morgan and his crew and that is because they came from the Cayman Islands and the Cayman Brac not so long ago.

When Morgan died, the King of England promised to look after the island. Then, when Colombia was free from Spain after fighting, Queen Victoria gave the island to the country as a freedom gift. But she said you must treat the people fair and look after them, else we shall take it back. Now it is certain that the pays have not treated us fair and it is time for England to take us back.

At least one islander, with the backing of others, had sent a letter and petition to King George VI with such a request, and one of the many speculations as to my own presence was that I was a spy from Scotland Yard come to check up on the facts preparatory to reclamation of the island by Her Majesty's Government. When I was cast in this role, fieldwork went splendidly; but I was also suspected of being an agent whose mission was to prepare the way for the reinstatement of slavery —which was rather less helpful!

This history is usually amplified with lurid accounts of Henry Morgan's swashbuckling deeds, tender anecdotes of his love life, and adulation of his ability as a sailor. Islanders generate hypotheses concerning the whereabouts of the treasure with as much facility as an anthropologist accounting for "culture change"—and about as scientifically. These and similar tales are recounted at wakes, weddings, dances, and in rum shops —whenever people congregate for good company, and become "learnedly introspective."

As just a glancing comparison of the two histories will reveal, the second history, even given its romantic and ideological bias, contains some rather ornate elaborations and some surprising omissions. Morgan, who probably spent no more than a week there and, for all we can tell, never really left anything behind, is given center stage, while Luis Aury, a real rascal who spent three years on the island comparatively recently. is never mentioned. What is more, there is every likelihood that Aury and his men, riffraff recruited from Europe, New

Orleans, Haiti, Jamaica, and St. Thomas, did leave behind some progeny. It is most unlikely that any offspring of Morgan or his crew could have engendered the present population.

A comparison of these two characters, hero and antihero, reveals the ideological message of the history. Islanders could only have become acquainted with Morgan, directly or indirectly, from books; but clearly they prefer their own version of the story. Of the two figures, of course, Morgan is the more illustrious; and if honor and reputation are qualities for a "founding ancestor," Morgan has all and Aury nothing. Morgan is first and foremost an "Englishman," and more than that, an Englishman who walloped the Spaniards. Who else but an Englishman could be an ancestor of the islanders? Certainly not a Frenchman such as Aury. Then, Morgan was a sailor par excellence, and are not Providence people the finest sailors in the Caribbean, if not the New World? Aury gave no evidence of his sailing prowess and considered himself a soldier. Who on the island is proud of soldiers?

Morgan does not seem ever to have died. What happened to him after burying the treasure on Providence is left completely up in the air. Aury died most unheroically as a result of a fall from his horse, which is certainly no way for an ancestor to go. Though Aury plundered for booty, and the few gold coins that have been found postdate Morgan's time, Aury is not known to have carried off a spectacular treasure or to have pulled off an operation comparable to Morgan's sacking of Panama. In short, Morgan exemplifies in mythical proportions the qualities that islanders, the men at least, would like to see in themselves. He is certainly more consonant with their present situation and characteristics than Aury, even though the latter is "historically" a truer figure with respect to the island.

The ruins known as Morgan Fort were in all probability never used by Morgan. They stand where the original Warwick Fort was built by the Puritans. This became the Spanish Fort St. Theresa rebuilt by Aury during his stay. The site is impressive: it commands the harbor and its approaches and today, in addition to its ruins, it is marked by a large statue of the Virgin and a flagpole. All national and island celebrations begin with an observance at this site, which takes on many of the attributes of a "sacred place"—adding credence to the notion that Morgan is a sort of founding ancestor. Not surprisingly, the "treasure" is buried beneath Morgan Fort.

The two histories of Providencia clearly show a sense of selective adaptation—the first to a sense of temporal order and idea of social structure, the second to a contemporary environment calling for particular moral generalizations. Each emphasizes in its own way themes that help point a contemporary observer in certain directions and not others. If geography has made Providencia an island, history has given it insularity. Its people display a fierce sense of independence and of their own unique identity. Whether this is because they are descended from Morgan or because they have had to fend for themselves does not matter. Each history points in the same way.

In this independence and insularity Providencia resembles other Caribbean islands. For example, a recent writer surveying the Caribbean scene refers to the "notorious insular prejudices still characteristic of West Indian communal psychology" (G. Lewis 1968). For Providencia we can pin down some particular causes, but we must also investigate specifically the sustaining bases of this independence and insularity. By so doing we will, I hope, not only come to understand the particular instance of Providencia but be able to suggest, by analogy, a foundation for a more general understanding of the Caribbean.

All island peoples, having a clear view of their physical boundaries, can be said to manifest what to mainlanders appear as nonconformist traits: the British, on their sceptered isle, are stubborn and incomprehensible to their European peers, for example. It seems as if certain generalizations about insularity are attributable not to idiosyncrasies of history or quirks of morals but to the physical fact of living on an island. The island not only provides and defines but also serves as the symbol of the qualities it generates. It takes on pragmatic and emotional values in the beliefs of islanders.

3 Living on the Land

In a short but sensitive article the geographer David Lowenthal observes that in the Caribbean "land is seldom mentioned (save by tourists) except as a commodity" (1961 : 1). Having explained why this is so, he then shows by a judicious and wide-ranging selection of examples that in fact the people of the Caribbean value land in a "philosophical" and "sentimental" sense: land connotes freedom, a deeply felt attachment, security against economic vicissitudes, community solidarity, and individual prestige (ibid., pp. 4–5). "Caribbean land and Caribbean people," he concludes, "belong to each other more than at any time for centuries past" (ibid., p. 5). In chapters 3 and 4 I shall explore and analyze in detail this twofold relationship of man to land—the sentimental or philosophical relation and the economic relation. Such an exploration is fundamental to any understanding of Caribbean social life.

SENTIMENTS

The Sudanic Nuer, who from a European point of view live in a land with no favorable qualities, retain an unshakable conviction that they live in the finest country on earth (Evans-Pritchard 1940 : 51). The people of Providencia have the same opinion of their island, but happily a European's credulity and comfort are not as strained as they must be in Nuerland. By anyone's standards, except possibly those of the Nuer, Providencia must be accounted utterly beautiful. Islanders are appreciative not only of the scenic beauty of their land, but also of the fertility that supplies them with an abundance of fruits, vegetables, meat, and poultry, to which must be added the bounty of the sea.

Affectionately called the Rock, the island is personified in any number of ways: it is peaceful, moody, *tranquillo,* reposeful, vexing; it possesses its own spirit and it harbors the spirits of those who have lived and died there—"duppies." The quirks of its topography are recognized in the local names bestowed by people, which may also commemorate persons and events of bygone days. A complete list of place names would fill a chapter, but a sample of the most colorful might include Far-enough, Big Well, Kitty Wharf, Joe Hole, Pull-and-be-damned Point, Morgan Head, Durkin, Bum Hill, Touchmenot, Spring, Rock-for-Nothing, Loma Frijoles, Wormwood Valley, Swamp, Goat Hill, Nancy Clark, Bat Yard, Provision Ground, Mara-caibo, Dispute, Bunchee, Black Bay, Coffee Piece, Content, Plantation, and Horse Pen.

When men gather together, especially if an outsider is pres-ent, the talk invariably encompasses reference to land. Within any group there is claim and counterclaim—who owns most pieces, whose land has been longest in the same family line, whose land is of better quality, whose land is better worked, which parts of the island produce better crops, where the sweetest mangoes come from. Nor is it an exaggeration to say that every islander is thoroughly familiar with nearly every rise, fall, and twist of the landscape, with every clump, outcrop, spring, hole, ditch and hummock, tree and bush, if not over the whole island, then certainly in those parts of it where he lives and gardens. A man glows with pride and waxes eloquent when he has occasion to speak of his plots of land and their crops: "My yuccas are soft, my yams delicious, my oranges vitamise and strengthen. My pumpkins are large, for my seeds fall on good ground. My melons delight your eye for they become beautiful red—their colors are green on the outside."

In their eulogizing over the island, islanders implicitly and often explicitly have in mind another part of the world for com-parison, for all of them have been abroad at one time or another. Most often the comparison is with nearby San Andrés, which is flat and relatively infertile and now, with tourism and free trade, compares most unfavorably with the tranquillity of Providencia. A comparison of islands is also an implicit com-parison of people, so that the superiority of Providencia is also a claim for the superiority of its people. Living on and owning part of Providencia is what makes a person different from every-one else and at the same time identifies those who are like one-self. To own a piece of land is regarded as a birthright, particu-larly for a man. It ensures a source of livelihood and acceptance by a community—a place to lay one's head in peace. When living overseas, where he does not belong and where he is often not accepted, this knowledge that he owns a piece of land on Providencia is perhaps the single most important factor in the preservation of a man's identity.

That land is the most signal factor in confirming identity as an islander, as one who is like oneself, is confirmed by recognition that the most meaningful gesture of acceptance of an outsider is the proferring of a piece of land as a gift or for sale. This is generally no more than a gesture, for the outsider is not expected to accept unless he fully intends to settle down on the island. So, in fact, there are very few "outsiders" living on Providencia and even fewer who own land. The recent moves by one or two wealthy islanders to sell land to outsiders for speculation or commercial development met with considerable resentment and opposition by the majority. They succeeded in persuading the principal landowner to withdraw from his negotiations. The arguments advanced in public were that such sales would stop islanders from having access to their own land and that foreigners (notably panyas or Colombians) were too different from islanders. It is not without significance in this respect that certain families who came to Providencia at the turn of the present century from the Cayman Islands are still identified as Caymanians as frequently as they are acknowledged to be islanders.

The outsider, be he San Andrésano, Colombian, or American, is the "being-that-one-is-not." What one is, viz. Providencian, is expressed positively through identification with all those like oneself who own or have the right to own land and hence the island. For, in a sense, to own land on Providence is to own the whole island. "Providence is mine" is the ever-echoed sentiment. And if the land belongs to the man, then the man belongs to the land. These sentiments are reexpressed in the idea that everyone who is an islander is an equal. All islanders are equal, all islanders through common possession of their island belong together. They have, to use a well-worn sociological phrase, social solidarity.

This affirmation of equality is made constantly in the course of daily interaction. It is loudly protested to the visitor that "we is all equal" or "we is all one family"; and as we shall see later in this study, it is a principle invoked in situations where the parties are blatantly unequal. However skeptical the outsider might be of the equality of islanders, such a sentiment is a positive force whenever that outsider confronts the island. It is a principle not so much of structure as of sentiment, or, to use Turner's term, *communitas* (Turner 1969 : 127). The question is, then, how far such sentiments may be said to be "grounded" in the facts of land ownership and use, since land is the means through which equality and solidarity are claimed.

THE STRUCTURE OF SENTIMENT

Association

Table 3, outlining the general pattern of land ownership on the island, reveals some interesting features. Of a total of 605

TABLE 3. Land Ownership *

Acreage		Male	Female
0–1		99	53
2–5		178	67
6–10		73	33
	Subtotals	350 (77%)	153 (87%)
11–20		52	18
21–30		18	2
31–40		5	–
41–50		3	–
51–100		1	–
100+		2	1
	Totals	431	174

Total Registered Landowners = 605

* Based on the land register and my own survey and therefore only approximate. This table does not include all absentee landowners.

registered landowners, 431 (71 percent) are male and 174 (29 percent) are female. Land ownership, it is fair to say, is primarily a male matter. These figures refer to a total adult population of 455 men and 597 women, meaning that almost 95 percent of adult men but only 29 percent of adult women own land. Though fewer women own land, the percentage is great enough to suggest that they may well have equal rights to ownership but less opportunity. This matter will be taken up later. What concerns us immediately is the subtotals given in the table, which indicate that 83 percent of all landowners have less than ten acres, and 65 percent own less than five acres. Most people do not own much land, and the majority of the population differ little from each other in the amount of land they own. Most of them do not own enough land to permit them to "take off" to a better economic status. It is a fact that most adult men own land, but not enough, and that they equal each other in the amount owned. There is, then, a material foundation for the sentimental claim of the equality of all islanders through their common interest in land.

This sense of equality and cohesion is further enhanced and supported by recognition of the continuity of association between men and their land. Different parts of the land have remained attached to the same families over a number of generations, thus providing a basic pattern of settlement throughout the island. Each of the fourteen communities is dominated by one or two surnames or "titles." Thus the people of St. Isabel are predominantly Howard, Free Town is mostly Barker (who also live in Old Town, which, however, is overwhelmingly composed of Hawkins, Dawkins, and Sjogreen). Most of the people of Lazy Hill are either Watler, Bush, or Robinson, and all the island's Huffingtons live in Freshwater Bay. Virtually every one in Bottom House is a Livingston or a Henry, while in Rocky Point the Brittons, Bryans, and Hookers predominate. The Taylors are concentrated in Bailey and the Archbolds and Newballs in Smoothwater Bay and Jones Point. Since they are numerically dominant, the Archbolds and Newballs, like the Robinsons, are found living throughout the island. Not only are these names clustered within communities, but they are also associated with cultivable lands in contiguous areas.

This present-day pattern of concentration is but the continuation of the pattern of association begun in the time of Captain Francis Archbold's settlement in 1788. A reconstruction of the division of the island amongst the major estate-holding families at about 1830–50 (see fig. 3) shows how closely the

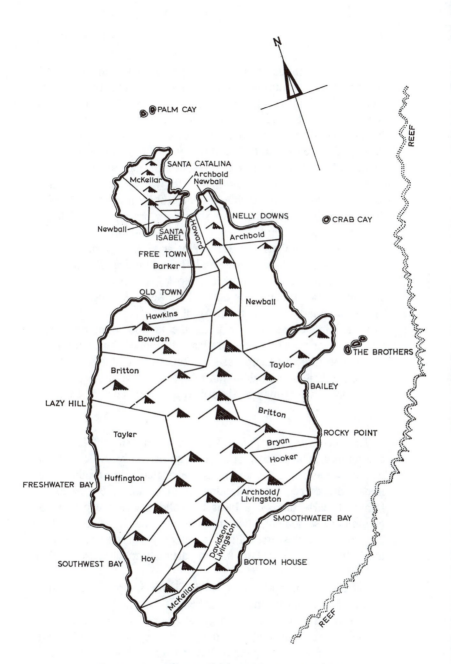

Fig. 3. Approximate division of land ca. 1830–1850.

contemporary model has held to the original, which in turn
testifies to the continuity of association, the effectiveness and
steadiness of ideas of inheritance, and the fact that other
forms of land transfer have remained more or less within the
boundaries of the prototype. The major differences between the
pattern depicted in figure 3 and today are: the Davidson, Archbold, and McKellar estates in the southern portion of the island
were given over to the slaves, most of whom bore the names
Henry, Livingston, or Archbold. The Robinson and the Rankin
families, neither of whom are shown as present in 1830, acquired extensive lands throughout the island after 1900, and
the Britton estate around Lazy Hill has been partly divided
among the newcomer Watler and Bush families. Bowden and
McKellar are names that have almost become extinct; at the
time of fieldwork there was one old McKellar spinster, and one
old Bowden lady married to an Archbold.

Remaining constant over time, the identification of people
with land has thereby gained a sense of sanction. But underlying
and supporting this temporal sanction is a set of attitudes and
habits characteristic of this kind of spatial association, an entire
social process that may be described as the system of tenure.

Tenure

The sketch map in figure 4 shows the division of land in a
community. The striped pattern is immediately evident. Most
of the owners are male, and most are related to each other. The
houses are owned by the landowner or a close member of his
family. Clearly there is a basis for solidarity in the pattern of
community settlement where most of the land is owned by kin.
The nature of this association is not only sentimental but also
legal, thence formal. This has important implications which I
will consider below.

Let us look next at garden land. Figure 5 shows the division
of a lower hill slope among members of four families. The area
shown amounts to about twenty acres and is homogeneous in
the sense that it is surrounded by relatively uncultivable land.
The owners cannot expand beyond their boundaries. It is
claimed that members of these families have been gardening
neighbors for many generations, and every effort is made to

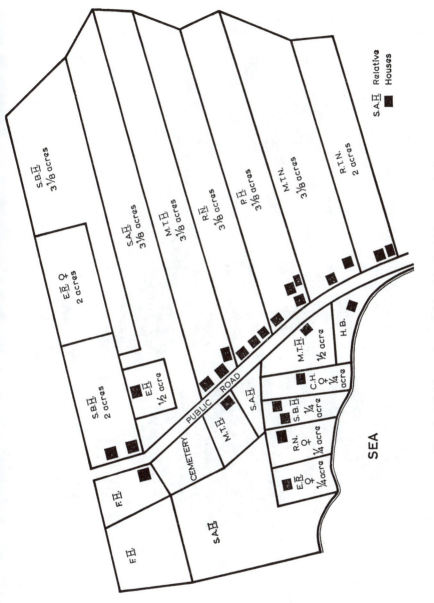

Fig. 4. Division and ownership of land within a community.

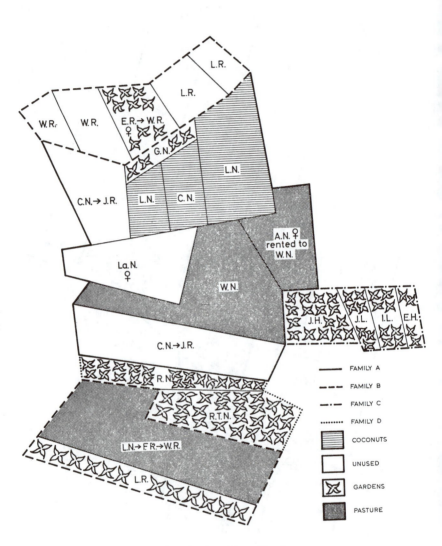

Fig. 5. Partition of land.

preserve this unity. When *AN,* for instance, wanted to rent her land, there was considerable pressure put upon her to rent to one of her neighbors. They in turn put pressure on *WN,* the wealthiest among them, to rent the piece.

Finally, the sketch map in figure 6 shows the arrangement of gardens in terms of crops grown. Here again, among neighbors there is a certain amount of cooperation and synchronization that leads to a sentiment of harmony. Neighbors attempt to plan their gardening so that, for example, an entire hillside may be burned at the same time. They try to plant sugar cane so that it will be ready at the same time, thereby allowing the millowner to come and grind all the cane grown in one area. Generally speaking, only those with relatively large plots of land plant one crop. The usual custom is to mix crops.

Thus the sentiment of solidarity is principally the product of continued association of kinsmen with land. Having described the features of this association as they have evolved through time and as they operate in a particular place, we must consider a third set of factors: the practices that govern this association, or the practices of inheritance.

Inheritance

Superficially the ideal of inheritance—the equal inheritance of land by all full siblings—appears conducive to an egalitarian ethos. But the assumption of equality in inheritance is challenged by the jealousies and rivalries of heirs so that it is with inheritance that the ideal of solidarity and equality begins to crack.

Most islanders die intestate. Many, however, leave behind a grubby piece of paper on which they have stated their desire concerning the division of their property, and this "will" is followed as nearly as possible by those responsible for the division of the estate. The custom is for all lands to be divided equally among a man's children, and this task is carried out by one of the two "surveyors" on the island—Mr. Alpheus Archbold, Baptist minister at Smoothwater Bay and the recognized authority, and Captain Sheridan Archbold.

All sorts of difficulties attend this division. There is no question about a man's children by the woman he was married to,

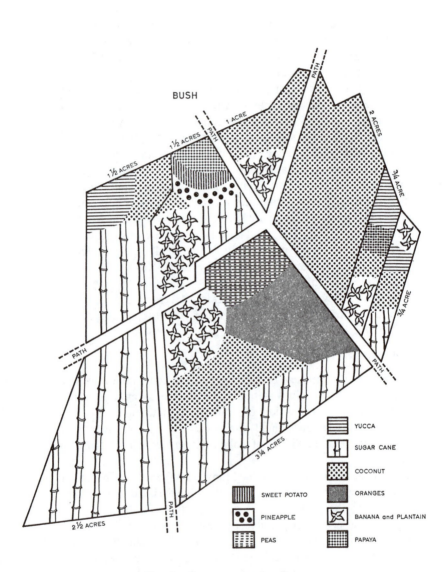

BUSH

1½ ACRES

1½ ACRES

1 ACRE

2 ACRES

¾ ACRE

¾ ACRE

PATH

PATH

PATH

PATH

PATH

PATH

3¾ ACRES

2½ ACRES

	YUCCA
	SUGAR CANE
	COCONUT
	ORANGES
	SWEET POTATO
	BANANA and PLANTAIN
	PINEAPPLE
	PAPAYA
	PEAS

Fig. 6. Arrangement of gardens.

but there is always a problem concerning the rights of a man's children by other women, particularly those born before he was married and those "outside" children born while he was married but to a woman other than his wife. His proper children are entitled to equal shares, and the claims of other children are customarily left to be recognized only if they come forward, in which case they are accorded one half-share, provided the full heirs consent. This was nowhere stated as a rule and is simply my own generalization from a few observed cases.

If there is a widow the land is left undivided and in her trust until she dies. Sooner or later, though, the task of division must take place. Mr. 'Pheus tramps over the land with his instruments and collects whatever documents, such as ground plans, exist. In making the division among the heirs he must take into account not only the quantity of land but the quality, topography, and siting. He usually has to argue with each of the heirs in turn to convince them that what he assigned as their share is right and proper under the circumstances. In their turn the heirs argue among themselves. Eventually—and the process often takes up to five years—the land is divided. The heirs frequently try to buy and sell parcels of their inheritance, usually to prevent excessive fragmentation. Especially do brothers try to buy out their sisters, and this common practice is the main reason why fewer women than men own land. Some women, though, enjoy owning and buying land and there is nothing in island law or custom that prevents them from so doing.

Those who die intestate generally do not own large amounts of land. Those with sizable plots make every effort to draw up a legal will and to secure legal title to their lands. Dividing the estate is a tortuous and heart-searching procedure that begins more or less as soon as a man's sons are grown up. Mr. Randall, for example, a retired schoolmaster, owned about forty-five acres of land. He had two grown-up sons, one of whom had failed in business, while the other had failed at school. His two daughters were married and living in Venezuela and Japan. He had decided to divide the land equally among all four children, but the daughters had written back that they wanted their share to go to their orphaned nephews and nieces—children of the fifth but deceased son of Mr. Randall.

For ten years or more, Mr. Randall, then about seventy-three and crippled with arthritis, had been poring over the deeds and maps of his land trying to divide it up. From time to time he called in one son and, showing him his latest plan, asked him what he thought. Each son, being jealous of the other, constantly tried to change the will to his advantage, and as far as I know a final decision was not reached—nor would be until Mr. Randall died, when the will would stand as it was last altered. Even then, Mr. 'Pheus would have to make the actual measurements and there would still be time for disagreements!

It is often the case that a man will make special provision before his death for his "outside" children, particularly his sons. Usually he provides them with a house site, or money to buy one, on the understanding that this will offset any claims the child might think of levying against his estate and heirs. A similar sense of obligation toward daughters does not appear to be so evident.

FAMILY LAND

The continuity of the relationship between kinsmen and land is more deliberately expressed in the idea and reality of family land. This category of land has been found elsewhere in the Caribbean: it is described in most detail by Edith Clarke in her examination of Jamaican land tenure (Clarke 1957), but it has also been noted in other, widely separated islands such as Andros in the Bahamas (Otterbein 1966b) and Carriacou in the Grenadines (M. G. Smith 1962b). It is quite likely that, on Providencia at least, the pattern of family land originated in Jamaica, since that is where the early settlers came from.

In Jamaica, family land is inherited land, as distinct from "bought" land, and it particularly involves land granted originally to the emancipated slaves (Clark 1957 : 36). This is not the case on Providencia. Here most of the "family land" is located in the interior of the island, which, during the time of the original estates, was left unclaimed, and still is regarded, in parts at least, as "empty" land. In both societies the land in question is land that has been cleared or staked out by an ancestor and explicitly designated by him as being for the exclusive use of his descendants, male or female, full or outside. Anyone can so designate his land—it does not have to be a long-dead ancestor. Such land is no longer subject to the dividing process described above. It remains forever undivided and available for the use of descendants.

Should a man wish to cultivate family land he informs the co-owners. As soon as he has harvested his crop the land he used goes back into the pool. He may neither sell nor rent any portion of family land, except with the consent of all the co-owners, and the sentiment is strong against such a practice. Even so, when many of the owners are living half a world away, it is difficult to get consent or even to consult on matters of family land. There have been one or two cases known to me personally where a man simply fenced off a portion of family land and sold it as if it were his own. Also, because there is always a percentage of people living away from the island, the actual number actively concerned with family land at any one time is relatively small. Since it is located in the hilly interior it is not entirely suitable for cultivation or even pasture. So family land on Providencia is at best an emergency pool of land where a man, otherwise landless, can affirm his sense of belonging to the island and, if need be, can support himself.

There are other, secondary uses of the term *family land*. Sometimes it denotes land that has been left to be divided but, perhaps because the widow is acting as trustee, must remain integral for a while. It also applies to all the lands left by a man until they are divided. The same rules apply, however: an heir may cultivate any part with the approval of his co-heirs, but when the crop is harvested, it reverts back to family status. This goes on until division.

As noted above, inheritance is an elementary part of the social process where competitive sentiments are mustered; where ideals must sometimes give way before circumstance. People quarrel and spend a lot of time and effort maneuvering for an advantageous position for themselves, especially in respect of land. This sort of behavior is a sufficiently conscious aspect of reality that it has a special name: *crab antics*.

CRAB ANTICS

Crab antics is behavior that resembles that of a number of crabs who, having been placed in a barrel, all try to climb out. But as one nears the top, the one below pulls him down in his own effort to climb. Only a particularly strong crab ever climbs out—the rest, in the long run, remain in the same place.

Thus in spite of the ideal or even the reality of equal inheritance, the way is always open for some to acquire more land than others. This in turn inspires a reaction on the part of those others to stop them. It might be argued that if, as I have maintained above, land is a primary basis of social identity and of belonging to the island, then owning more of the island is indicative of a greater sense of belonging and ownership—a sign of wealth, power, status, and prestige. The connection between land ownership and structural ranking will be considered in detail in chapter 4. But first we must examine, in specific examples, the disagreements, quarrels, and maneuvers that go by the name of crab antics, particularly as these relate to land.

Crab antics manifest themselves in two attitudes toward land that islanders suggest are ingrained: covetousness and contentiousness. Court records seem to bear out this opinion. For the year 1958, the only year for which I was able to obtain figures, the municipal judge and the alcalde adjudicated 114 cases. Forty-seven of these (41 percent) were disputes over land; 34 (29 percent) were over debts, some of which involved land matters; 14 were about breaches of the peace and quarrels, some of which arose over land matters; and the remaining 19 cases may be listed as miscellaneous. The following cases give some idea of the operation of these attitudes of "covetousness" and "contentiousness" and the part they play in crab antics.

Randall and James

Randall and James are cousins—sons of a brother and sister. Both of them are well into their seventies and, incidentally, in the opinion of their respective wives, ought to know better. For more than twenty years they have had nothing good to say of each other, and each takes any and every opportunity to malign the other, to spread a rumor imputing some crudity to the other, or to accuse the other of some misdeed. Of course, most of the island knows all about their relationship and doesn't believe a word either has to say about the other.

Their quarrel dates back to their inheritance of land from their grandfather. According to James, Randall inherited a plot promised to him. Things did not start to get serious, however, until Randall bought a plot of land from James's sister (now deceased)—a plot she had inherited. At least, Randall claims he bought it. James argues that Randall simply moved in one night and fenced in his sister's plot of land, making it his own. Randall usually replies "rubbish and nonsense" and that James is simply an idiot. Then James claimed that Randall, if he did not secretly take over the land, has in fact inherited more than his share of their grandfather's estate while he, James, has less. After many years of this allegation, Randall said, "All right, we'll call Mr. 'Pheus and have him make a measure of the land."

After the measurement, Randall claimed it was he who turned out to have *less* than his share! This only made James become more and more vexed and keep up the quarrel, which Randall says is nonsense. James still claims that Randall has cheated him out of one of the best pieces of land in his grandfather's estate. The quarrel shows no sign of abating and has been taken up by the sons, all of whom are grown up and are jockeying for position in their own claims to inherit land.

Comment. Typically, the details of this case are quite confused and nobody will ever know what really happened—not even the two principals who have by now talked themselves into their own versions. However, this particular case does have a number of features that make it typical. The bitterest and most protracted quarrels usually arise between coheirs, who are inevitably close kin. Such quarrels are commonly between men, and, putting these facts together, one can state that kinship relations between men tend to be limited to their mutual involvement in legal matters, above all, land, and hence confined to a somewhat formal conduct which deteriorates rather more easily into bitterness than it rises into amity. Kinship for men, on Providencia, is not a principle of amity (cf. Fortes 1969, chap. 13). The nub of the problem of land, well illustrated

here, is the difficulty of dividing land equally—which really
means to the complete satisfaction of all the heirs. James, to
put it mildly, was rather peeved that he did not receive the very
piece he most wanted.

Astie and José

Astie and José, two young men of rather colorless personality,
had just begun to settle down with wives in their own households, and so were at the particular point in their lives when
they had to expand their resources. Astie claimed he made an
agreement with José to swap a piece of land for a colt. José
delivered the colt and proceeded to cultivate the land. After
two years he took the horse back, but continued to use the land.
Astie wanted to sue José for the sum of one peso for each day
he had used the land, from the time he claimed their agreement
was broken.

José agreed he had given Astie a horse for the use of a portion of land called Rickett, up on Peak, which land, as it turned
out, did not belong to Astie at all but to his wife. José claimed
he had actually bought the land outright, which he wanted to
do because he already owned some land up there and was trying
to consolidate a sizable plot. However, when José turned over
the horse, Astie had not handed over the title deed. "So,"
claimed José, "I was forced to call back for my horse which
was the payment I give, so you can see, Mr. Judge, that he is
the one who has fail his agreement." José then compounded
matters by going on to say that Astie had actually sold the land
to someone else before he made his agreement with José "so
the whole business is only fraud from the commencement."

Astie reaffirmed that he had received a horse as payment for
six months use of the land. Witnesses were called in, and the
parties agreed to compromise. José agreed to pay Astie seven
pesos for the time he had used the land and he kept his horse.
Astie accepted the payment on behalf of his wife. The judge
rebuked him for misusing his wife's property in this way.

Comment. Again, charge and countercharge only serve to
confuse matters. José was probably trying to pull a fast one at
Astie's expense, and Astie had behaved opportunistically in
taking the horse for use of land that was not his. Astie was in

fact only the common-law husband of his wife and did not have powers of trustee. Though the renting of land is common practice on the island, it is customarily done for short periods covering the growth cycle of the particular crop to be planted. Only pastures are regularly let out on a long-term basis. It is more usual to rent for cash these days, though payment in kind, whether an animal, as here, or a percentage of the crop, is not uncommon.

Relations between José and Astie did not become too strained, for as soon as the case was settled they resumed their friendship while at the same time going their separate ways.

Serasto and the Demon Rum

Serasto is just a born loser. He is a small, gentle man, simpleminded perhaps but always happy and optimistic. Now about forty-five years old, Serasto is addled with rum and averages only an hour or so a week sober. He owns seven small parcels of land, of which he rents out four and from the remainder manages to procure a bare minimum for the support of his wife and five children. He is also trustee for his mother's land while she is living in Panama. One of the pieces owned by his mother was particularly choice and Serasto had been approached about it by a number of people on several occasions. After several years standing steadfast against temptation he finally succumbed and sold the land, for he desperately needed cash to pay debts and buy more rum.

When his uncle, his mother's brother, heard what he had done he made a "denouncement" and tried to stop the sale. Cables went back and forth to Panama, but Serasto's mother did not appear too concerned and gave her consent to the sale. The uncle was furious. He would certainly have liked that piece, and what was more, he could have bought it, though he would probably not have offered Serasto such a good price.

One evening Serasto, hopelessly drunk, came wobbling down the road singing at the top of his voice. His uncle and cousin suddenly jumped him and beat him to the ground. There they left him, bruised and bloody. The attack was seen by several people, one of whom reported it to the alcalde. At the hearing the uncle explained how angry he was at Serasto's action in

selling a piece of land which he, as kin, should have received—
his "daddy had intentioned it" to him, he told the alcalde, but
somehow, when the time came, his sister got it. The alcalde
made them sign a bond of peace not to molest each other, and
he gave Serasto a short sermon on the evils of rum. Duly con-
trite, Serasto agreed wholeheartedly with the alcalde but was
drunk by next morning.

Comment. The strain of kinship and land is again apparent,
this time in the uncle's violent reaction. And had Serasto's
mother not been quite so accommodating to her son, things
might have been worse, for Serasto had certainly abused his
position as trustee. Most islanders will affirm that one should
not appoint kinsmen as trustees because it is too easy for them
to take advantage and too embarrassing to go to court. A
trustee is usually a nonrelative and disinterested party. The
matter of trusteeship is raised again in the next example.

Carlos and Family Land

Carlos was a tall, gangling man who loped rather than walked
and amused everybody with the high-pitched voice that issued
shrilly from his toothless mouth. His string bean appearance
belied a shrewd, and some said mean, character. He, his brothers
and sisters, and some of his cousins all had the right to use of
a large tract of family land in the interior, left to them by their
grandfather. For some years no one had made any use of the
land since the entire family was reasonably well-off. Then
Carlos decided to clear about one-third of the tract and plant
it with fruit trees. Having done so, he left the island for about
ten years and worked in Panama as a clerk in the Canal Zone.
Upon his return to Providencia he surveyed his planting, which
was doing quite well, and decided to fence in the tract and
register the land in his own name as legally his, though what he
had done ran quite counter to island custom. There was nothing
anyone could do about it, though when members of his family
heard about it they were furious. His action was something of a
cause célèbre among islanders, who admired his effrontery but
at the same time disapproved of the act and the precedent it set.

Comment. Taking advantage of the absence of landowners
is a common occurrence, as we see both from the present in-

stance and from the previous example of Serasto. Because of the particular circumstances of the co-owners, who were well-off and who for the most part were living away from the island, nothing drastic happened. But the vulnerability of customary land tenure is clearly evident, and in other instances more unfortunate consequences may result. When, for example, a poor landowner who has no more than a crumpled piece of paper with a few lines drawn on it to show the land is his suddenly finds that a ruthless and wealthier neighbor has fenced in his land and taken out a legal title to it, he is left without any redress. Fencing, which is expensive, is often necessary to prevent trespass, particularly of animals, and a man is more or less obliged to fence his land if he wishes to maintain his sovereignty in a court of law.

The First Murder on Providencia

This story differs from the others in that the principals were of vastly different economic status. It is a famous island story, and perhaps because it is, it might just be apocryphal. I tell it here because it makes a point.

Captain Fred Robinson owned more land than anybody else on the island. Only a small two-acre piece prevented his lands from meeting and stretching from coast to coast. These two acres were farmed by José Gomez, who said they belonged to his wife, who had received them as servant wages. Therefore he could not sell them. One morning Gomez was found in his field with a bullet through his head. In due course Captain Fred and an accomplice were arrested, tried, and sent to prison. There the great Captain Fred, known throughout the island as the *cacique* or chief, rotted away to his death.

Comment. I have greatly abbreviated the story, which is told in lurid detail. For people of the island it points up in vivid terms their greatest sin—covetousness of land. There is a factor beyond the economic which makes owning land and then more land a goal of life that here dramatically ends in death. That factor is the power derived from land ownership.

In all of these examples except the last, the participants have all been of equal social and economic status: Randall and

James were comparatively well-off, the same age, and of the same standing; Astie and José, less well-off, younger, and of a lower but equal standing in relation to each other; Serasto and his uncle, though differing in age, still had the same rather low social standing, although Serasto's alcoholism was gradually removing him from any but the status of an outcast. Carlos too would be classed in the same social bracket as his siblings, though his idiosyncracies made him somewhat abnormal. The motive behind such crab antics is not then solely economic but is partly the desire for prestige—to own land for its own sake, or because it is particularly beautiful. Land in this capacity has about it the same quality of ritual prestige as Trobriand arm-shells and necklaces.

Far from denying the economic importance of land, a matter I shall document in the next chapter, these anecdotes serve rather to affirm that even in the structural realm, where relations between people become formalized and specific, sentiment is a dynamic factor.

TRESPASS

Trespassing on land is a major irritant to social relations. Though of less consequence than questions of tenure, it reflects from a slightly different angle the conditioning of relations through people's close identification with land. Trespassing on someone else's land can be seen as a first step toward coveting that land. It can also be viewed as a prelude to stealing from that land. In both cases trespass on a man's land is a sort of infringement on the actual person, since land is so much a part of a person's identity.

Some question to do with trespass comes up every day. Life and conversation on Providencia would be inconceivable without trespass, and I can probably best convey this aspect of things by quoting verbatim, and more or less at random, from my field notes:

Sitting on the porch rocking and chatting with Lynd when Jacob Garcia rushes up, dribbling, sweating, panting: "Ho, Missa Lyn', Missa Lyn'. Cayetano cows is in the sugar piece na' Gully."

Lynd asked him how long they had been there. He says he

doesn't know, but it look like they have eaten all the young cane shoots. Lynd gets furious but miraculously avoids swearing, good Adventist that he is. Just a couple of weeks ago he had been breaking his back clearing and planting the cane and talking with loving anticipation of all the syrup they would get.

Lynd thanked Garcia and went off to tell his father, but the old man says not to do anything because he doesn't want trouble with Cayetano. He will go around and speak to Cayetano himself. Lynd is all for getting a machete and chopping up the cows, or at least catching them and putting them in the pound.

The fact of the matter is that for some time Cayetano has been trying to get Lynd's father to sell him a certain piece of land; but so far he has not succeeded. For the past few months he has been trying to provoke Lynd's father by letting his cows out, possibly to convince him that the piece of land is badly situated for the father's purposes.

Some time later Lynd, Henly, and I went down to Cocopiece to pick some coconuts. As we were walking through a spot called Lena, Lynd spotted some cows in the gardens munching away at the bean tops. We rounded them up and took them to Isaac, in Bottom House, who was keeper of the pound. There they'll be kept, at the expense of the owner, until the damage is paid for.

For about two years, certainly ever since I have been coming to the island, Alfredo and Baldwin have been quarreling. Alfredo says that Baldwin's cows keep breaking through the fence onto his land and eating up all his cane and yucca. Baldwin counters with the allegation that Alfredo's horses have grown fat eating his grass and that "they doesn't even know what 'Fredo's grass taste like." One day the pair of them got so noisy and abusive toward each other that a crowd started to gather. Now that they had spectators their game became serious because they felt they could not back down. Manhood at stake! After about ten minutes cussing, Baldwin challenged 'Fredo to a fight. Baldwin is about seventy years old with a bent back and 'Fredo looks like the first puff of wind will blow him over. Elwin comes to the rescue by suggesting they go with him to the office and let the alcalde decide who is right. Since this saves them

*both from an embarrassing situation, they agree to go along.
I tagged along too.*

*Richie (the alcalde) nods away as they go through their
familiar routine of accusation and counteraccusation. As they
start to heat up again, he intervenes by giving them eight days
to repair all their fences. He tells them to keep their animals
penned and makes them sign a bond of peace. "I don't mind
as how you molest each other," says Richie, "but you molesting
is molesting all of us."*

*Alfredo and Baldwin are first cousins on the father's side
and both have ample land and other sources of wealth.*

*While I was working in the alcaldia at the census records,
Granville Hooker came in to complain that two cows belonging
to Captain Britton had been grazing on his land for the past
week. He and his son wanted to impound them but did not do so
because they did not have the necessary two witnesses. Britton
admitted that the cows were on Hooker's land, but adamantly
maintained that they had done no damage. Hooker, who is a
poor man, says he needs this land to pasture his own animals
and his sister's cow and he just can't afford to let Britton's cows
take his grass. He wants Britton to make restitution by allowing
him to pasture his animals on Britton's land for two weeks.
Britton refuses and begins a countercomplaint. He tells Richie,
in melodramatic tones, to send for Granville's father and a
nephew. When they arrive he accuses them of trespassing on
his land and damaging the corn and hints that they "might be
a tiefing something."*

*The old man vigorously denies he had anything to do with
damaging corn, and in fact does not recall ever having been
near Britton's land. He concludes his tirade by saying he
"thought there was only two madmen on the island, but is like
there is three." Richie, the alcalde, put an end to the slanging
and said he thought they were all being foolish. He suggested
that they all sign a bond of peace, and that they promise not to
go near each other's land.*

Trespass and the accusation of trespass demonstrate how
sensitive are people's feelings about their property, and this
sensitivity in turn is an index of the closeness of identification
between people and land. The strains of social relations be-

tween people can also be expressed through trespass and accusation of trespass because a man is vulnerable through his property. Trespass is a way of niggling at the inequities, real or imagined, that exist between people, and in this sense, it is very close to praedial larceny, which is rampant throughout the island as it is throughout the Caribbean. But it is far more difficult to substantiate charges of stealing from gardens than accusations of trespass, and the implications of such charges are rather more drastic and damaging. Given the scale of praedial larceny it is surprising how few people are accused. This suggests that accusations of trespass serve in their stead to help maintain a social balance. Stealing is a crime, trespass but a misdemeanor, and one is very loath to send one's "own people" to prison. What is more, in the few cases where a man has accused another of stealing, it is he, not the thief, who suffers social degradation from the disdain of his fellow islanders.

In other Negro populations of the Caribbean, in Guyana, for example, "the very strong feeling against alienation of permanent rights over this [village] land to 'outsiders' is a reflection of the social solidarity of the village group" (R. T. Smith 1955 : 81). The same sentiments exist on Providencia; but, as I have tried to show further, such feelings are born of a sense of common possession of and by the land. The island exists not merely as a source of subsistence but as a symbol and integral part of existence, giving each islander his identity over against the rest of the world. Derived from this is the fact that part of an islander's identity as an individual is gained from his ownership of, and his belonging to, a specific part of the island. In this rather abstract sense man and land are indivisible.

At this plane of living, all who own land or have rights to own land are "islanders"—people of the Rock. Likewise, all islanders are those who own a piece of the Rock, no matter how small. It is in this sense that one must interpret the moral cliché, which for all its platitudinous quality is nevertheless real, that all islanders are equal or that the people of the island display strong social solidarity.

Squabbles about tenure and trespass are expressive of this sense of common interest and they actually occur most frequently between people of equal social status. This does not mean, however, that land cannot also be the source of both social and economic ranking, and the next chapter will show in detail that such differentiation is a hard fact of Providence social structure.

The sense of ethos and identity of man with land which I have tried to analyze in this chapter is one that has received scant attention in Caribbean anthropology. Apart from Lowenthal's fine article, reference to which began this chapter, there are only the barest hints of this meaning—just enough, though, to suggest confidently that what I have described for Providencia may be true of other populations. The association between land and social solidarity in Guyana has already been noted, and in Jamaica Edith Clarke writes of the "nostalgia in the tone of a sugar worker who longed to 'go home' to his mother's land in a distant parish" (Clarke 1957 : 54) and of the solidarity that results, even out of conflict, from family land (ibid., p. 56). As Lowenthal points out, owning land was the most tangible expression of freedom from slavery throughout the Caribbean. To have a piece of land meant the achievement of autonomy, a sense of being that not only liberates the individual, but by extension has come to mean the independence of a people. "However barren, useless, or pestilential a tract may be, the passion for sovereignty renders it precious" (Lowenthal 1961 : 6).

Providencia may not have suffered from colonialism and slavery as did other Caribbean societies, but its historical and contemporary situation makes it an apt model of the more general and varied condition of these societies.

4 Living off the Land

So far I have concentrated on the common interest of all islanders in their ownership of land, arguing that this is the basis for the sentiment of equality that pervades much of the island social life and relations. But land is not only to be valued for reasons of sentiment; it is also the basis of subsistence. From this economic point of view the social equivalence of all islanders through their common ownership of the land disappears. Land must be seen also as a focus of social constraint and competition, as the infrastructure of social relations based on production, and as a backing for social stratification.

To support the recognition and interpretation of social equivalence I emphasized the fact that 65 percent of all registered landowners owned less than five acres; the most important fact now is that only 5 percent of landowners own twenty acres or more. Five acres or less is not enough to meet the continuing needs of adults and their dependents throughout the year, every year. Twenty acres or more, on the other hand, seems enough not only to meet subsistence requirements but also to permit the production of a surplus of either crops or livestock. Or, by freeing a man from dependence on the land, having such an acreage enables him to achieve a cash surplus.

Thus we have a situation which has become structured. By virtue of their relationship to land people on the island come to have extremes of a single life style and enjoy different life chances. By these very differentia that define the terms of their daily existence, a new form of conflict arises, one in which ambition is let loose and where a sense of the status quo slips away. Instead of homogeneity, a prizing of difference or a resentment of it activates social relations.

In the present chapter, then, I shall detail these differences as well as attempt to give some idea of different life patterns. I shall also open a subject that will be expanded in the following chapter: the institutionalization of these differences into structured relations and rationalizing values. Rather than write about islanders anonymously and try to re-create some composite, hence lifeless, typical case, I prefer to keep uppermost the fact that the subject of anthropological investigation is real people, lively, dull, idiosyncratic, or colorless. My discussion of social stratification in terms of life style and life chances therefore takes the form of a series of portaits of selected households.

POOR PEOPLE

Isaac and Lena

Isaac and Lena live in Bottom House, the island's "poorest" and "blackest" community. Isaac is about thirty-four years old, and what strikes one immediately about him is an idea of precision. His speech is fast and clipped, his walk brisk, his appearance neat. His hair is close shaved, his moustache meticulously trimmed, and his steel-rimmed eyeglasses so clean that sometimes I used to wonder whether there were lenses. This whole impression was completed, for me, by his mannerism of slowly drawing his lips over his teeth to a final close whenever he finished a sentence. He had had a few years of schooling and was able to read English fluently, but his writing was hesitant and he avoided it whenever he could. He loved to read—adventure novels if they were available, otherwise comics.

Lena, about twenty-eight years old, is soft, quiet, and flowing in her presence. She never raises her voice, her smile, ever present, is never too extensive, and even when she laughs she laughs quietly, so that her laughter is most evident in the cocking of her head to one side. Laughter is a keynote for this family, because Isaac is a great joker, delighting in puns (a delight he shares with most islanders).

Together Isaac and Lena are a handsome couple, and she, dressed up, could be quite stunning with her hair drawn back, her smooth, coffee-colored skin contrasting with Isaac's rich blackness, and always her half smile.

They had been living together in common-law union for eight years and they now had five children. Lena had lost another before it was born. One of Isaac's daughters by another woman lives with them, a lively, laughing sixteen-year-old, a great help with the younger children, but unbelievably clumsy according to Isaac—who may be more critical than most.

Isaac had built their home before they had begun to live together. It was a small, two-room house made out of wood that he had imported, using money he had earned when working in Panama. There was also a small thatched kitchen standing separate from the house, and this is where Lena spends most of her day. The house stands on about an acre of land that Isaac inherited from his father. Only a small part of this is level, the rest being a steep, rocky slope. Still, Isaac planted yucca on the slope and also tethers a goat on the grass. Lena cultivates a garden around the house—squash, melons, cucumbers, beans, peas, and yams grow healthily, while in one corner of the property are a couple of banana and plantain trees. She uses all she grows and doesn't remember ever having sold produce. Isaac bought a cow and pastured it on land he rented. He reckons on using the milk, possibly even selling some, but eventually making some money by slaughtering it when it is fat enough.

Isaac loves to fish and he goes out to the reef at least twice a week in his homemade canoe with its floursack sail. He uses nets that he has woven himself, and he weaves nets for sale—if somebody asks him to. He sells most of what he catches straight from the boat, keeping aside enough for his household and always making sure they have some dried fish, which he not only enjoys for its own sake but which stands them in good stead when the weather prevents him from going fishing and which Lena can use when he is away on one of his "trips."

Isaac likes to talk of his trips with the same air of excitement and indifference assumed by the modern businessman-cum-husband. These take place on an average of every eight months or so, when he goes to San Andrés or Panama to work. He likes to sign on as crew for one or two voyages with one of the small boats that ply the waters of the southern Caribbean. This provides him with some cash, perhaps a hundred pesos, which, though useful, is not much. More to the point, it gives him the opportunity to do a little trading of his own. Isaac enjoys a good reputation among his neighbors in Bottom House as being trustworthy and intelligent, so before leaving for a trip he solicits orders from his friends and neighbors for any goods they might want that he can buy for them. When he comes back it is usually with an assortment of goods: a bolt of cloth, a sewing machine, a bedstead, a chest, tinned foods, tools, spectacles, and so forth. For each item he receives a small commission. The most lucrative source of cash on these trips, however, is smuggling. While abroad he will procure a few thousand American cigarettes or a case of whisky. Sometimes he gets these from San Andrés, the free port, but most often they come from a "friend" in Panama, an agent for stolen goods. He sells them either in Cartagena, or, if he has procured them cheaply enough, to tourists in San Andrés.

From such activities Isaac clears as much as five or six hundred pesos, a little less than a hundred dollars U.S.; but this will be sufficient to purchase the needs of his household (matches, soap, kerosene, sugar, salt, meat, sewing cotton, etc.) as well as keep him solvent enough to buy rum and keep gambling with his friends.

Isaac prefers to leave the island often but for short periods (his trips last about six weeks). In other instances men and sometimes women leave the island for several years, sending remittances back to the island or trying to accumulate enough in savings to see them through a period of many years. Isaac did this before he built his house.

Lena sews all the family's clothing, using an ancient Singer that Isaac bought for her when they first settled down together. Isaac likes to bring back new shirts and pants for himself when he goes on a trip—especially to Panama, which has the latest "American" styles. He also usually treats himself to a new item such as sunglasses, a wristwatch, or a pen. At certain times of the year, when their garden is not in yield, Lena has to buy island produce, and at all times she has to buy coconuts, cooking oil, and eggs (since Isaac can't abide chickens they don't keep them, though most island households do).

Isaac controls the money. In his precise way, he likes to be in charge, and Lena, in her quiet way, acquiesces. Since Isaac is not mean, though he is sometimes careful, and since good humor prevails, there are no difficulties. Lena spends most of the money that comes in and Isaac holds back enough for cigarettes (he doesn't like the American cigarettes that he smuggles, and there is no point in smuggling Colombian *Pielrojas*), rum, candy for the children, and gambling. He also gives a little money now and then to a sweetheart—a girl with whom he enjoys a sexual but not a domestic relationship and who has borne him a child.

Lena is in complete charge of the house, and if she says she needs something for it, Isaac never questions her. When he is in the house he does what she tells him, though she, in turn, treats him with deference, serving his meals whenever he calls for them, seating him at the table and usually alone. She is also the real source of discipline and socialization of the children, for, on the whole, Isaac spends little time in the house. He is usually away fishing, tripping, or passing the time with his group of friends. He insists on respect from his children; but when he is at home he indulges them far more than he chastises. Very occasionally he will bring some of his men friends home for a meal and a good time. When he does, Lena sets to. Most of the visitors to the house are women friends and kin of Lena, most of whom live nearby. Lena leaves the house mainly to visit these friends or to make a quick purchase at the store, where she may stop for a chat with a friend. On Sunday she and some of the children dress up and go to the Baptist church in Smoothwater Bay. Once in a while she prevails upon Isaac to go along, but most often he responds by saying that church is woman's business.

Isaac works hard to provide for his household and Lena backs him up. They respect each other and have great affection for one another and for their children. Consequently they appear quite happy. But were it not for Isaac's trips abroad and their hard work, the family would be in dire straits. As I was leaving after my last visit, a possible crisis was looming. Lena was pregnant, but she was anemic and had kidney trouble. There was fear of complications and expense ahead.

Neither Isaac nor Lena talks much of being able to "improve" their social position. They are sensitive about their poverty, shy in the face of outsiders, and very reticent in any dealings they may have with "big men"—the doctor, the administration, sea captains, and so forth. In private Isaac can be quite scathing in his resentment against the wealthy people of the island, asking what makes them go about so high and mighty when he knows, and they know, they only got their money through stealing or worse. For the most part, though, they acquiesce in their situation, attributing it to God's will and pointing with pride to their children—"poor men's riches." What is important to both of them and what compensates greatly for their poverty (though in being poor they are no different from most other islanders), is their commitment to a certain moral standing among those "others." It is their own self-respect, and the respect of others.

What Isaac does, he does well—or tries to—whether it be fishing, shopping, smuggling, net-making, or drinking. He is not quarrelsome, but neither is he a coward. He is not a spendthrift, but he is not tight and does not avoid his obligations to his friends: he readily buys rum, and he as readily drinks it. Though somewhat resigned to his own lowly position, he has ambitions for his children and says he wants to give them whatever chance he can for them to improve on his position. What is more, by his skills, his confidence, and his virility, he has proved himself a man. In short, he enjoys a good reputation among the people of Bottom House and this, in its turn, gives him a sense of self. Furthermore, these qualities are ones to which all island men aspire, no matter what their economic standing and social status, so Isaac gains respect as a man from those of higher status even though they may never regard him as an equal or treat him with any intimacy.

Lena, too, in her demeanor and interests conforms to a generalized pattern common to the island as a whole, though again, her economic and social status prevents her from meeting all island women on an equal footing. What Lena strives for and upholds is respectability: she keeps to her house and to her female friends and kin; she is loyal to Isaac; she presents herself and her family in public as being well cared for; she supports the church and, presumably, believes in God. She would like to be properly married to Isaac, but he does not wish to be married yet. By comparison with some "high class" women she is not yet as respectable as she might be. But until she had been living with Isaac for about five years or so, she did not wish to marry either—waiting to see that everything worked out well between them and keeping herself "free" in case it did not.

Isaac, then, has a good reputation, and Lena is a respectable woman. This serves to establish them as being in harmony with the ethos [9] of Providencia's culture and places them as individuals vis-à-vis that ethos. Reputation and respectability are terms encompassing a number of "values" that as ideals are held by the entire society and as behavioral qualities are manifested, with varying degrees of fullness and fulfillment, by all (cf. Wilson 1969). But not all people, not even all poor people, are "good" people like Isaac and Lena, though Isaac and Lena are as representative of their class as any I knew. Contrast, however, makes for clarity, and I will now introduce Lerio, who is in fact quite atypical statistically, but who is an all too familiar type on the island.

Lerio

Lerio gives you the impression of a man prematurely old: he stoops and is hollow-chested but does not seem as frail as a truly old man might be. His skin, which is quite fair, is lined, and though his eyes peek out of their bags, it doesn't sag as much as an old man's skin. He has a long face, thin lips, thin nose, and long, thin, silvery black hair. He wears grubby, torn clothes that are always dark; in fact, so nondescript is his clothing that it never occurs to you that he actually is dressed. He is about forty years old.

Lerio lives in Southwest Bay with his mother, sister, and the sister's three small children. Their house is much shabbier than Isaac's: there are gaps in the wall planking, the shutters do not close properly, and the gutter pipe leading rain off the roof into the barrel has rusted through. The water barely makes it into the barrel. There are a few sticks of furniture: the remains of a table, a three-legged chair, a sagging cupboard, a bench, some shelves on the wall, and a large iron bedstead. The house is reasonably clean, though because of its condition it looks dirtier than it really is.

Lerio's mother and sister garden two plots of land amounting to about three-quarters of an acre, and Lerio has a plot of about one-half acre, which he says is really family land left by his father's father. He hardly ever goes to the gardens, leaving the cultivation to the two women—though now and again he gives them a hand if they ask him to. His mother says he is just too lazy. The land is not particularly good land and only cassava grows really well. The household, in short, is able to supply itself with only a fraction of its needed supplies.

Lerio cannot work as a sailor because he gets too seasick and has a fear of water that is apparently quite genuine. There are precious few jobs available on the island, and the way things are, no one is likely to give one of them to Lerio. As a young man, in his early twenties, he did go to Panama, where he worked for a few years as a laborer. But he has not been able to face traveling on the sea since he got back to the island. His sister manages to earn a little money by doing laundry for a household in Smoothwater Bay, and she occasionally receives small sums of money from the father of her children, who is at present working in Barranquilla. She keeps all she earns, using it to buy food for her children, and she saved enough to buy an old sewing machine. She also helps to support her mother, but she vehemently insists that nothing of what she earns or receives goes to her brother. Once she hit him over the head with a shovel when she caught him stealing a tin of sardines she had bought as a treat for the children.

Lerio eats most of his meals at home, but now and again he eats at the house of a "girlfriend" who lives in Bottom House.

Here is a household on the margins of existence. How does it survive? Lerio makes an occupation of stealing from gardens, which, of course, is why he is looked on as such a pariah. He rarely steals alone but goes with his close friend, Clarence, a distant cousin and member of a "crew" [10] with which Lerio is loosely associated. They make their expeditions at night, going some way away from any community. Since most gardens are located a distance from communities and are never guarded at night for fear of duppies or ghosts, stealing is reasonably easy. Lerio does the actual stealing while Clarence keeps watch. Clarence is really along to give him courage, though he does not hesitate to accept his share. In this way Lerio more or less keeps the household supplied with such items as yams, beans, and fruit.

He makes a specialty of stealing coconuts, which he can sell around in St. Isabel for cash, no questions asked—or could until the island council passed a law that said all sellers of coconuts had to have a witness to certify who had produced them. Lerio would take a few coconuts at a time from different stands and pile them in a hiding place. Then, when he had a good number he would rent a horse from Clarence and take them around to St. Isabel, to Jenkins, the merchant who asked no questions. The latter shipped them to the lard factory in San Andrés. With the cash that he made in this way Lerio was able to keep himself supplied with cigarettes, rum, clothing, and chance (lottery) tickets. Occasionally he gives his mother some money, thereby mollifying her and preventing her from being too influenced against him by his sister.

The two households I have described so far could not survive on their land holdings and so must look to other means of subsistence. Isaac takes his trips and Lerio is a full-time thief. There are not many full-time thieves on the island, but given the scale of praedial larceny, as indicated by the complaints made by people of the loss of their crops and the lengths they go to protect their gardens with fetishes, part-time stealing is the occupation of many and should probably be counted among the normal means of subsistence. What also seems evident is that, with such a small amount of land, and lacking any other advantage, households such as those of Isaac and Lerio are caught in a cycle of bare subsistence. They are unable to build up a cash surplus, to secure an education, or to gain access to a more rewarding means of support, which would permit them to improve their life style and the life chances of their children.

Even so, within the constraints implied by their "class," one can see by comparison that the quality of life lived by these households is quite different: contentment and good humor, even a relish for the future, marks the outlook of Isaac and Lena. But Lerio is a miserable soul, and strain and ill-temper mark the relations in his household.

Isaac is a confident man, cocky to some, while Lerio is jumpy and nervous. Wherever Isaac goes he at least receives the respect due to a man, even though he is poor. But Lerio darts furtively in and out and has the respect of no one but a few cronies like Clarence. Though not outcasts, Lerio and his like are regarded by the majority as beneath their notice. He is sometimes taunted and insulted by young men, usually when they are drunk, and though he may lose his temper and chase them off, he can expect no sympathy from anyone. Only if a nonislander, especially a mainlander, assails or insults him, will he be able to rally support, though clearly this will not be for him personally but for him as an islander and thereby an equal. The reason for all this seems clear: even though other people may steal, they are discreet about it, whereas Lerio is shameless. He makes little or no apparent effort to appear a man and thereby undermines the values of reputation and respect that are the basis of island ethos. Such shamelessness, interpreted as blatant disregard for what everyone else considers right and proper, is a form of threat which can be countered only by disdain and disregard.

Cayetano and Rosalia

Our next couple, Cayetano and Rosalia, are representative of that 29 percent of all landowners who have between five and twenty acres, an area usually adequate to meet all subsistence needs. These are still "poor" people in island eyes, in the same broad social category as Isaac and Lena and Lerio. But they are a sort of "subclass" made up of those in a position to "take off" economically and, perhaps, with luck, better their life chances and those of their children.

Cayetano is about thirty-eight years old, a short, squat, powerful man distinguished by a mop of almost golden curly hair —burnished copper perhaps. He lives with Rosalia in common-law union, though technically she is his "sweetheart" because he was once properly married, in church and civilly, to another woman now living in Cartagena, from whom he was never divorced. With Cayetano and Rosalia live his eldest daughter, about seventeen years old, with her baby, and four boys and three more girls whose ages range from two to fifteen years. Rosalia, a merry, roly-poly woman, is pregnant again.

Cayetano tends a little toward dourness, but Rosalia chatters away all day with her children or her lady friends. If you pass her house, you are bound to hear her uninhibited laugh rushing out of the window. She is one of those women who manage to do everything while seeming to do nothing. Cayetano has two children by another woman living in Bailey whom he visits occasionally, taking her small sums of money and odd presents. The relationship is purely a sexual one and has no domestic implications, so it is no threat to Rosalia or her household. As soon as this girl "keeps" with a regular man, Cayetano will no longer visit her.

Cayetano and Rosalia live in a single-story, two-room house painted white with a red tin roof. It is on the beach at Rocky Point and stands high off the sand in case of too adventurous tides. Cayetano stores his canoe, fishing nets, traps, tools, and a bicycle underneath the house. Inside the rooms are subdivided by partitions and furnished with a low table, some plastic flowers in a vase, and a few upright chairs, companions to two rocking chairs that are usually kept on the veranda. A glass-fronted cupboard occupies pride of place opposite the front door, and in it one can see assorted photographs, cups, glasses, spectacles, plastic flowers, cosmetics, letters, and knickknacks. The walls are decorated with pages from magazines, travel and religious posters, calendars, and fading photographs. There are two cots for children and a large brass bedstead that, together with a huge wooden chest, takes up an entire room. Clothes hang from wooden pegs on the walls or lie bundled on top of the chest and in a hammock suspended from the ceiling. Across the roof beams lie canoe paddles and assorted timbers, some of which are for a coffin, since this is the accepted island custom. The kitchen is a separate thatch hut.

Cayetano owns almost fourteen acres of land, split up into five pieces and each situated in a different part of the island, though all are within approximately forty-five minutes' walk from his house. Rosalia has two pieces of land totaling about three acres, but these are in Lazy Hill (where she comes from) and at present they are rented out for twenty pesos a year. One of Cayetano's pieces is large, almost five acres, and on it he keeps six cows and two horses. He also rents a neighboring pasture from Jenkins that costs him ten pesos a year. Another plot of about three acres is sown with sugar cane, and he expects to get about two hundred gallons of syrup, some of which he

will sell and keep some for his own use. A third piece is planted
with vegetables, banana, plantain, and breadfruit; and a fourth
piece, a stretch of beach, has some twenty coconut palms. These
yield enough for his household and give him a surplus that he
can sell. The fifth piece of land is small and has a little corn,
some melons, and a few pineapples. Cayetano has to leave his
land fallow every couple of years, and he has begun to notice
that the yields, of late, have not been very good. Like everyone
else, he has started to realize the effects of erosion and over-
cultivation.

The two older boys, thirteen and nine years old, take care of
the animals, leading them to the pasture first thing in the
morning and then back home at sunset. Sometimes they stay
with them all day. Rosalia and the other children do most of
the gardening, visiting the gardens on an average of two or three
times a week to weed and harvest. Cayetano takes care of the
sugar cane and does the heavier clearing and burning. He also
takes great and loving care of the melons.

His chief interests and occupations, though, are woodworking
and fishing. He is not considered as being among the best carpenters on the island, but he is adequate for relatively minor
house repairs and boat mending. At fishing he excels. His specialty is crab fishing, which is done at night by torchlight. He
also makes his own lobster pots and often sets as many as
twenty at a time—more than anyone else on the island. He sells
most of what he hauls, and whenever he can he sends a catch
down to San Andrés, where there is a constant demand and
where the price is far above that on Providence.

Whenever a boat arrives at the island, particularly if it is
going back to San Andrés, Cayetano gets frantically busy. First
he sets his pots for as big a catch of crayfish and crab as he can
manage. Then he gets together whatever copra is ready, which
he augments by buying up whatever his neighbors might have
available. In this way he can accumulate enough to enable him
to sell directly to the ship's captain, who pays a better price
than the merchants in St. Isabel. If his melons are ripe he har-
vests them to send to San Andrés, adding also to these whatever
fruit he can pursuade his neighbors to sell him. He also aims
to sell at least two head of cattle a year—usually to San Andrés,
for it is here, thanks to tourism, that the demand and the

price are so high that having to pay freight charges is more than adequately compensated. Usually when he sells a cow he himself sails to San Andrés, where he buys supplies and odds and ends that he resells to his neighbors in Rocky Point. He is in short a middleman in the sale of island produce, serving Rocky Point and nearby. But note the limited scope of his trading—he confines himself to selling island produce, mostly his own, and does not import goods to the island except when he takes a trip. He does not think of himself as a trader, and is not so considered by his fellows.[11]

Like most island men, Cayetano loves the sea and gets restless if he is away from it for too long. From time to time he gets the urge to "take a trip" and signs on with a vessel for one or more voyages. This happens about once every two years, and, as might be expected, he takes the opportunity to exercise his trading talents, coming home with a tidy sum.

Cayetano is an agent for Mr. Ling, who runs the main "numbers" game on the island and also sells tickets for the national lottery. Cayetano gets his supply of tickets each week to sell around Rocky Point, and every Sunday makes his way to Mr. Ling's store to get the results, hand over his takings, and collect his commission. Mr. Ling, or his son, gets the results via the radio operator at the telegraph office.

When Cayetano is away on a trip Rosalia in her effortless way takes over everything—except the fishing. She collects produce and has it taken around to St. Isabel for sale. On one occasion she collected nearly 2,500 coconuts from all around, far more than Cayetano had ever managed. She also sells produce from her gardens to neighbors because very often too much ripens all at once. The money she gets from this she keeps, and Cayetano also pays her for anything he sells from their gardens (only the sugar cane and melons are his crops). At sugar-boiling time she, like many other island women, boils up fruit in the molasses, some of which she sells. Most of her time, though, is taken up with the house and with her many friends who are always popping in and out. There is invariably a niece, nephew, cousin or other relative from Lazy Hill spending a few days "on a visit," and once in a while she goes "home" to Lazy Hill.

Cayetano was a little reticent about divulging his income from all his activities, and the fact is that he had probably never totaled it. I reckoned he made about five thousand pesos a year (about seven hundred dollars U.S. in 1960). Given a general island tendency to underestimate one's income and plead poverty, this figure should be regarded as a very conservative estimate.

Most of the cash comes to Cayetano, but he gives Rosalia money whenever she asks for it. He stores the cash in various hiding places around the house and in secret places elsewhere on the island. Rosalia also hides money. Sometimes their ingenuity gets the better of them, as when Cayetano hid a hundred pesos in a lamp and Rosalia filled and lit it!

This household, then, comes closer to being able to feed itself from its own land resources than the others we have discussed. At the same time, by raising cash crops (sugar cane, melons, and coconuts) and keeping cattle, as well as fishing for profit, Cayetano earns a fairly substantial income without ever having to leave the island. And with this income he cannot only purchase material items that enhance his life style, but he can think seriously of being able to save enough money to send some if not all of his children to high school or even university. And he is indeed thinking in these terms. Thus can the household begin to improve its life chances.

In tempo and in temper the life style of Cayetano's household differs little from that of Isaac's. But there is a noticeable sense of "expansion," of variety, and of quality. This shows up particularly in the foods they eat, which include a far greater portion of imported items even though they are able to better supply their own needs from their land. Imported rice, for instance, is the staple in the household, whereas it is manioc for Isaac and Lena. Rosalia also buys such items as cocoa, Nescafé, and canned soups and meat; she makes bread with imported flour and uses packet pepper.[12] She has more cooking utensils, and her family eats off cheap china plates rather than the enamel ones used by Isaac and Lena. The children attend school rather more regularly and have a larger wardrobe, while two of the younger ones, who show particular scholastic promise, will likely go to high school. At least that is what Cayetano wants and what he is saving up for.

Comparing these households allows us to see that while the conditions of life style are similar, Cayetano, owning much more land, is freer to expand his activities, to earn more cash without always having to leave the island to do so. Having the land, he is, paradoxically, less dependent on it than either Isaac or Lerio. Nevertheless the most important resource, outside of the land itself, is cattle. These serve as a sort of capital that, through breeding, reproduces itself. Selling a cow brings in the single largest sum, and though much of his energy is taken up with fishing and trading produce, cattle remain the backbone of Cayetano's "take off."

In life style and life chance Cayetano is representative of a significant segment of the population. If the people themselves recognized a "middle class," Cayetano would exemplify it. But such a segment is not so distinguished, and we should think of him and his family as perhaps the upper echelon of the mass, the "others," as members of the "high class" call them. Many of these people trade in exactly the same way as Cayetano, though perhaps not as regularly, and all of them may be characterized by the fact that they own enough land to meet their needs for subsistence. Others in this bracket include small storekeepers, of whom there are one or two in most communities. Their stores are usually only a room in a house given over to a few shelves of goods, articles of daily use such as matches, kerosene, soap, rice, salt, cigarettes, cotton, lard, and the like. Such stores are as often as not kept by women, and they yield an income of between twenty and fifty pesos a week.

The other occupation of this segment of the population is rum distilling, which, though illegal, is carried out more or less openly. There are fourteen distillers on the island, of whom seven might be considered "full-time" while the rest do it as a hobby. The full-time distillers buy up as much syrup as they can at harvest time but have as the basis of their livelihood their own canefields. Their stills are hidden, some in the house, some in the bush. Since the demand for rum on the island is constant and heavy, they are assured of both good protection and a regular and adequate income. This in turn facilitates the carrying on of other activities: in one instance a distiller bought a sixteen-foot boat in which he transported produce and people around the island. In three years the boat had paid for itself.

Cayetano works hard, but he enjoys what he does; in fact he does not really make the distinction between work and enjoyment. But because he does work so hard, and because he does what he does well and with a sense of ambition, he earns and keeps the respect of all those around him. He is a Seventh-day Adventist, but something of a backslider since he does not go regularly to church. Like Isaac in conforming to island ideas about how men should behave, Cayetano too enjoys a good reputation. Rosalia, who is Baptist by persuasion, is about as lax as her husband in her attitude toward the church. But she runs a good house, looks after her children, is fine company for the women around her and a good hostess to her kinswomen from Lazy Hill. She rises to the occasion when Cayetano is away and so, in all these ways, she is a respectable woman among her peers. What is more, her standards do not depart from the social standards associated with the church, so her nonattendance is not very serious socially. That she is not married is something of a disadvantage to her self-esteem, for among other things she cannot call herself "Mistress"— though this does not bother her much. She does get a bit annoyed at some of the talk from others less well-off about her lax church attendance, an annoyance which suggests a slight chink in her social armor. But on the whole, the fact that they have not achieved a certain level of "ideal" prestige is not a problem, for Cayetano and Rosalio are economically and socially secure enough to laugh.

THE HIGH CLASS

Ever since the first settlement there have been some islanders who own large amounts of land. Only the lineage of large landowners has fluctuated—the direct descendant of a landowner is not necessarily himself a large landowner, though one of his kinsmen may be. We have glimpsed the mechanism of land accumulation through acquisition of the patrimony of siblings, especially sisters, and through purchase. The money for such purchase is gained through trading activities like those of Isaac and Cayetano.

Most of the islanders depend on their land for subsistence.

Even those like Cayetano, who gets most of his income from activities directly associated with the land, are free to do so only because their minimal needs can be met by the land. Beyond a certain point, people who own plenty of land are independent of the land and are quite free to devote full time to either another occupation or activities that may be considered more lucrative or more prestigious. This group includes the 5 percent or so of island households whose members, in their own eyes, comprise most of the "high class" on Providencia. They are certainly the wealthiest and most influential islanders.

Mr. John and Miss Ray

At sixty years of age, Mr. John is one of the wealthiest and most influential men on Providence. He owns one of the two large stores, which occupies the ground floor of his large house, and he owns nearly fifty acres of land. He has other assets which I shall mention in a minute. Mr. John moves slowly and deliberately, speaks in the same way and softly, and with his pear-shaped body and large head, gives one the impression of ease that is almost torpor. He always wears a large, flat porkpie hat and glasses that seem about to slip off the bridge of his rather flat nose. His features are rather heavy, especially his mouth, which has thick, flat lips, and his whole face screws itself up with a fantastic, mask-like effect when, every fifteen minutes or so, he either sniffs or harks up phlegm with great vigor.

Miss Ray—tall, thin, and angular—has somewhat more regular Caucasian features, but her habit of pressing her nose flat with her forefinger suggests sometimes that she is not too pleased with her appearance. Whereas Mr. John speaks in slow, soft, and measured tones, Miss Ray has a hard, piercing voice and a laugh that can be heard halfway across the island. She loves to joke, and whenever she does she lays her arm affectionately on her listener. But underneath the joviality she is a hard and determined woman whose pungent opinions, particularly of her fellow islanders, will often be quoted in this book. If Mr. John is all piety and stodge, Miss Ray, in spite of her sometimes quite outrageous prejudices, is fun.

Mr. John is an only son. He inherited nearly twenty-five

acres of land from his father when he was quite young. Much of this was a hillside used as a pasture. Another five-acre plot was good garden land. His father kept a small store in St. Isabel, and Mr. John took this over and kept the house. Later on he pulled down the old house and built a new one. This in turn was demolished by a hurricane, but with the insurance money (he was one of the few people to be insured on the island), he built the present beautiful house and store.

With the pasture he also inherited a small herd of cattle. He sold off half the herd, about six head, and with the proceeds bought a one-third share in a boat—the eighty-ton converted schooner *Elizabeth,* which he renamed *Ray,* after his wife. His partners were his cousin, the captain, and an uncle who, after a year, sold out to the other two. For nearly ten years Mr. John sailed as the supercargo on the *Ray,* traveling between Cartagena, San Andrés, Panama, and Providencia, with an occasional visit to Barranquilla. Within three years he had recouped his investment, and since he was able to supply his store quite cheaply, this enterprise began to expand and show a good profit. After the hurricane and the decision to rebuild the store, Mr. John gave up going to sea and sold his share of the *Ray* to his cousin the captain. He still maintained an arrangement that gave him priority for shipping any goods in the vessel. He had also bought himself into a wholesaling agency in Cartagena and through this was able to keep effective trading links with the mainland. In addition to retailing goods in his store, he imported building materials and made, by his own admission, a near fortune after the hurricane.

He bought land regularly and over the next twenty years or so added another thirty acres to his holdings. This enabled him to expand his herd to about forty head, a number he considers large enough. From these he obtains milk for his household and meat that he sells from time to time on the island. He exports cattle on the hoof to San Andrés quite regularly, about once a month.

Miss Ray also owns land that she inherited. It it situated in the vicinity of Jones Point, where she grew up. For some time after her marriage she allowed her brother to use the land rent free, provided he kept her supplied with vegetables and fruit.

This arrangement came to an end when the brother left the island to live and work in Panama. For a while Miss Ray's eldest son and a daughter worked the land, but when they left to go to school in Cartagena, they had to give up. Now the land is idle.

By the time he was about forty-five years old Mr. John was a wealthy man by island standards—in fact, by any standards. Competition from other stores did not affect him, mainly because he had managed to become the supplier to the government of everything from stationery to road-mending materials and refreshments for official functions. He was also paymaster, handling the government payroll, since there was no bank on the island. This meant a more or less captive clientele at his store, for he extended credit liberally to government employees. In this way he was soon able to control much of the cash circulating on the island.

He did not always have it his own way, however. His archrival, Jenkins, began a rise to prominence soon after World War II. Mr. Jenkins had worked in San Andrés for Mr. Rubinstein, a Russian Jewish refugee who had succeeded in building up the largest retail business on that island. Rumor had it that Jenkins set himself up with what he managed to siphon off from Rubinstein. Rumor also said that he had made a fortune ferrying German spies, selling oil to U-boats, and so forth. Be that as it may, Jenkins opened a large store right opposite Mr. John, and within a year or so had also acquired a small fleet of four boats with which he managed to monopolize the carrying trade to and from the island. Since Mr. John had sold his interest in the M.V. *Ray,* and Captain Julio, his cousin, was no longer so reliable or beholden, he had to rely more and more on Jenkins's boats to bring in his supplies.

The rivalry became a political one, too. Mr. John became head of the island Liberal party and Mr. Jenkins headed the Conservatives. Their rivalry was conducted from the relative safety of their respective cashier's cages, for they never confronted each other face to face.

Unlike his rival, Mr. John did not continue to enlarge his landholdings but invested his money in mainland businesses and combined on occasion with his half-brother in San Andrés. He also dabbled in new projects. When, for example, the government built the road around the island, he was the first to import a motor vehicle—a three-year-old pickup truck that did good business for the short time it ran. It was brought to the island, incidentally, on Jenkins's boat.

As Mr. John grew older his health and blood pressure declined. He spent much of his time poring over his ledgers and began to leave more and more of the day-to-day running of the store to his youngest son. His two daughters were married, one to a mainland Colombian who lived in Barranquilla, and the other to a sea captain, an islander. These two had lived for some years in Cartagea, but when I was there they were about to return to Providencia to live.

Mr. John and Miss Ray are Roman Catholics. Together they go to church each Sunday morning for Mass, but otherwise he plays little part in church affairs, remaining on good terms with the priest for political reasons by making a more than adequate contribution to collections. Miss Ray, on the other hand, is the leading lay member. She is a chairman of all the committees and organizer of all the notable events.

By comparison with the other households we have discussed and even with non-island households, the life style of Mr. John and Miss Ray is lavish though not ostentatious. The most significant indicator is perhaps the daily menu for the household which always contains a great number of imported foods and is of considerable variety (see the Appendix for details). True, most of these items are obtained wholesale since all Miss Ray has to do is send downstairs for a tin of this or that. Nevertheless, it remains an impressive and elaborate set of menus. Part of the reason for the preponderance of imported foods is that the household grows nothing of its own. Not that Miss Ray does not want to or that Vidi, their youngest son, is unwilling to garden. It is simply that, had they tried to grow anything, it would have been stolen before they had a chance to pick it. Their only chance for fresh food is when someone comes around, someone like Cayetano, offering produce for sale.

Miss Ray does all the cooking, and she is never happier than when she is making the week's bread, baking a wonderful assortment of cakes, puddings, and pies, boiling jellies, and preserving fruits. If she is not cooking she is sewing clothes, and the entire household is kept clothed in the styles of a backdated Sears Roebuck catalog. She has help with the housework and the laundry, and a water boy keeps various pots and jugs full.

The house is fully furnished with a dining-room suite, bedroom suites, fine linens, good English china, and sterling silver cutlery. The paintwork, inside and out, is immaculate; there is an indoor flush toilet and shower, both fed from a gravity water tank. A huge concrete cistern catches all the rainwater from an extensive expanse of roof. The kitchen bristles with utensils and pans. It also contains a kerosene stove, a charcoal stove, and storage cupboards. There is a large kerosene refrigerator in the dining room, and in the store another refrigerator and a huge freezer powered by Mr. John's diesel generator. This generator also provides power for electric lights and a radio.

The children of Mr. John and Miss Ray had all received a high school education, and they could have gone to university had they wished. All the grandchildren too will receive a higher education. The children had all been brought up according to rules and standards that closely approximated British middle-class ideals of the 1930s or American Southern middle-class ideals of the 1950s. Children were taught "manners" and were kept in line with a "beating" or a "flogging." They had to respect their elders and conduct themselves with due restraint. Miss Ray is bringing up two of her grandchildren in the same way. It is she who gives greatest voice to, and assumes responsibility for, the respectability of the household and all its members. In addition to disciplining the children, she is very careful whom she admits into the house, always expressing concern about the people with whom her children and grandchildren are associating and voicing her opinion in public as well as in private as to the conduct, manners, and standards of others. She directed her children in their choice of spouse and was at the time of my field work very concerned and active in arranging the betrothal and subsequent marriage of her son Vidi to the alcalde's daughter. Fortunately the girl was Vidi's choice too.

Mr. John remains in the background in such matters but always backs up his wife. For his part, he shows constant concern for his reputation as an honest man, a good businessman, and an upright citizen. He talks of the good deeds he has done, of the people he has helped, and of the unselfishness of his motives. He is most sensitive to talk about himself in the community—and quite rightly so, for his wealth and power render him vulnerable. As the island saying goes, "The higher a monkey climb, the more he expose himself." Mr. John never drinks, condemning the foolishness that rum lets loose: "When the rum is in, the wit is out." Until his own daughter and son-in-law gave a housewarming party he was never seen to dance in public. He studiously avoids getting into any arguments in public and roundly criticizes others who demean themselves by getting involved in shouting matches.

Yet neither he nor Miss Ray are deadly puritan. Mr. John fondly recounts some of the exploits of his youth, especially those as a sailor, letting the listener know that he too is a man, though now he has come to repent of his sins and to see the foolishness of his old ways. Miss Ray shows a mother's pride in the successful amorous exploits of her son Vidi, getting worried only if they seem to be getting too serious. It was with somewhat mixed feelings that she received the gossip that her son-in-law was paying rather frequent visits to a certain household in Bailey; it was good to have a son-in-law who was *macho,* but it comes a little hard when it is one's own daughter who is affected!

This household represents an extreme in island living style. There are others who approach it, though: certain administrators, traders, and sea captains—in short, those who are wealthy. Almost all of them attained their occupational status and cash income by having a springboard in land that they either acquired themselves or inherited. Through this, the life chances of members of their households were enhanced: they could afford a higher education, hence access to more prestigious and remunerative occupations; they could also afford better medical treatment, thereby improving their life chances in another sense.

Such households, which together form the best part of the social stratum known as the "high class," enjoy a status and a standard which is a model for all, though something to which few can attain or even aspire. Such households represent the apex of the moral community of the island, as that is defined particularly by respectability; they are where economic success and ethical standards come together. Where such does not happen, where for instance a well-off household is not also respectable, "high class" is not achieved. This I shall discuss at greater length in the next chapter. What must be affirmed here is that Isaac and Lena, Lerio, Cayetano and Rosalia, and Mr. John and Miss Ray are all subscribers to the same views and standards, but that they differ from each other in the degree to which these are fulfilled and the degree to which it is considered necessary to fulfill them. Mr. John and Isaac may never mingle socially or intimately, but each will demand and receive from the other a mutual respect and deference which stems from factors quite independent of their economic standing.

ECONOMIC STANDING IN OTHER CARIBBEAN SOCIETIES

By means of these household sketches I have tried to indicate the extent and scope of economic differentiation on the island. In discussing such matters as reputation and respectability I have also given some indication of the moral basis of social differentiation. One might well ask to what extent the sort of economic differentiation found on Providencia is evident in other Caribbean societies. Ethnographic studies of Caribbean communities have conveyed an impression of great social and economic homogeneity and egalitarianism; but if the present findings are anything to go by, this is a most misleading picture. It is quite clear that considerable economic differences exist within the population of Providencia. If such differences exist elsewhere, then they need to be properly reported, and existing accounts and analyses must be revised. I am not, I hasten to add, referring to a well-defined "class" situation in such societies as Jamaica or Trinidad, where economic differences can be clearly discerned on a society-wide basis and where, incidentally, there are no accounts of the "well-off." Rather I am concerned with differences within a community. Providencia, with two thousand people, is not much larger than most of the communities that have been the subjects of other anthropological investigations.

A brief survey of the literature should indicate whether the findings of the present chapter are indeed pertinent to other Caribbean communities. Virtually every major study gives some indication of the existence of economic differences within the community, though very little is said about the nature of these differences or their consequences. In Jamaica, Edith Clarke writes that in Sugar Town there is a middle-class section with better housing than that of the majority, who are said to be unable to enjoy a decent home life (Clarke 1957 : 23). In the village of Mocca everyone is poor, but in Orange Grove most people are relatively well-off, though there is within that community a distinction between the well-off and the poor (ibid., pp. 27–28). We are told of some people who are especially respected (p. 47), and of others who are "descendants of an old family [which] has prospered and moves in a social group within which a different set of ideas is operative" (p. 49). A distinction is made between middle- and working-class homes, and living on family land is said to confer status in a community (pp. 150, 153).

In another Jamaican community, Rocky Roads, described by Yehudi Cohen, we are informed that land is the "mainspring of life" and that, as the main avenue to the accumulation of wealth, it affords to some the chance of "setting themselves up as richer, and enjoying greater prestige," while others, without land, are driven to poverty (Cohen 1954 : 107).

In the Guyanese Negro villages studied by R. T. Smith, economic differentiation is correlated with ethnic differences, a situation consonant with the ethnic pluralism of the society as a whole. But even so, there are slight hints of economic and social differentiation among Negroes. For instance "a constant complaint is that if you are black, other people in the village don't like to see you doing well financially" (Smith 1956 : 208), which suggests that some people do in fact prosper, or at least have the opportunity to do so. This in turn gives rise to a certain dynamism in socioeconomic relations which might bear some resemblance to crab antics. Such feelings lead people to seek status through occupation, and this occupational elite maintains its prestige by lavish spending, for "to spend money has much more social approval than to accumulate money, and giving lavish parties is common practice" (ibid., p. 209). And even though he maintains that land does not confer status, Smith records in his paper on land tenure that at least one individual owned more plots than others (1955). This is hardly enough evidence to affirm that economic differentiation among Negroes in village Guyana is highly significant, but it is enough to make one wonder.

Turning to M. G. Smith's study of the tiny island of Carriacou, not much bigger than Providencia, the ambiguity concerning economic and social differentiation is even more apparent. In general terms, Smith informs us that "almost all the land is now held by islanders as peasants: there is no local elite class stratification or cultural plurality (1962b : 4). And yet "until 1946 approximately a quarter of Carriacou was held by about seven landowners" (ibid., p. 19). Men who own stock in greater number and variety than others are envied locally (p. 49), and there are also "fairly prosperous people who build distinctive kitchens" and "successful men who build themselves larger houses" (p. 51). What is more, "prosperous married men enjoy certain sexual privileges" (p. 190). For a scholar who has made such a detailed statistical examination of social stratification in his study of Grenada (1965b), Smith seems to have mislaid some sensitivity to the topic when moving a few miles to Carriacou.

There is similar fleeting evidence from other societies such as Barbados, Andros Island, and Trinidad, but it is enough to let the present examples suffice. They go some way to suggest that land ownership and life style may be closely linked in these so-called homogeneous Caribbean communities, and that, in turn, these are the supports for social status and differentiation. What is more, such differentiation, both economic and social, not only takes its own particular form as part of a culture but provides us with certain of the fundamentals of structure in its dialogue with sentiment.

5 Putting on the Style

I have gone almost as far as I can in describing the direct relation between the physical environment, especially land, social sentiment, and structure. Land, I have argued, is the springboard to wealth; but once a man generates a surplus that he can translate into cash, or once he is free to earn cash beyond the amount necessary for his subsistence, he becomes independent of land. Economic differentiation is primarily a function of income, even though for many people land still retains a function as security and capital. In the event of government development of the island, the latter function of land will fully assert itself.

Economic differentiation becomes a public and social matter through the assumption of a life style, marked in part by the acquisition, use, and display of goods. Economic differentiation facilitates, and hence is indicated by, an improvement in life chances. One who is better-off can provide his children with the opportunity for a more remunerative and prestigious occupation. In turn, economic differentiation is often signified by occupation.

Since life style is an important factor in translating economic differentiation into a public status, wealth does no good "squatting," as islanders say. It must be spent, freely but wisely, first on the accouterments of a desirable life style, then, periodically, on entertainment, and finally in a judicious way through gifts, loans, and by employing others. Unlike the Jamaican villagers of Rocky Roads described by Cohen (1954 : 110), the way to status for Providencians is not through hoarding. Neither, in the long run, is too much generosity an advantage, for that can quickly lead to ruin. Those who acquire wealth become vulnerable: "The higher a monkey climb, the more he expose himself" is once again an apt island summary of the situation.

Economic differentiation is clearly a large and vital part of social differentiation—the reclassification of people in terms of their status, and thence the broad grouping of these statuses into classes. Exactly how this transformation is made is the question I will try to answer in this chapter.

COLOR

In addition to the supporting and constraining function of land with respect to social sentiment and structure, certain circumstances of history (another facet of the environment), have provided elementary conditions of differentiation. From the time of Francis Archbold's settlement there have been white Europeans and black Africans living together on the island, but not as equals. Until 1853, the official date of emancipation, whites were economically better-off and socially superior, standing as masters to black slaves or virtually propertyless freedmen.

With the abolition of slavery, black Africans were allowed to own and inherit land. Though obviously at a disadvantage vis-à-vis white landowners, they now had at least the possibility of achieving wealth and thereby blurring the equation of white skin with prosperity, black skin with poverty. Even so, the nature of the model, which has been vaguely retained until the present day, was a simple transposition from white master, black slave to white upper class, black lower class.

Another blurring of these categorical lines began before emancipation but increased considerably afterward. Black and white mated and their issue confused the synonymity of white with upper and black with lower. There have come to be all shades of color in all social positions. Even so, in the most general statistical terms as well as in the minds of the people themselves, there persists a correlation between white, better-off, and "high" class; and black, poor, and "other" class. To some extent this is reflected in the bisection of the island, for the southern part, specifically Bottom House, is called the "other side" by those living elsewhere. The association between "other side" and "other class" is clearly intended. Not too great store should set by this, however; it is not a dual society, and this is strictly a manner of speaking. The social categorization of islanders is a more subtle business.

Color plays an important part in the view people take of each other. To use Anselme Remy's telling phrase, it is part of a person's "credentials of identity." In this and in its particulars, color on Providence is thought of more or less in the same way as in other formerly British Caribbean societies (cf. Hoetink 1967 : 43 ff.; Henriques 1968 : chap. 2). "Fair" or "clear" skin is socially and aesthetically preferable, with the aesthetic really providing a rationale for the social. Most people on the island, however, are of some shade in between "black" and "clear," so that in actual fact skin color per se is of less selective importance than facial features for many purposes. A long, thin, straight nose with a high bridge, thin lips, straight hair, and a flat rather than a prognathous face are the aesthetically appreciated features, which, if they accompany a fair skin, make for a beautiful person, particularly in a female. Such ideals, however, are not taken too seriously in the context of everyday life. To have such advantages is indeed to be fortunate, but how many can be so lucky? One who is "good-looking" has more reason to be proud and, in sexual matters, has good grounds to be more choosy. But few lose much time in admiring such features for their own sake.

On the other hand, particularly when islanders go to Panama or the United States, they are quickly made conscious that their color and features place them at a disadvantage before any other qualities can be mobilized to identify them as persons. Nowadays, as more and more islanders go to work in Cartagena, with its large Negro population, the Iberian "somatic norm image" prevails (Hoetink 1967 : 120), and they encounter less prejudgment and discrimination on the basis of color. Instead they encounter other difficulties, in particular, the anomaly of being English-speaking Protestants, and yet Colombians (who are by definition Spanish-speaking Catholics).

There is still, then, an imprint of historical origin which conditions the acceptance of color as a criterion of social classification. Actual circumstances often give the lie to this historical sanction—people achieve eminence or degradation in spite of their color. A prevalently endogamous mating pattern has led to the situation of people of all shades being members of the same family, or sharing the same name, and not simply because they are descended from slaves who adopted the names of their masters. The result is that while white European features may indeed be aesthetically preferable, there is a vagueness, often an ambivalence, as to the social significance of ethnic phenotype. Few people are constrained by race, but no one rejects it out of hand as a principle of classification.

The following example is interesting because it is an extreme, not because it is typical. Hamwell, with clear skin, red hair, and "good" features (but considered by most to be a homosexual), publicly avowed to the amusement of those who listened that he would never marry an island girl because there would always be the chance that the children would turn out black. Did not everyone on the island have some black in him? (That he was subject to his own generalization did not occur to Hamwell.) Very well then, he was going to Cartagena for his wife and "even if she is poor and stupid, it no matter so as she's white." In fact, he did exactly as he said he would, and his baby was indeed fair.

The notion of its being lucky (rather than an imperative) that one should mate with a lighter partner is illustrated by the example of Betty, a tall, fairly clear-skinned girl who was otherwise quite remarkably ugly and who, being over thirty years old, looked like she would never catch a man. Then, lo and behold, Betty fell in love with a particularly fair-skinned, blond policeman who had come to the island for a tour of duty. He fell in love with her, resigned from the force, married her, and took over gardening his father-in-law's land. There was, as can well be imagined, a lot of talk. The gist of it was that the union would not last, but that she was lucky because he would give her white babies.

Color is no barrier to mating, but marriage can be another matter, especially when social status is involved. I shall discuss the subtleties of status in a moment, but just to illustrate the way in which color comes into people's thinking in the matter of marriage, I shall quote a snippet of conversation between Miss Ray and Mr. John. At the time, Miss Ray was most concerned that her youngest son, Vidi, was showing too serious an interest in Benny, a girl with whom he was having an affair. Miss Ray was afraid that he might wish to marry her when her own plan called for him to marry the alcalde's daughter:

"Tscha! Mister John, man! I tellin' you her skin right, yes, an' her nose good, an hair O.K.—fuzzy but O.K. But me no want a girl from a house like she keep. Tscha, them all a' sleep on the floor man, an' is no matter who come."

"Yes, Ray, you is right," replied Mr. John.

The really important point, of course, is the matter of respectability that is here raised. But it shows that color plays some part in defining the acceptability of marriage partners.

In fact, Vidi had fathered a daughter by a very black woman, and Miss Ray, far from showing any disapproval, fostered the child. Though she spoke of her disparagingly whenever she was angry, she was raising the child as if it were her own.

Quoting Miss Ray's opinion on a suitable match for her son raises the matter of respectability, and thus brings us to the discussion of perhaps the most crucial as well as the most subtle criterion for social differentiation.

RESPECTABILITY

When some people in a society become and remain wealthier than others, or when they occupy positions of power and prestige over others, they must establish a right to such advantages. Why should they, rather than others, be so well-off? Innumerable doctrines in various societies of the world develop rationales to answer this question: the rich and powerful may be descended from first settlers or mythical ancestors; they may simply be more devout in their worship of God, so that their prosperity is no more than a just reward; they may be superior human beings because they are white, or Chinese, or civilized. On Providencia a large part of the rationale, which is itself a form of social value, is bound up with the idea of "being respectable."

Such a rationale, it must be emphasized, is put forward by those in the superior position; and they thereby retain the right to define the conditions of their own identity. For not only must they justify their position, they must preserve it, keeping themselves exclusive. These rationales draw boundaries, and thus serve the dual purpose of boundaries—inclusion and exclusion. Since these rationales are offered by the privileged ones, those excluded are under no obligation to conform to the provisos unless they desire admission to the privileged stratum. They can accept the definition and by their very contrast help to maintain it. They can also remain largely indifferent to it, going their own way and allowing the privileged ones to go theirs. Or they can reject it by refusing to respect it or by revolting against it.

On Providencia the terms *high class* and *others* are used principally by those who consider themselves high class. The term *respectability* is used primarily by high class people to describe themselves and to characterize others as not respectable. But other people are relatively indifferent to these niceties. They accept that they are not high class but do not characterize themselves by applying another label, unless they refer to themselves as being *poor people*. They make no pretense to being respectable in terms to rival the respectability of the high class; nor do they regard themselves as being *not respectable*. But their aspirations are manifest relative to the ideal standards of respectability. This rationale divides but does not separate the people of the society. The values and standards that make up respectability are subscribed to, *in varying degrees,* by everyone, so that there is a continuity: they are emphasized according to particular social circumstances and life-cycle situations.

One other feature of this ideological aspect of social differentiation is that while each criterion is recognizable, even definable, it is not measurable in any objective sense. Therefore those employing this rationale in a positive sense, to include themselves and exclude others, can manipulate the ideals to suit their own purposes and the immediate circumstances. In this way a person who conforms to all the other clear-cut criteria of status —wealth, life style, education, and color—can still be refused admittance to the high class because he or she is "not respectable enough." What Miss Ray was claiming, by her criticism of Vidi's girlfriend, was that she and her family (i.e. those living in her household) were not respectable. She singled out two aspects: that the girl was promiscuous and that the house and manner of living were disheveled. With such a background a wife would not know how to bring up a family and keep a house respectable.

Sexual propriety and household "manners" are not only important dimensions of respectability, they are also the indexes of less immediately obvious qualities of honesty, considerateness, discretion, and demeanor. They should also indicate a God-fearing attitude, real or assumed, and such an attitude takes us to the very source of the rationale of respectability—the church.

The mores advocated by the church, including especially monogamous marriage, are the ultimate referent for respectability. From this follows the emphasis on the nuclear family household as the ideal, not so much from the angle of composition as from the point of view that such a family is the indivisible unit of the society. Premarital chastity for girls, sober living for men, self-improvement for all, are the other ideal standards of respectability borrowed from the church.

The role of the church on Providencia is essentially a secular one. In all respects what goes on within the church is concerned with ideals of daily living, while the actual function of the church in bringing into sharp focus the degrees of respectability is most pronounced. Simply to go to church is a mark of being respectable; but it is important that those who claim greatest respectability attend church as a family or household. Thus the ideal and the fact appropriate each other. High class people attend church as a family, and the children go to Bible school as well. This assumes (but does not necessarily require) that the parents have been married in church, and church marriage is itself a major index of respectability, as it is in most other Caribbean societies (cf. R. T. Smith 1956 : 180–81, Clarke 1957 : 70, Gonzalez 1969 : 62, Greenfield 1966 : 117–18). Premarital chastity, strongly advocated by the church, is duly accepted as a mark of respectability not only for the girl, but as a responsibility of the family and household. Consequently high class families strictly chaperone their daughters to ensure that this ideal is met—at least insofar as public appearance goes.

The church advocates abstinence and restraint during the course of daily living. Its standards are revealed, unintentionally perhaps, in the various publications sent to all three of the island's denominations from conference headquarters in the United States. The image presented by this literature clearly reflects the life styles of middle-class midwestern or southern Americans. It offers pictures, real and in words, of neat well-furnished households, of neat, well-groomed children. It condemns all departures from the ideal without seeking for causes other than the ignorance of God, loose living, broken homes, squalor, and antisocial behavior laid at the foot of alcohol. The stories and articles offer vignettes of the good life, how it was found, and the bad life, how it was conquered. Testimonies from those who once trod the paths of evil but have now found the right way abound in every issue. Furthermore, implicit in these teachings is the idea that by following the ways of the church, one will achieve worldly success.

The sermons preached in island churches are directly influenced by this literature; indeed it could sometimes be said that they are direct plagiarisms. This is neither surprising nor to be condemned since all but the Catholic pastors are islanders whose education has not been extensive and whose imaginations are not so creative that they can be original every week in a foreign idiom. It is through sermons that the message of the church is most influentially put across, and their pattern is well standardized. The sermon is introduced by a text from the Bible, followed by lengthy quotations from church publications and then a translation of these sentiments into the everyday idiom. The themes center on examples of bad living—drunkenness, the depravity of towns, in which dancing is frequently singled out, the tragedy of broken homes; or examples of good living—the family which stays together through adversity, the family that abstains in the face of temptation and eventually comes to reap its reward, the young man who resists the challenges of his peers to illicit adventure. Such stereotyped examples are fleshed out as recollections from the actual experience of the pastors, or as people actually known to him, or sometimes they are reported as actual cases that happened in America. But in every sermon judgment is passed by the pastor in accordance with the values approved by the church, the values of respectability. Since people also seek advice on their personal problems from the pastor, these standards of judgment are applied in more intimate and specific situations as well.

Church literature and sermons are then almost exclusively

concerned with domestic matters rather than, for example, with
political, economic, or world affairs. Child-rearing, household
organization and family management, marital and parental relations, sometimes set in the context of an evil or heathen
world, are the stuff of these magazines and sermons.

Such literature appeals to women, for it is for such matters
that they are usually most responsible. Not surprisingly, most
Providence men think of the church as the women's affair.
There are, of course, men who can and do look to the church
for occupation, for this institution is one of the few that the
poor and one must say black man with intellectual aspirations
can enter. Nor, at another level, would it be true to say that
men totally ignore the church, for it is necessary that men with
claims to high status attend church simply because their respectability is a function, in part, of the total respectability of
their households.

Not only is the church the ultimate authority for the definition of respectability, it is, outside the home, the principal
public domain of sociability for women, who more or less control the activities of the church even though such key positions
as pastor and deacon are held by men. By far the largest proportion of the congregation in all three denominations is made
up of women and their children. In a choir of twenty in the
Baptist church in St. Isabel, only two were men. In the various
semicharitable societies attached to the church, women dominate the committees and take full responsibility for fund-raising
activities such as bazaars, concerts, bake sales, and sales of
work. Lest it be misunderstood, this is not to claim that the
church is exclusively a female affair but only to emphasize that
women dominate, that the church as a societal institution is
tied closely with secular and domestic life, and that it encourages
the opposition between the sexes in that much of the behavior
it condemns is male behavior, over which it has little control.
It places the blame for poverty, misery, and difficulty on men,
while exonerating women. This is not quite as true of the
Seventh-day Adventist church on Providence, for Adventists in
many ways form a closed community. Membership requires a
far more all-inclusive submission to church demands than in
either the Baptist or Catholic churches. This closed character

is most strongly affirmed by the very strong insistence that all Adventists settle their quarrels through the arbitration of church elders and avoid as far as possible calling upon the secular authorities.

The closer one comes to the definitions of the church the more completely one is respectable, and to be high class demands the fulfillment of at least minimum requirements. All islanders, however, stand somewhere on the scale of respectability and may thereby be identified with a community of values. Depending on the nature and scope of their ambitions, they render themselves amenable to judgment, acceptance, and achievement. Thus Lena is a respectable person within the limits of her total socioeconomic status; her respectability, manifest in her home, her children, and her churchgoing, is consonant with the expectations of respectability among high class people, and because of this she is accepted with respect by high class people, though in all other ways she is not high class. Part of her respectability is knowing when and how to keep her distance from high class people. On the other hand, Lerio, his sister, and his mother are in no way thought of as respectable people.

If a woman is ambitious to improve her social standing through her children, she must encourage the economic careers of her sons—and enhance the respectability of her daughters. For the latter there are certain prerequisites, since basically this is to be done first through marriage, preferably to a higher status man. Color is a great help as a first step, and some women have been known to give themselves to clear-skinned men in order to have lighter colored children and thus accomplish the first, relatively simple step up the ladder. It is also necessary that the girl be kept respectable, which means she must conform as far as possible to the provisions established by the church. A girl who becomes pregnant before marriage has simply destroyed the chances of a shortcut to an improved social position. The mother frequently reacts quite violently, often beating her daughter for "shaming" her, which means simply that the girl has now spoiled her easiest and best chance for gaining respectability. Not only does a daughter who becomes a respectable wife improve her own position, she improves that of her mother, who becomes a mother-in-law to a respected family. Even if the girl has let her mother down, the damage is not irreparable and not all ambition is thereby thwarted. For when a girl has a baby her mother becomes a grandmother, and once the new statuses are familiar, all are reconciled. The advent of children, is, as far as I know, never an event to be regretted; in fact, a "woman must have as many children as are in her belly," and unless a woman has a child she never really achieves proper female status. For the sake of prestige, however, it is better to wait.

Something of the same aura of respectability attaches to schooling, though since education is also a major avenue to occupation and income, it takes on other values too. To have a good education implies automatically that one has acquired certain of the manners, good taste, and moral sensibility that respectability insists on. Though this is only an impression, it was my sense that women far more than men were keen on their children going to school, and girls were given every opportunity for an education. The schools themselves are closely aligned with the churches: the Baptist and Adventist churches run their own secular as well as Bible schools and the Catholic church runs a convent school on the island. State schools throughout Colombia are dominated by the Catholic church. While sending one's child to school is by and large taken for granted, not to send a child to school is a mark of ignorance and lack of respectability.

I have argued that the cluster of values making up respectability has its terms set through the church. I would go so far as to say that, apart from the function of consolation, this is the church's principal role in island life, and as such it is a secular one. In this respect I have pointed out that the church is the representative or vehicle of values which originate outside the island—notably in certain parts of the United States. Though it would require a full-scale study to substantiate this point, I would like to suggest that throughout the Caribbean, the role of the Christian church, the *white* church if you will, is much the same as that described here, and that it contrasts with the *black* cults which coexist or have syncretized with Christianity. Whereas the white church in addition to being a secular church is also female-oriented and focuses on the domestic domain of social life, the black church has far more of a sacred character, gives far greater play and emphasis to the male, and concerns itself far more with matters of power (though in this latter respect it is often thwarted). The extreme example that one could cite in support of this suggestion is the Ras Tafari church in Jamaica, which is almost exclusively male, exercises complete control over its members and has become a political force, partly through its political ideology of seeking a return to Ethiopia (Barrett 1968).

PARTIES

Wealth, color, and respectability are the means by which social ranking is defined on Providencia. Of these, respectability is the most subtle and pervasive, the farthest removed from the ecology of environment and people, the most purely social. It is a quality shared by all islanders but in varying degree. To be respectable is essential if one wishes to be accepted as high class, while being respectable in general earns respect throughout the whole society. Some people, though, are indifferent to being thought respectable, others find themselves in circumstances where respectability is difficult to maintain, and for others respectability is not a matter to which one's entire life need be submitted.

Social ranking is a function of three criteria that are applied to make generalized classifications among the population as well as to assign individuals a place in a class. As I have pointed out above, such a classification is insisted upon by those in higher positions, and it is they who affirm through their behavior such a class division. There is one activity above all others which publicly marks this division, and that is the party.

The most frequent social function on the island is a party, to be distinguished from the rather more informal and spontaneous *spree*. A party is organized and, since it takes place in someone's home, is initially exclusive. Three types of party are recognized: the *invitation* party, the *paid* party, and the *public* party. Of these the invitation party is the one most pertinent to our present concern with social stratification.

An invitation party is always given by a couple or a household, and the guests are invited not as individuals but as a couple or household. The hosts prepare a list of the guests in English or Spanish, usually in alphabetical order and in this form: Mr. and Mrs. Archbold invite Mr. and Mrs. A. Gomez and Family. . . . At the head of the list is a statement of the time, place, date, and purpose of the party. This list is taken, usually by a small boy, to all of the proposed guests in turn. Each guest carefully scans the list; if all meets his approval and the guests are able to attend, he signs O.K. by his name. Otherwise he writes "sorry." It is readily admitted that the purpose of sending a complete list is to allow all to see who is coming. One does not go to parties that might not be respectable, where people who are not high class have been asked to be present, or, of course, where one might meet one's enemies.

Time after time the lists include the same names, with omissions resulting most often from personal, often temporary, animosities. And only the people mentioned on these lists hold such invitation parties. Now and again a new name appears and in this way the high class officially accepts or rejects a new member. If certain key islanders accept an invitation which includes a new name, all is well. These lists, then, which are made up largely of people from St. Isabel plus a few from Lazy Hill, Bailey, Rocky Point, and elsewhere, are virtually a social register of the island. The only high class absentees are certain Seventh-day Adventists, who because of their religion do not attend parties. Most of them live in Smoothwater Bay.

The invitation party is said to have originated with an immigrant Swedish family, the Sjogreens, who gave fine parties and who compiled a document known as the "Golden Roll." They left the island after many years' sojourn, though there are still some less fortunate Sjogreens living in Old Town. During their stay on the island the Sjogreen family appear to have been the primary social arbiters.

These parties have their own style, quite different from other forms of the party.

Mr. Richie gave a party in honor of his wife's birthday. It was held in the area underneath his house, which formed, in effect, a large patio that was very pleasant. It was decorated with streamers, knickknacks, and electric lights. Mr. Richie had

*arranged to borrow the alcaldia's portable generator. All invited
had agreed to come.*

*On one table, with a suitable white cloth, stood an array of
bottles—Johnny Walker, Black and White, and William IV
scotch, Hennessey cognac, and a Mexican brandy. There was
also, for the ladies, a rose-colored, peppermint-flavored rum,
the specialty of Jack Tree, the finest island rum distiller. Inside
the house was a supply of island rum, known variously as Jump
Steady, Jom's Toddy, or Cumfia. Another table was set with
plates, cutlery, and bottles of soft drink.*

*Promptly at 7 P.M. the first guests arrived. The ladies went
straight to their seats on the edge of the patio while the men
gathered at the table of drinks. Each having taken his lady a
glass, the men ceased serving for the rest of the evening. In a
shadowy corner sat a trio of three young men playing an accordion, a guitar, and a jawbone. They provided the music for
dancing, which was not too enthusiastic at first. Within thirty
minutes all the guests had arrived. There were a few couples
on the floor dancing and conversation went on freely.*

*At 8:30 there was a surprise: spaghetti and tomato sauce
with meat—the new island favorite and still very much a
novelty. One or two ladies had minor mishaps as they balanced
the plates precariously on their laps and tried to eat the spaghetti politely, but this was cause for laughter as well as embarrassment. After supper the trio was given a break and Vidi's
phonograph supplied the music. This too was a novelty, since
portable, battery-driven phonographs were very new on the
market. With the latest music—Elvis Presley—and the spaghetti
supper, this was for islanders an* avant garde *event.*

*By 11 P.M. the older people had almost all left. Some who
were chaperoning younger girls insisted that their charges leave
too, but others, particularly close friends of the family, remained,
as did one or two younger couples. With most of the guests
gone, the party became more informal. Men removed their ties
and began some serious drinking, though most were already
rather tipsy. The few women remaining drifted inside the house,
and the spectators looking in from the yard all disappeared.
By midnight only the host, his son, and a few close friends—*

members of his crew—were still in evidence. They stayed until
the early hours of the morning talking and drinking, dispersing
only when the drink finally ran out.

A paid party is also private, but admission is charged and
anyone who pays can go in. Giving such a party is a popular
way of making money. The host supplies the house, music,
food, and sometimes drink and hopes to make a profit out of
the charges for admission—which varies from fifty cents to
three pesos. Invitations are not sent out, but the word is spread
around. People rarely come in couples and never as a household. Men and women attend as individuals, though usually in
company with a "best friend" or with other members of a crew
or peer group. High class men, whether married or not, do
attend such parties, but high class married women would never
attend such functions, and unmarried high class girls go but
rarely and at some risk to their respectability.

A paid party is held indoors so that those who do not pay
do not party. At one typical party the house was quite a small
one, comprising one room to which was attached a small
kitchen. There were benches around the walls and in one
corner sat the band, teen-age boys playing guitar, accordion,
and maracas. They sat expressionless, glazed perhaps by the
hypnotic effect of their music, the rum with which they had
been liberally plied, and the hot, heavy atmosphere of a packed
room. The dancers crowded the floor swaying their bodies but
barely moving their feet. Little children, some hardly bigger
than the babies they carried, darted in and out of the crowd
to fetch and carry refreshments. Overlooking the whole scene,
eerily lit by by the white glare of a Petromax lantern, stood the
hostess, arms akimbo, now and then turning to one of the men
standing nearby to make a remark, or perhaps to direct them
to calm a rather too excited or drunken guest.

The atmosphere was noisy, smoky, stuffy, and hot, but completely relaxed. Now and then people would detach themselves
from the crowd to catch some air, or sneak away for some
love-making. For such parties are an excellent way for the sexes
to meet in public and retreat in private.

The third type, the public party, is one usually given by the
government in celebration of a national holiday. Refreshments

are provided and high class people are served in the alcalde's and adjoining offices on the second floor of the alcaldia. Everyone else remains below on the ground floor. Some public parties, for example official receptions for visiting dignitaries, which are few and far between, are in effect invitation affairs expressive of the same social hierarchy.

The social gatherings so far described are primarily recreational, but at the same time they express certain purely social differences between people. They are to be distinguished from those social gatherings which mark life crises—funerals and weddings in particular—where lines of social demarcation become blurred, though they are still retained in a subtle fashion.

Most "other" people live in common-law union. They are "married but not churched" as islanders put it. If a couple decides to marry in church it is usually after they have had several children, when their life situation is relatively firmly established. In such cases the reception is held at their own home, less often at the church hall-cum-school, and largely at their own expense. High class people, on the other hand, encourage their sons and daughters to marry before setting up a household, and the wedding responsibilities are assumed by the respective parents.

Members of the families of both bride and groom attend the ceremony, while onlookers remain outside the church. The bride and groom lead the procession to the house of the bride's parents, where the reception is to be held. Only immediate members of the families, plus all the high class people invited, are asked to go inside the house where they are served a fancy meal and refreshments. They are joined by the priest or pastor. If there are "other" class members of the family and they are not first degree kin, they as often as not remain outside the house with the onlookers, receiving only the same light refreshments offered for general consumption. After the reception there is usually a dance which, as much for convenience as anything else, is held outside. At this time everybody mingles.

At high class weddings, in fact, only guests whose names appear on the "register" are invited, plus close kin if they are not high class. Other class weddings always invite members of the high class, and the newlyweds show great delight and deference if a high class person attends. Getting married is among other things an assumption of a new level of respectability, a way in which poor people demonstrate to their "betters" their improvement. The presence of high class people at such a wedding is taken as a sign of recognition, not that the new couple is now high class, but that they are now better than they were, since they now more nearly resemble their betters.

Funeral wakes, or *sit-ups,* by their very nature are less organized and less deliberate than weddings. Though the people of nearby San Andrés observe the Jamaican nine-night wake, the people of Providence do not (cf. Price 1954). Some people mentioned that this was the practice in the old days, but nowadays a wake rarely lasts more than thirty-six to forty-eight hours, the exact length depending on the time of death.

When death appears inevitable, or even when a serious illness reaches a climax, relatives abroad are notified by radiogram, and they make every effort to return to the island as quickly as possible. As a body hovers close to death, a noticeable pall comes over the community. As the final moment clamps down the priest or pastor administers the last rites and the doctor confirms the death. When this happens a young man, known as the rider, circles the island on horseback calling out the name, time of death, and time of burial of the deceased. Thus within a few hours the entire population is informed. The church bell rings out the number of years lived by the deceased.

At the house of the dead mirrors are covered, windows closed, clocks stopped, the corpse washed, orifices plugged, and the body redressed. Close relatives of the same sex as the deceased carry out these tasks while close kin—mother, wife, father, or husband—keep watch by the bed and lead the moaning and mourning. Neighbors and devout members of the congregation to which the deceased belonged arrange benches, chairs, and tables around the yard. Others prepare urns of coffee and bake biscuits to accommodate those who come to pay their last respects to the dead, first by walking past the body and then by sitting up through the night to sing hymns, drink coffee, and above all to tell stories and reminisce. Meanwhile, unobtrusively in a corner of the yard, the local carpenter and his assistants make the coffin or "box" using wood set aside by the deceased during his life for that very purpose. The carpenter works for a supply of rum and food. At the same time, or at dawn if the death occurred at night, the grave-digger begins his work in the cemetery.

The sit-up, though a solemn affair and clearly heart-rending for those close to the deceased, is also a time of good fellowship for those on the periphery of the bereavement. It is a time when people from all over the island come together. Once arrived they are not ready to leave immediately, and after the funeral procession has escorted the coffin to the grave, many of them return to the house of the dead for more talk, to offer further comfort and consolation, and then to visit kin and friends living nearby. Whether the deceased was high or other class, high class people do not tarry after they have paid their respects, and they spend no more than an hour or so at the sit-up, returning later on to join the procession to the cemetery. The only high class people who remain throughout a sit-up are the close friends and relatives of the bereaved, and especially the women.

At social gatherings, then, the generalized social differences are made apparent. What appears only fragmentarily, often only as nuance in the intricate interactions of individuals, is summarized and in a sense ritualized in such gatherings. The division of the population into two "classes" does not necessarily pervade all facets of social life, for there are other matters to be taken into account, which I shall discuss in later chapters. But clearly such a division offers a basis for the allocation of power and authority: members of the high class are in control of the economic and political domains of life.

Social demarcation as between individuals and as a general classificatory phenomenon is not fixed. There is scope for mobility between the two classes, and the existence of such a hierarchy provides one of the arenas within which social relations can assume a dynamic form—*crab antics* again.

CRAB ANTICS: MOBILITY

Social status, in terms of class, is a matter of wealth or occupation, color, and respectability, which last is closely dependent on life style. An acceptable combination of all criteria is neces-

sary for acceptance into high class, but not necessarily an absolute combination.

A man becomes wealthy by gaining sufficient independence
from land that he can accumulate cash by various other means
such as trade, smuggling, entrepreneurship, sailing, or a profession. But he is born to his color and to his respectability, while
some are born to wealth as well. Wealth can be achieved; color
can't be changed, but can be overlooked. Respectability, inherited primarily from one's mother and the household she
maintains, remains unchanged in the eyes of others—unless one
goes away from the island. If a person stays on Providencia the
transition in his life is too gradual for others to be able to recognize any real change; he remains what others remember him to
have been, not what he wishes to be or become. But if he goes
away for a sufficiently long period of time, he can present himself as a new man. He can be granted respectability on the evidence of his new life style independently of his past and that of
his family. This is especially true if he can secure a respectable
wife.

Mr. Garcia is a case in point. He had worked for some time
aboard a boat that plied regularly between Panama, Cartagena,
and the islands. Consequently he spent part of each year on
Providence. Through trading and a great success in smuggling,
he had managed to accumulate a tidy fortune within the space
of fifteen years or so. He bought several acres of land, including a new house site on which he built a small but modern and
expensive villa. What is more, he was able to realize the ambition of many islanders and buy his own boat—a forty-ton vessel
which soon yielded him a good return. For twenty-five years he
prospered, marrying his common-law wife along the way. By
the time he was forty-five years old he could give up sailing the
boat himself, employing others to do this business. Having given
up the energetic side of his enterprise, he sought to take an
active part in island politics and in the affairs of the Baptist
church, of which he became a deacon.

Mr. Garcia assumed all the marks of respectability, even to
the extent that, though phenotypically he was a black man, by
the way he dressed and by his activities and life style he became
white—culturally at least. Yet he was never accorded the re-

spect he claimed. On one occasion, for example, he had con-
sulted with the alcalde and tendered advice on certain matters.
As he left the alcalde's office, the alcalde turned to the secretary
and together they burst out laughing. Later on in the rum
shop they recounted the meeting, observing how Garcia had
become "big ass and swollen head," and concluded the story
with imitations of his talk and swagger. But Miss Ray summed it
all up, turning to Mr. John to observe as Garcia walked up the
street: "Hoo! Him a think him a sa' holy now. Tscha! 'Member
when him a walk by every night drunk as a Bush Indian?" She
also commented on his wife, saying she would never let the likes
of *her* in the house. Mr. Garcia was simply around too much
and never away long enough to allow people to forget what he
had been. So they could not see what he had become.

In contrast there was Tulio. Like Garcia, Tulio was "black"
and born into a poor household in Bailey. At sixteen years of
age he left the island to work, first in Panama, then in the
United States. He was away for twenty-seven years, during most
of which time he was a sailor with Standard Oil of New Jersey,
working his way up from ordinary seaman to second officer on a
large tanker. He managed to save a lot of money, having some
kept back for him and saving up the rest himself, as well as
sending his mother a regular remittance. In New York he had
met and married a girl from San Andrés.

At the age of forty-three, with his savings and a pension, Tulio
returned to Providence to retire. He built a small but modern
Spanish-style house with modern furnishings. Before he actually
returned he had purchased a total of twenty-five acres of land,
most of it from Jenkins, and on this he intended to pasture a
herd of beef cattle.

Tulio and his wife regularly attended Mass at the Catholic
church and sent their youngest children to the Bible school
(their adolescent children were at school in the United States).
They always appeared well dressed, even when going into the
bush, and they were never, for example, seen to go barefoot.
Tulio visited the rum shop regularly, where he struck up friendships and impressed others with his tales of experiences all over
the world as well his general air of sophistication. His wife,
through the church, came to know women like Miss Ray, with

whom she sat on a number of committees. Within a year their names appeared on the invitation lists to parties. They in turn gave their first party, to which all the notables were invited— and more important, to which they came.

Another example is Mr. Forbes, whose story clearly shows the role of respect and respectability. Mr. Forbes's story is very much like Tulio's. Forbes left the island to work as a sailor, serving in the Gran Colombiano merchant fleet. He too worked himself up to become a ship's officer and eventually retired with savings and a pension. He had married a Colombian girl and they returned to the island to live in their new house. But there the resemblance stopped. Forbes spent most of his time getting drunk, getting into arguments and fights, mixing with the younger, unmarried, and other class men of the community. He was often heard to bemoan the backwardness of Providence people, their stupidity, and the lack of good bars and night clubs on the island. He became so quarrelsome at one point that he had to appear before the alcalde, where he was made to sign a bond of peace. Clearly he was making no attempt to achieve respectability or to become accepted as a higher class person.

A good part of this respectability, of living right, is in fact conforming to a pattern of behavior, of having certain social skills and graces which are "modern" and "cosmopolitan"—and white. These are acquired by living abroad in a metropolitan center, most advantageously in the United States, but also in Panama or a Colombian city. Or they are acquired through education, which in any case must be gained in similar urban centers. This is especially important for men, since knowledge and urbanity contribute to aspects of their reputation, which others respect and which complements the moral respectability guarded by women. An educated man, for instance, does not act so foolishly as to drink himself silly night after night like Forbes.

The reference group, then, for high social status and for respectability is the urban middle-class Afro-American and white community of the United States or the Panama Canal Zone. This is the model where proper English is spoken, where manners come naturally, where a house is immaculate and furnished in the best taste to the utmost convenience, where sophistication has its roots and modernity its zenith, where God and the church are an integral part of daily life, and where morality is impeccable! It stands to reason that if a man brings back a wife from such an environment she will be thought of as an asset—as soon as she can convince the rest of the island of her authenticity. Otherwise, marrying anyone from outside the island, unless from San Andés, is a risky undertaking.

Nowadays there is a glimmer of change. The Colombian government has, at last, begun to show something of an interest in the welfare of the island, beginning with the provision of scholarships for further education. Though this is generally recognized as a measure to convert islanders to Catholicism, they are taking advantage of such opportunities—becoming "job Catholics," in their words. Work in the United States and Panama is no longer so easy to come by, and, not being nationals of these countries, islanders face aggravated immigration problems. They can migrate freely to Colombia, however, and since they must go away to earn cash, Colombia, particularly Cartagena and Barranquilla, is where they go.

This in turn is changing the cultural reference group from English-speaking America to Spanish Colombia. Mainland spouses are more and more coming to be accepted, the Spanish language is less and less decried, books in Spanish are beginning to exercise their influence, and Colombian music had almost completely won the day by 1961. Only Colombians themselves are greeted with hostility and thought of in terms of a gross stereotype as cunning, vicious little men, too handy with the knife and only too ready to kill for a purse or the church.

CRAB ANTICS: SHAMING

Social ranking is not something one just nods one's head over. There is not only acquiescence and acceptance that some are better-off than others, there is resentment that "some think they are better than others." People of equal or unequal status take whatever opportunity they can to pull another down or keep him in his place. Since such goings on are a constant, albeit visceral, ingredient of social relations, this chapter concludes with some account of them.

I have already had occasion to mention the fact that those

who are well-off and who own a lot of land do not expect and
are not allowed to grow their own food. If they attempt to do so
their gardens are either vandalized or the crop stolen. Better-off
people are expected to buy their supplies from those who are
less well-off. Since such supplies are irregular, whenever people
come around with produce for sale, the well-off almost fall over
themselves to buy. But though some try, customers for this
produce cannot secure any guarantee of supplies nor can they
make any arrangement with a producer for a regular supply or
for preferred treatment. If you are well-off you cannot get what
you want when you want it, though sometimes you can send
around for what is needed. The same is true of fish. No well-off
person fishes, and so all are dependent on "others" for their
supply. But it is hard to get a fisherman to save a piece of fish
—you have to be there, like everyone else, on the beach when
he gets back.

These are not just accidental circumstances. They are the
results of a deliberate, open means of asserting "equality" or
"independence," and those who are well-off must go along
with the situation. Incidentally, such a relationship explains, in
part, why it is that so many well-off people must rely on imported foodstuffs.

Those who own land are expected by those who own little
or no land to provide work, and at the convenience of the
laborer rather than the owner. Otherwise, when the owner needs
help, for example to harvest sugar cane, it will not be forthcoming. Furthermore, once he has been hired, a man does not
consider himself under much obligation to work to the full
or even to do things the way the employer would like them
done. Relations between employer and employee on the island
are always strained and riddled with mutual suspicion.

Here, from my notes, is a partially reconstructed scene at
which I was present. It shows quite vividly just what things are
like.

*Laredo is a high class man who owns about forty acres of
land. He had a piece of about seven acres under sugar cane,
which was now ready for harvest. He went to Bottom House to
recruit some help, and among those willing to work was Frank
Livingston.*

On the first day Frank arrived two hours late and rather drunk. He spent the rest of the morning finishing his rum. On the second day he did not turn up at all, because his hangover was too rough. On the third day he was late again. Laredo told him to be sure he came on time in future, otherwise he would not be paid. Laredo then proceeded in the customary island fashion to lecture Frank on his drunkenness and irresponsibility. This led to a heated argument, the last part of which went as follows:

Frank: *What de goddam you tink you are, heh? Listen man, nobody tell me what fe do. If me wan' tak' life easy man, der ain't no goddam black arse nigger tell me no. Fuck.*

Laredo: *Don' use that language man. You is worse than a Bush Indian. You kind is all the same. All you want is money for you Jom's Toddy an' you children running around in rags.*

Frank: *What de fuck! You insult my children man? Tscha! I make more children in one fucking week than you got hairs in your arse. We not all rich like you. An' don' you tink me no know how you get all dat money—you goddam teef. Me no forget how you teef day money fe my mother, and she you own sister fe de same goddam belly.*

Laredo: *Tscha man! You da talk a pile o' foolishness. I is too busy to listen to you foolishness.*

Laredo asserts the idea of "place"; Frank invokes his superior manhood and implies, by his reference to Laredo stealing money, that there is a skeleton in the closet, of which Laredo and his family should be ashamed. The invocation of kinship as an equalizer is an important and widespread feature of island social relations which I shall take up in detail in the next chapter. This example, though, illustrates how even when apparently personal animosities are being worked out, social criteria are the means by which they are expressed.

The idea that the better-off are in fact no better is the rationale for such behavior as store assistants filching from their employers, and quite openly too. I was able to watch Septimus drain soap powder from cartons in Mr. John's store and remove bottles of soft drinks from their cases. Septimus then sold these privately.

Most shaming or denigration does not take place before the person's face but behind his back, though still publicly, as gossip and in the circulation of stories detrimental in some way or other to people's respectability and reputation. Ridicule is the main ingredient of these stories and serves clearly to suggest to those less well-off that, in fact, their betters are no better.

One night Dolfo (minister of the Baptist church) was asleep. He awoke suddenly thinking he heard the shutters bang. This was strange because they were always tightly locked at night. Thinking it must be a thief, or possibly an animal, Dolfo climbed out of bed to take a look-see.

It was a thief all right.

"Aha! You teef my daughter!" yelled Dolfo, giving chase to the intruder and running bare ass down the road—an' him a minister.

Certainly an incongruous situation for a pastor—but the insinuation that, through his daughter, the respectability of the household was not all it was supposed to be is not lost on the audience.

Mr. Jenkins is reputed to be the wealthiest man on the island. But everyone knows how he got to be so—certainly not because he deserved to be. When his employer, the old Jew Rubinstein, got old, Jenkins simply took what he needed and came quickly to Providence. Then there was all the money he stole from the German spies he drowned, after promising to smuggle them into Panama in the war, not to mention the proceeds from his other smuggling activities. Nowadays Jenkins hardly ever comes out of his store, preferring to sit behind his huge rolltop desk, from which base he conducts his many affairs.

A lot of gossip centers upon the real or imputed sexual indiscretions of "respectable" people: Miss Ray's son-in-law was sweet on the two Hernandez girls around in Bailey; Bradley got surprised with his trousers down in Bercita's house; Miss Gloria was not in when Miss Ethel paid a visit, but her children were there and they said their mammy was around seeing Miss Ethel. And what was one to make of Harris, who came back from

Barranquilla not with his own wife but with his brother's? Alfredo and his wife were looking a bit bruised one morning, as if they had been fighting, and that is no way for such people to be carrying on.

It is impossible to describe all the subtle ways and means, the nuances of conversation, the innuendos in a tone of voice, by which people's images of themselves are tinted and tainted by those around them. Those higher up are of course more frequently the butt of such behavior (the higher a monkey climb the more he expose himself), but putting down is an island-wide trait. It is, for example, the chief means of punishing a child and is practiced far more often than the constantly threatened flogging. The net result of such antics, however, appears to be the preservation of a sense of balance between differences, a constant interweaving of the public and private images of status.

I would like to conclude this chapter with a short account of the rise and fall of Napoleon Coleman. It incorporates and summarizes many of the points I have tried to make in the last two chapters.

Napoleon was "black as a Bush Indian" and "ugly as an African" and he came from Southwest Bay. He was big and strong, rough and ready, but a good soul with the laugh of a free man. He was not well-off, but he had some land with plenty of coconut trees. Having decided to leave the island to sail and work, he left his wife to harvest his coconuts and sell them while he was away.

With good fortune assisting his undoubted talents he began to make money. He took a job sailing with a boat owned by a Colombian who lived in San Andrés, and while working for this man he did well trading and smuggling on his own account. Winning the trust of the owner, he became the supercargo and further improved his fortunes.

In five years he was able to buy his own small boat, doing so well with this that four years later he had five boats trading for him as far afield as Miami. During the twelve years or so that he accumulated his fortune at sea, he came back only once or twice to Providence, though each time he bought land. At last he handed over command of his boat to another and settled back on the island. He moved from Southwest Bay to St. Isabel, where he built the largest house on the island, and in which he opened its grandest store. He took on a partner, a Jamaican, to run the seagoing part of his enterprises, while he attended to affairs on the island and set about transforming his advantageous economic position into a socially privileged one.

He and his wife were married in a no-expenses-barred ceremony. They gave lavish parties, dressed in the latest finery imported direct from the United States, and their house was by far the grandest, inside and out, that the island had yet seen. Withal, Napoleon was a most generous man, and there are today many who remember with gratitude his generosity.

Napoleon's partner, however, was eroding his business, cooking accounts, siphoning off cargo which he then sold in his name, running up debts, and the like, so that slowly it began to appear that Napoleon's empire might be crumbling. Eventually Napoleon found out what was happening, sued his partner and succeeded in having him put in jail.

That, said most people, was his worst mistake.

The partner, like all Jamaicans, was a great obeah *man. Soon after their quarrel came to a head, three of Napoleon's boats sank with no apparent explanation and under circumstances that stalled the insurance company. Napoleon himself fell mysteriously ill (which could have been a consequence of his worries). The doctors could do nothing for him, but meantime he could not shore up his business, and there was no one who could take over for him. Creditors began to pressure him, debtors reneged, and others proved not to be as generous to him as he had been to them. Within eighteen months he was dead. His business lay in ruins, his fortune had disappeared and his family was shattered.*

Today the same house, its dimensions now superseded by houses of the more recently rich, stands a sad, sagging relic of former glories. His daughter, its sole occupant, lives there a virtual recluse, making what she can out of letting the rooms to visitors, especially policemen whom she supplies with young girls and other refreshment.

Not all lives on Providencia conform so neatly to such a melodramatic plot, but the life of Napoleon sums it all up. The black man transcending his color; the poor man become rich; the Bush Indian becoming the leader of society and arbiter of taste. Here, too, is the wise man turned fool, the victim perhaps of himself, but also of crab antics.

6 Sentiment and Structure: Kinship

Social ranking is a development of economic differentiation and, as such, it is defined not merely by material factors but also by rationalizing and sentimental considerations. Those better-off include, in their image of themselves, a justification for their advantage—that they are, in fact, better people. This is expressed and rationalized in the idea of respectability which in turn confirms that there is a thoroughgoing and justifiable inequality between islanders. It is not a matter of luck or fate that some people are better-off than others, but a matter of the innate superiority of total persons. Inequality and inequity, for those in superior positions, are the pillars of a doctrine of social stratification. Those less well-off are confronted by the physical and material facts of inequality and, as we have seen, find various ways and means to try to negate it, or accept the premise and work for improvement accordingly.

But the doctrine of inequality is contrary to the universally held sentiment that all islanders are equal. We have already examined the way in which land is defined according to this sentiment and, in turn, defines the sentiment. I will now examine the principal response made to the fact, and doctrine, of social stratification and inequality. The "handle" used to operate a purely social doctrine of equality is kinship.

Kinship on Providencia and in most societies of the Caribbean does not have a discriminating function, as it does in most so-called primitive tribes. Different classes of kinsmen are not defined in contrast to each other, nor are certain principles of genealogical connection emphasized so as to direct specific political and legal matters, giving rights to some and not others. Instead, kinship exercises a generalizing function summed up in the Caribbean-wide saying common in most communities: "we is all one family" (R. T. Smith 1956 : 51). Kinship is invoked at a general level to emphasize the equality of all members of a population and at a specific or interpersonal level to counterargue assertions of social inequality.

122

If kinship itself is not a cognitively discriminating principle, there is a very definite sense in which the population can be differentiated according to the use of kinship in organizing social relations. For men kinship is a means of expressing sentiments of equality in the politico-jural domain; for women, kinship is a means of organizing and expressing emotional (or sentimental) ties in the domestic domain (cf. Fortes 1969). This does not mean to say that men have nothing to do with the domestic domain or that ties of kinship are never affective, nor does it mean that women are excluded from the politico-jural domain of social relations or that they never can mix kinship with a political or legal role. The question, as we shall see, is one of emphasis.

KINSHIP AND RESIDENCE: THE MALE

Each of the fourteen communities, except such small ones as Jones Point and Freshwater Bay, is informally divided into sections. Each section bears a name, usually that of the family that is or was the original owner of the land. In Old Town, for example, there are Dawkin, Bowden, and Sjogreen sections; in Rocky Point we find Hoy, Britton, Hooker, and Bryan sections. Still other sections may be unnamed, though the people living there as neighbors, who are also related, recognize a boundary between themselves and others. In addition to this system of named sections, there is a preponderance of family names or "titles" in given communities: Archbold and Howard in Nelly Downs and St. Isabel; Henry and Livingston in Bottom House; Watler, Bush, Robinson, and Hawkins in Lazy Hill; and so forth. These sections and the concentration of families are a direct consequence of the inheritance of land, in this case, house spots, by males. Every father will do his best to ensure that his sons by the woman he considers his permanent spouse will receive a house spot. Preferably this should border his own house, but if this is impossible, then a site is acquired as close as is feasible. Many fathers also consider it a matter of paternal pride and duty to provide either the land or financial assistance to purchase a site for their "outside" sons. Daughters too may inherit a house spot, as they may inherit land, but most often this is by default—if a man has no sons, for example, or if a girl

remains unmarried or otherwise can find no place to live but
in her parents' home.

To comprehend the relationship between kinship and residence, let us consider in detail the history of two sample sections. Dawkin Town, in Old Town, comprises houses built on
land first cleared by William Dawkin, the first to bear his name
to the island. When he died, the land was divided among his
children, to be used by them as house spots. But when these
children died there was not enough land for all their heirs, so in
some cases the houses and land were left to youngest sons
or, in two instances, to daughters, while others built houses elsewhere, though within the limits of Old Town. The process of integration and dispersal has continued since then and all males
bearing the "title" Dawkin, still live in Old Town.

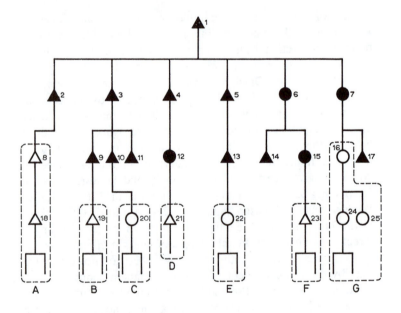

Fig. 7.   Inheritance of house spots: Dawkin Town.

Figure 7 gives the details. When Dawkin died there were
seven houses in a cluster—six for his children and one his
own. Upon his death his eldest grandson (no. 9) took over his

house. All the others left their houses to their youngest children, except no. 7, whose daughter never married, having devoted her life to looking after her father in his invalid old age. She did, however, have three children; her son left the island permanently, but the daughters stayed with her and the house will pass on to one daughter (no. 24) and her husband.

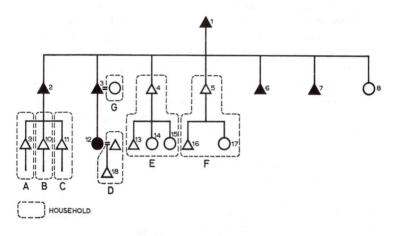

Fig. 8.   Inheritance of house spots: Nelly Downs.

In Nelly Downs, James Archbold left each of his five sons a house spot (see fig. 8). There was enough land in every spot to allow for further division in the succeeding generation. But now Edward (no. 9), John (no. 10), and Robert (no. 11) do not have enough land in the section to provide for all their sons. They will have to look elsewhere in the village.

There is, as far as I know, no political significance to these sections. They are not inviolate, for there is buying and selling as well as renting of house spots within villages. And although preference is usually shown to a kinsman in such transactions, non-kin quite frequently move in. Such sections, however, do give form to neighbor/kin relations, a form that is far more the consequence than the cause of inheritance norms.

To own a plot of land on which to build a house is considered a cultural imperative for a man. This more than anything else is the plot of land that gives him title to an island identity. On it he will build the house that signifies to the world at large that he is now mature, competent, and solvent enough to provide for a wife and family—and that he wishes to do so. Few women will live with or marry a man who cannot provide them with a house. When a young man goes abroad to work, he does so, at first, to accumulate funds to begin building his house. Very often it cannot be built all at once, and a demonstration of the intent to build is considered acceptable as a "permit" to cohabit. So it is not unusual to see throughout the island half-completed structures or even a pile of building material marking the spot where eventually time and money, as well as inclination, will raise a dwelling. In other circumstances a man, usually the youngest son, cares for his aged parents, becoming actual if not titular head of the house while one or both are alive, then inheriting the house as his own.

With preference given to males, we find the coincidence of fraternal ties with residence, but on a formal, legal basis. The relationship between brothers is bound up especially with their economic and legal status vis-à-vis each other in respect to land. Kin who are neighbors, then, are at the core brothers, while parents and grandparents become more and more loosely attached as they get older and sisters most frequently are physically and legally removed, since they go to live with their husbands. In addition to this basically formal, legal interest of brothers in each other within the community, there is the important factor that the domestic life which centers on the household and is conducted within these sections is the province, the true domain, of women. Men hardly interfere unless as arbiters, and in a completely social sense they remain on the periphery of domestic affairs.

This formal, detached relationship and status is manifest in other small but meaningful ways. A man is usually fed separately and alone (though this is true less often of high class households). Though children always take the father's title, fathers have comparatively less intimate relations with their children, but rather relate to them as objects contributing to their pride. The father frequently shows off his children, and he indulges them rather more than he disciplines them. True, a mother may threaten a child that "when you pappy come back he gwan' flog you"; but this very "bogeyman" role indicates the detachment of the father. In some cases, admittedly exceptional, fathers refused to allow the mother to carry the new baby in public. Children are evidence of a man's virility, for to their conception he has contributed the blood and the soul. Hence children are part of oneself—a part to be proud of. They are also "an insurance for old age" and "poor man's riches," conceptualizations which, for all that they have much truth in them, also betray a sense of distance in relationship. As a child grows up, and becomes a person in his own right and less an object that can be dandled, he moves farther and farther into the emotional orbit of the mother, coming under her sway and returning intense loyalty. When the father of a child no longer lives with the mother, the intensity of their relationship fades almost away. Fathers do not necessarily lose all interest, however, and I heard of a number of instances in which a man, upon learning of the unhappiness of his child in his mother's household (usually with a stepfather), made arrangements to look after the child. Fathers try to contribute to the upbringing and education of their children, particularly sons, even if they have severed all relationship with the mother.

However many exceptions may be instanced, though, it is plain that by comparison with our own culture, even with the suburban commuter variant, the man in Providencia and in the Caribbean generally if other accounts are to be accepted, is marginal to the household, formal in his standing as a neighbor, and detached in his role of father. His greatest involvement, which increases directly with status, is in maintaining the respectability of the household, with the result that the domestic role of high class husbands is far more integrated.

KINSHIP AND RESIDENCE: THE FEMALE

As has been repeatedly pointed out, females dominate the household and domestic life in Caribbean societies. In fact, by far the greater proportion of anthropological literature is devoted to the "female-centered family," or the household variously called matrifocal, matricentric, conjugal, and so forth. Most theories have been directed toward "accounting for" the prevalence of such a form (see Whitten and Szwed 1970, Greenfield 1968).

In outlining the male's standing vis-à-vis kinship and residence above, I indicated his marginality and his lack of complete involvement, thereby confirming the general Caribbean situation. This very emphasis, in observation and theory, raises an important question that has gone unrecognized, which I shall confront in the following chapter. How does a male achieve social identity and existential fulfillment if he is peripheral to domestic life, especially if, in turn, the household is to be characterized as the basic unit of the society? (Greenfield 1968, Gonzalez 1969 : 68).

As a young girl grows up she assumes more and more responsibility for household affairs. She looks after younger children, keeps the house clean, helps in the cooking and laundry and runs errands. Running counter to this heuristic involvement is her emotional development, for as she approaches adolescence her interests and emotions extend to others outside her household. She seeks the friendship of girls of her own age and she begins the fulfillment of her sexual desires. The result of this tussle of competing interests is an increasing strain between a daughter and her mother, which culminates with the girl's first pregnancy. When the condition becomes obvious a violent quarrel often ensues, climaxing with a beating—behavior that Madeline Kerr, writing about Jamaica, observes "is so general that it is almost a ritual" (Kerr 1952 : 11, 62). Since in the previous chapter I suggested that this is connected with certain ambitions a mother has for improved respectability, let me give a typical instance.

Gilly, a widow with two daughters aged fifteen and thirteen years, had herself borne two children before settling down with Lysandro in common-law union. The eldest girl began to show obvious signs of pregnancy and, living next door, I could not help overhearing what went on one morning.

First, there was the verbal lashing, with much talk of the shame the girl had brought to her mother. Now everyone on the island would be talking about her "scandal." And all this in spite of everything Gilly had tried to do to bring the girl up decent. While she was talking and getting more and more excited, she began cuffing the girl; then, almost as if she did not know she was doing it, she picked up a broom and beat the girl while shrieking uncontrollably.

The girl finally ran out of the house screaming "She a gwan' kill me," pushing her way through a small knot of people attracted to the house by the noise. The girl made her way to her grandmother's house in Mountain, and there she stayed for nearly five weeks. The grandmother, acting as go-between, tried to mollify the mother and convince the girl she should apologize for "cheeking" her mother. Eventually Gilly came around to fetch her daughter. There was a reconciliation and in a month or so the baby was born in Gilly's house. Gilly proudly bore the new baby, her first grandchild, around to Mountain to show her friends and relatives. Mother and daughter, now grandmother and mother, adjusted with pleasure to their new relationship and from then on grew closer together. On my next visit to the island the girl had moved out to live with the father of her child, though she remained emotionally close to Gilly.

With the birth of the first grandchild, we may say that the relation between mother and daughter is redefined and the closeness but asymmetry of the mother–daughter relationship is transformed into a close but far more symmetrical relationship.

The relation between sisters also follows a pattern of development closely correlated with sexual maturation, though I hasten to add that the difficulties of the relationship vary greatly with individual personality, a reservation that applies to any structural generalization. Young girls in a household are commonly occupied in performing household tasks that they share; they also find time to play children's games and later, to go to school. It is at adolescence that the greatest strain can become apparent, for unmarried sisters living in the same house are often rivals, not simply for the same man (which sometimes happens) but for the resources of the household that are needed for subsistence, entertaining, dressing up, and so forth. Such strains last until one or all of the girls moves out to live with a man. Some of the bloodiest quarrels on the island have occurred between two sisters.

'Poldo's eldest daughter had been living in common-law union with a man, but now they had separated and she returned to live at home, where her younger sister was living. She soon took an interest in the younger girl's boyfriend, and the quarrel erupted

*one day when the younger girl accused the older one of stealing
her man—and that when she couldn't keep one of her own.
Words gave way to blows, as charge and denial rushed vainly
to and fro. In the end, they both hauled off at each other with
machetes.*

*The very next day, I was witness to another bloody affair.
Sam had brought back a bride from Panama, and they were living in his mother's house while he made his own house habit-
able. Sam's sister was also living there, with her two small children, and a quarrel arose over the cooking arrangements. It
had apparently been brewing for a long time and at last it had
come to a head. People tumbled out of their houses to witness
the bloody, clawing battle.*

While a girl remains a distinctly subordinate member of her
mother's household, but is on the threshhold of securing mature
female status through motherhood and eventually marital union
(not necessarily "legal" marriage) where she has a household
of her own, there are various courses open to her to find emotional and convivial fulfillment. The most dramatic of these
severs the physical ties of a girl to her household. She leaves the
island to work, usually as a domestic, in one of the metropolitan centers; the motives are mixed—a desire to see movement,
i.e. modern life, a desire to earn money, and a desire to "catch
a man," are the most frequently cited. If she remains on the
island she "keeps company" with other girls of approximately
the same age and marital status, usually schoolmates. These
"sets" (Curtin 1970 : 27) of girls go on picnics together, take
trips around the island, take walks from one village to another,
go to church and school together, and stand around giggling
and ogling, especially when a boat arrives and St. Isabel bustles.
Basically these are casual peer groups with nothing like the
intensity of involvement and commitment typical of male peer
groups. They provide an addition to the sociability of the household for some of the time; they are not an alternative or a
substitute.

In some cases these sets of girls may be "patronized" by an
older woman who allows them the use of her house and who
perhaps provides them with money, food, and so forth to en-

courage their conviviality. Frequently such patronage is associated with a distinctly amateur form of prostitution. In return, say, for allowing a girl to use her house to entertain her boy-friend, the patron might require the girl to sleep with a customer —usually, in Providencia, a policeman, or perhaps a visiting seaman. Because this does sometimes happen, and because sets of girls openly seek to flirt, high class parents are particularly anxious to prevent their daughters from "keeping company" and insist that they be chaperoned (cf. Kerr 1952 : 162).

It is the aim of most women to become "mistress" of their own households, and no woman will consider living with a man unless he is willing and able to provide her with a house. Once he has done this, even though he is the legal owner and head, he in effect turns over all authority and control of the house, its affairs, and its personnel to the woman. He may, indeed, be accorded nominal authority and respect, but as Kerr puts it for Jamaica, he is "only ostensibly head of the house because of the patriarchal eidos of the culture pattern" (ibid., p. 60). As far as I could tell, even the most forceful males deferred to the woman of the house on domestic matters or, more usually, simply left them to her.

When a woman settles with a man in a house of her own, she moves from her parental household. Such a norm, together with the pattern of male house-spot tenancy, results in certain consequences and impositions on the relations between households in a section. For if men have little else but a formal, legal interest in the household and in any case spend most of their time away, the social life between households and on into the community via sections, is dominated by women. But since women move in, they are not kin, although the men are. The basic social "cell," centering on the section, is a woman and her daughters-in-law; the generalized structure is a hierarchical one based on age: women of the generation of mother-in-law, of daughter-in-law, and of grandchild. The ethos within a section is that of authority and respect based on seniority between affinal generations and within each generation, that is, daughters-in-law who have been resident longer have more authority than those more recently arrived.

We find then that between households daughters-in-law assist mothers-in-law in daily chores either directly or by sending a child in to help. Sisters-in-law [13] help each other and defer to each other in terms of seniority. In return mothers-in-law "mind" children, indulge them, and play a large part in their general socialization. The houses of sisters-in-law are always open to each other and they and their children pop in and out. The older a mother-in-law becomes the less she seeks to impose her ideas on a daughter-in-law and the more easy the relationship becomes until, in fact, it sometimes reverses itself, as when the one looks after the other. In any case, if the mother–daughter-in-law relation becomes too strained, the latter can always retreat to her own house, where, if she so chooses, she can remain exclusive.

Sisters-in-law are often though not always kin to each other in some other way, and this helps to strengthen the common bonds that result from their similar status vis-à-vis the rest of the community. Within sections there is frequently a strong spirit of camaraderie which develops among women who share the status of "wife" in the same generation, ranged against women who are mothers-in-law and elder sisters-in-law. In one community this sense of commonality went so far as to be expressed in the use of a common kitchen among a number of households. At the same time tensions can also build, particularly stemming from the wife's responsibility for the respectability of her household, to which is bound in some ways the status and prestige of her husband. Wives may try to outdo each other in presenting a "good face"; they may also be subject to the criticisms of their husband's mothers and unmarried sisters.

Such strains often reach a head in public quarrels, such as the two I will describe.

Bercita persuaded her husband to buy a new cupboard which would improve the tone of the home. Pretty well everyone in the village saw the piece taken off the boat and carried to the house. Many comments were made on how nice a cupboard it was, and Bercita certainly enjoyed installing it. One woman, Melita, went around protesting about Bercita: "Whom she a t'ink she is? Pretendin' she better than she born." She argued with several people about the merits of the cupboard, and whether it was indeed an improvement to the house. Most people thought it was and Melita was left rather isolated in her opinion.

It was, however, the beginning of a rather tense time between Bercita and Melita, who were married to two brothers.

Some weeks later, Bercita accused Melita of trying to shame her by cleaning out her house and putting up new curtains. Melita countered by accusing Bercita of trying to seduce her husband. Bercita screamed with anger at such "scandal" and "foolishness" and threatened to beat her. Bercita's husband's sister, who was in the house, came outside, and taking offense at Melita's accusation, accused her of flaunting herself in a way that was disrespectful to her, her brother, and their mother. In no time at all the three women were at each other, scratching and tearing until they were pulled apart. Melita, who was younger and more recently arrived in the community, went back home to her mother for a month or so, returning only when the two husbands had sorted out matters.

Melita's return to her mother brings in another feature of the pattern of women's relation to kinship and residence. Though she and her sisters move away from the household her mother runs, she never spiritually or emotionally loses touch, even though physically she may be distant. A woman always tries to have her earlier children, if not all of them, at her mother's house or with her mother present. She constantly visits her mother (if physically possible), often sends one or more of her children to spend some time with her mother, and may even provide a child to help the mother around the house and in the gardens. A mother may also visit a daughter. Likewise, though less frequently, sisters try to keep in touch with each other and periodically arrange visits to each other's houses. Similarly, a woman and her brother are effectively close. A brother is viewed as a protector, not only of his sister but of her children, particularly if she is not settled in a regular and independent union. Since property is a concern primarily of males, a brother also has a custodial interest. What is more, he is likely to remain in the community where his sister's property interests are concentrated.

In other words, though the range of kinship interests among

women is relatively narrow, it runs deep. Women keep in running order the ties of kinship that have their origin in the household of their childhood. As a result, women activate a network of kinship ties that transcends communities, although their community relationships are actually based on affinity. These latter, particularly when based on common-law unions, are frail—very often by choice, since men and women do not want to be committed to a relationship which might not work out. The ties a woman has with her mother and her siblings and her children always remain firm. Since, when a conjugal union breaks up, the children usually go with their mother, the kinship tie to the father attenuates and, in many instances, withers away. Consequently one can speak of women depending on kinship ties to preserve a constant and consistent set of persons with and from whom they derive emotional and physical satisfaction and existential identity. One can also claim that kinship, as a societal principle of interrelating, is preempted by women in all senses but the political and legal.

Furthermore, these close-kin networks, centering on mother and daughters, do get extended to embrace other kin, working out from mother's sisters and their children, working up to mother's mother and her collaterals and their descendants. Men are included in these networks through their position as brothers, thence as uncles, cousins, and nephews. But the degree of reckoning through males is in most cases foreshortened.

The nature of intracommunity relations, that is, where the placing of people in a community is relevant to the relationship, is primarily a female-oriented one and is based on kinship connections between specific households in different communities. Within communities there are sections, and the affective or sentimental ties between households are enacted by women, but on the basis of the formal legal tie of males to each other, and to property.

Sentiment and affect are achieved through the kinship of women to each other and to certain male kin. Kinship is a principle of social recognition in contexts essentially sentimental and affective and, in the main, involving only women. Such is the "model" or the "norm." This does not mean to say that men do not recognize and are not recognized in a sentimental way by kin; only that, compared to women, kinship ties for a man are limited and are of a politico-jural nature.

There is only one relationship which is ideally sentimentalized —a man's relation to his mother. Throughout his life he will maintain, if not actually observe, that he loves his mother above all else, and that he must show her the greatest respect. The gravest insult one man can offer another is to cast aspersions on his mother. Yet the very idealism of this relationship betrays something of its formal rather than spontaneous, dutiful rather than passionate nature. A man rather more genuinely feels a strong attachment to his children, particularly, as I already noted, when they are small. Otherwise, a man's existential reference group, his sentimental community, lies outside the realm of kinsmen.

One small modification to the distinction I have pursued above pertains to the high class household. As I noted in the previous chapter, a respectable household appears in public as a unit, in churchgoing, for example, or in attendance at parties. The husband-father is rather more closely bound in with the affairs of the household than the less respectable, other class males. Consequently, at least on the surface, the sentimental life of the high class male owes more to kinship and household membership. However, as I shall show in the next chapter, this is a minor modification.

The form of the household and family in the Caribbean is a subject that has preoccupied most investigators and theorists. Elsewhere I have published an account of household form on Providencia in terms of kinship composition (Wilson 1961) and tables 4 and 5 summarize the basic data. But the argument of the present chapter renders any further consideration of the form or structure of the household unnecessary, in my opinion, simply because the importance of the household does not lie in its structure. In terms of social relations based on kinship, it makes no difference whether the structure is conjugal or affinal, whether the family is matrifocal or nuclear. The domestic realm is the culturally defined province of the female no matter whether there is a spouse present or not, no matter whether he is a legal or common-law spouse. The societal relationships of women are built upon kinship ties, and all men are periph-

TABLE 4. Relationship of Household Members to Female Head

Relationship	St. Isabel	Nelly Downs	Old Town	Rocky Point	Jones Point	Smooth-water Bay	Bottom House	Total
Husband	–	–	–	–	–	1	–	1
C-L husband	–	–	2	2	–	–	2	6
Son of head and spouse								
under 14 years	–	–	5	–	–	–	8	13
over 14 years	–	–	–	–	–	–	2	2
Single father married	–	–	–	1	–	–	–	1
Daughter of head and spouse								
under 14 years	–	–	–	–	–	–	1	1
over 14 years	–	–	–	–	–	–	–	–
Single mother married	–	–	–	–	–	–	–	–
Son of head only								
under 14 years	4	1	3	3	–	–	6	17
over 14 years	1	2	8	3	–	2	–	16
Single father married	–	–	1	2	1	–	–	4
Daughter of head only								
married	–	–	2	1	–	–	–	3
under 14 years	2	–	3	5	–	2	4	16

							Totals
over 14 years	2	3	5	5	1	2	—	18
Single mother	1	1	4	6	—	—	—	12
married	—	1	1	—	—	—	—	2
Father	—	—	—	—	—	—	—	1
Mother	—	—	—	2	—	—	—	2
Brother	—	—	1	1	—	1	3	4
Sister	1	1	1	3	—	1	3	6
Adopted son	—	1	5	3	—	2	—	11
Adopted daughter	1	1	1	1	—	—	—	3
Son's son	—	—	3	5	1	—	2	11
Son's daughter	—	—	3	3	6	—	1	13
Daughter's son	2	—	3	5	—	—	—	10
Daughter's daughter	—	3	5	4	—	—	—	12
Son's wife	—	—	2	1	—	—	—	3
Daughter's husband	—	1	1	—	—	—	—	2
Brother's son	1	—	—	—	—	1	1	3
Sister's son	—	—	1	—	—	—	1	2
Sister's daughter	—	—	1	1	—	—	—	1
Sister's daughter's son	—	—	1	1	—	—	—	1
Sister's daughter's daughter	—	—	—	2	—	—	—	2
Son of spouse only	—	—	1	1	—	1	—	2
Unrelated	—	—	—	—	—	2	2	4
TOTALS	14	14	59	58	9	14	35	203

Source: Peter J. Wilson, "Household and Family on Providencia," *Social and Economic Studies* 10, no. 4 (1961).

Table 5. Relationship of Household Members to Male Head

Relationship	St. Isabel	Nelly Downs	Old Town	Rocky Point	Jones Point	Smooth-water Bay	Bottom House	Total
Wife	21	12	28	14	4	12	11	102
C-L wife	3	7	2	3	–	1	19	35
Son of head and spouse								
under 14 years	35	23	19	17	10	10	14	128
over 14 years	5	2	4	1	2	2	4	20
Single father	1	1	–	–	–	–	1	3
married	–	–	2	–	–	–	–	2
Daughter of head and spouse								
under 14 years	26	9	24	12	4	6	15	96
over 14 years	5	5	4	4	2	3	8	31
Single mother	–	–	2	2	–	1	–	5
married	–	1	2	–	–	–	–	3
Son of head only	5	3	10	1	–	–	4	23
Daughter of head only	6	6	9	–	–	–	–	21
Son of wife only	–	1	–	–	–	–	–	1
Daughter of wife only	2	1	–	–	–	1	2	6

								TOTALS
Son of C-L wife	–	–	–	2	–	–	2	4
Daughter of C-L wife	–	–	–	2	–	–	2	4
Son's wife	–	–	3	–	–	–	1	4
Daughter's husband	1	2	2	–	–	–	–	5
Daughter's C-L husband	–	–	1	–	–	–	–	1
Brother	–	–	1	–	–	1	1	3
Sister	1	–	3	2	–	–	3	9
Brother's child	–	–	1	–	–	–	1	2
Sister's child	–	–	6	2	–	–	–	8
Father	–	–	1	–	–	–	–	1
Mother	1	–	1	–	–	–	1	3
Son's son	1	–	7	3	–	3	5	19
Son's daughter	–	2	3	1	–	4	–	10
Adopted son	2	4	3	3	1	1	3	17
Adopted daughter	3	1	4	3	1	1	3	16
Wife's mother	1	–	3	–	1	–	1	6
Wife's sister	–	–	3	–	–	–	–	3
Wife's daughter's son	–	–	2	–	–	–	–	2
Wife's daughter's daughter	–	–	2	–	–	–	–	2
TOTALS	128	86	163	78	25	49	105	634

Source: Same as for Table 4.

eral within the kinship sphere. Because it is most convenient, the household is generally speaking a well-defined unit of consumption, but this is not hard and fast—consider the example above of the cluster of neighboring households whose women got on well together, who constructed a common kitchen and ate more or less in common. In terms of production the same holds—by and large most households support themselves, but an absent male may send a remittance to his mother (living in one household) and to the mother of his children (living in another household); a man who is "married" may cultivate land which he has not yet legally inherited, since his father is still alive. Some of the produce is for him to keep, but some also goes to his parents' household.

Since males are peripheral to household and domestic organization, the household is not a political unit; its integration into sections is a function of legal relations between brothers and the rules of inheritance, but the sociability and solidarity of these sections depends upon the age and affinal "structure" of relations between women. And this is complemented by the kinship ties that bind women (and certain men) closely to each other, but across community boundaries. Women living in the same community are not as closely related to each other as they are to women living in different communities.

I think this situation applies beyond Providencia, for it has generally been observed that there is a "weak sense of community" in the Caribbean (Wagley 1960 : 8). Community, or *communitas,* has other bases than the territorial, although, as I have tried to show, the sense of identity is indeed dependent on territory. Until the preoccupation with the household and family is reduced to a proper perspective, the mainsprings and wellsprings of Caribbean social life will never be properly understood.

MALES AND KINSHIP

It would be absurd to claim that kinship is meaningless to men. What we must try to do is to characterize the way in which it is meaningful, even though this is limited. A fair amount of "personal" trade is indulged in by islanders; people send to the mainland for certain goods they need, people need contracts and intermediaries to negotiate some of their transactions, particularly illicit ones, and others, particularly storekeepers, must depend on agents and contacts on the mainland to honestly attend to their orders. When a man goes abroad to seek work, a contact and a host is a great advantage; even if one merely goes abroad for a visit, having a house rather than a hotel to go to makes the trip more friendly and less expensive. In all of these situations the avenue of contact and communication often and most easily follows kinship relations. The kinsman overseas is more likely to help you and can be better trusted than the stranger. Such thinking is a good rule of thumb though it is by no means foolproof. But these are the contexts, all of them basically economic, in which males rely on kinship ties. The only tie that is more reliable, and thence preferable, is that between "best friends" or members of the same crew; and a man going abroad will go to a best friend rather than a kinsman if there is one living where he is going.

Given the irregular flow of cash in and out of the island and the fact that much that is there is hoarded as savings, many transactions are on a credit basis. All the storekeepers maintain large debit and credit ledgers, and some private individuals do so as well, for a lot of borrowing goes on, much of it small scale. Some 29 percent of cases that came before the municipal court concerned bad debts, and nearly all of these were between kinsmen. One feels free to borrow from kin because one can invoke the ideal of altruistic obligation thought to rest in kinship. But borrowing and lending create bad feeling, notably when the creditor tries to collect, and since kinship is irreversible (unlike friendship) the risk of hostility is easier to run when it involves kin. The nature of the problem between kinsmen is shown in the following letter, which I quote verbatim:

Colon, Panama, 1958.
Senor Judge Municipal District of Old Providence
Mr. F. Williamson

Dear Sir   I now inform you this few loins concerning to what I said to understand have taken place with my law-

full Wife it is to my surprise to no that my brother Artimas are now halling and pulling my wife to the offiss for
what she done him in my absent from home I dont like
that bisniss for this reason I am the husband of that lady
and I am risponcable for whatever bill she may contract
from anybody for if I didnt agree of such it would not
happen in my home we do not disaconalig [disacknowl-
edge] the bill but not manage as yet I am away now working to pay up all my bill as much as I can and furder
more I coindly ask you as the Judge to let that Business
remain as it stand untill I come home for this reason I
consider that my wife is the ears of Isaac Newton and said
Artimas Smith due the estate of one Isaac Newton. The
sum of $16.50 balance on arrange which he sold off. And
$8.16 for 2 tin of syrip—and according to Mr. Isaac New-
ton will my wife be intitle of those thing as I think. Or
ask you coindly to let the lawsuit business remain as it
stand till I come I will be there about two weeks more by
God help. Please act according to statement—we as
brother and must reason thing in an amiclable way. So I
ask you not to having my wife up and down to the offiss
in my absent for she have a husband. Furder more she is
not well. And no one would be satisfied to no that an ad-
vantig is taking of there wife in there absent from home.

                                                                J. Smith

Several standard island patterns are evident here: the man
working abroad for money to save or, as here, pay off a debt;
the quarrel between brothers as debtor and creditor; the insinuation that his brother is trying to take advantage of his wife
while he is away, emphasizing that men take care of economic
and legal matters; and disgust at his brother for going to court,
which is a violation of kinship "trust." Eventually John came
back and paid off the debt, but the brothers did not speak to
each other for over a year and relations were strained.

In this case the brothers were of the same social status. Kin
ties, however, cross over status lines, and as may be expected,
those who are better-off are most often approached for loans,
especially if they are kinsmen. All high class men are ap-

proached for loans on the basis of kinship—real or fictive. In fact it is often difficult to know whether or not one is related to a particular person, since the density of kinship ties on the island is so great. But apart from this, it indicates that the idiom of borrowing is drawn from kinship.

I was in Mr. John's store one morning when in came Reyaes. He stood momentarily in the doorway, darting a quick glance around the store to see who was there and to make sure that Mr. John was in his accustomed place behind the cashier's cage. He sidled over, put his hand in front of his mouth and murmured, loud enough for me to hear:

"Mr. John, I like a word with you. Now. You an' me is family, isn' so? Me remember as when you run aroun' this very floor, an' you wit' no pants an my mother to wipe and feed you. An' is a not true, Mr. John, like a say in the Bible: An I shall give you all as brothers, give you all as brothers, heh?"

Mr. John, very familiar with the tactic, just sat there blinking slowly, but otherwise expressionless. After the preamble came the request—which I did not hear because it was whispered. The preamble was obviously a semipublic appeal meant to place Mr. John in an awkward position in front of witnesses unless he made the loan.

When Reyaes had finished, Mr. John slowly gave his reply, prefaced with a similar homily:

"Well, you know, Reyaes, is true you an' me is family, but I is nearly as old as you man, and this floor is not here when I was a boy. Yes, we is family. But don't it show man, that you have jus' squander away your life while I have work hard to make a peso? I tried hard and I worked hard, and the Lord has helped me to provide. But He not give me much for left over."

There was more discussion, some a little heated, but in the end Mr. John agreed to loan Reyaes twenty-five pesos rather than the hundred he had asked for, and he was to repay thirty pesos in three months' time. The arrangement was recorded by Mr. John in a special book, which Reyaes signed. On other occasions when approached for a loan Mr. John, if he wished to refuse, invariably denied any kinship connection.

A further suggestion of the idiom of borrowing was evident

in my own experience, for what else could I have been but wealthy man? Who would have believed my claim to be an impecunious anthropologist? It was obvious that there could be no claim of kinship between me and the islanders, but all requests (averaging one a day, or so it seemed) were couched as follows: "Mister Pete! You know, we here on the Rock, we is all one family. Now you respects the island and you is like one o' we. Man, you an' me is like a brother. . . . Can you len' me a five peso?"

The somewhat formal, exploitative function of kinship for males is illustrated by the *compadrazgo* institution. This is recent on Providence and does not resemble, except skeletally, the institution found elsewhere in the Spanish Catholic Americas (Mintz and Wolf 1950). Some Catholic families, at the baptism of a child, invite a man to become the *compadre,* or godfather. To my knowledge, women are not asked to be *comadre.* It is expected that the godfather will take a continuing interest in the child, helping in particular with its education, and making whatever financial contributions are possible. In other words, being a godfather is primarily an economic relationship. Naturally the tendency is for other class people to flood well-off people with requests for them to become godfather. Most such requests are refused, although someone like Vidi, who finds it difficult to say no, was godfather to twenty-three children! Men who are best friends frequently call each other *compadre,* though they may as yet have no children. When they do, it is likely that they will become godfathers to each other's children.

The emphasis in the relationship between males and kinship appears to be primarily of a formal, politico-jural nature, in contrast to the sentimental, affective meaning of kinship to women. These are prevailing tendencies, not absolutes. Of course men may treat kinship ties or some kinsmen with affect, and women, especially as siblings, become involved in politico-jural affairs on the basis of kinship. Similarly, men spend some part of their lives in the household—of their mothers or of their wives—and some men may well be quite domesticated, just as some women may go into business and thus conform far less to the notion that a woman's realm is the domestic.

But if we are out to delineate the pattern, which in turn reflects not only general practice but people's own expectations of themselves, then we must draw a definite line between the importance of kinship to females and the relative unimportance of it to males. We must distinguish between application of kinship to the existential development of females and to the jural and economic roles of males. We might also note that certain of the consequences of these facts themselves have importance; for example, that while males control the legal aspects of residence (owning houses and land) they play little part in the social life and structure of the living community organized according to household and section; such a social life is dominated by women, but on the basis of affinity and domestic status rather than kinship. Their kinship ties bind them to a social network that crosses community boundaries without ever incorporating them into a given community. From this point of view, then, we can understand why the residential community is rarely an active structured entity or even a sentimental one. Only political considerations originating from outside ever treat communities as social entities—when baseball teams were organized or when schools taking the name of the community compete in drills on Independence Day.

KINSHIP IDEOLOGY

The question arises: What does kinship mean in the general ongoing process of the organization of behavior and values? In chapter 5 the inference is clear that stratification is an expression of a premise of inequality. Some people are not only better-off than others, but they are so because they are better. If we look at the context of kinship, the form of activities and relationships when kinship ties rather than others are invoked, it suggests an underlying premise of equality. Kinship may be considered a counterbalance to demarcation in the generalized framework of an island ethos.

The central relationship is that between siblings, especially brothers with brothers and sisters with sisters. They are the equals of each other, particularly in their relation to property. The relationship of brother is taken as the paradigm of equality, as it is indeed in our own society.

Invocation of kinship is explicit in situations where in-equality is most obvious and where the inferior seeks to estab-lish some claim over the superior. Borrowing is the chief situation where this applies, but all claims for help may be justified by claiming kinship and thence equality. Notice, for example, that John Smith appeals to the judge to help him "as a brother."

The claim that all on the island are "one family" is again an expression of the idea of both solidarity and equality. Actually in the case of such a small population as that of Providencia this claim may be literally true. It is the idiom of kinship that is used to assert common identity vis-à-vis the outside world as it is used to rationalize the common situation of all island-ers.

The application of kinship terms to non-kin gives more indi-cation of the idiom of kinship as an equalizer, as a device by which people who may be excluded from a social orbit can be drawn in. Old people in general may be addressed respectfully as *Aunty, Uncle,* or more rarely, *Grampa.* Not only does this reflect respect for age, it indicates that kinship can be used as a way of making "strangers" friends. Notice too that *Aunty* and *Uncle* are more commonly used as honorifics than *Granny* and *Grampa,* the former being ascending generation sibling terms. Likewise the kinship term by which most islanders conveniently identify each other is *cousin.* In fact, to say one is cousin to someone is the same as saying one is kin or family.

The contradiction between difference of status and equality based on kinship does not go without recognition on the is-land. Most high-class households employ close kin—particularly in the house. The reason for employing household help is usually "because of family." But the relationship is kept strictly formal. Miss Ray, for instance, had her laundry done by a first cousin. The woman was not allowed to come into the house but could only come to the porch or occasionally the kitchen. Miss Bernarda employed a half-sister to keep house for her while she minded her store, but as soon as Miss Bernarda came home, the sister left. They hardly spoke a word to each other.

The only time at which all kin, no matter what their social

status, come together is at sit-ups and weddings. But as I have already described, high-class people receive deferential treatment, and only when immediate kin die do they participate in full. For socially higher people to admit the equality of kinship is clearly threatening to their social position, but they cannot deny the bonds of kinship, and to that extent they must give way—by lending, by employing, by keeping company. Those of inferior status manipulate the possibilities of kinship as much as they can in order to counteract their status disadvantages.

To emphasize their equality with each other, and simultaneously their differences from the rest, high-class people tend to place a certain emphasis on kinship ties as a mechanism of exclusiveness. For them legal marriage at a comparatively early age is more desirable since it is more respectable, and the preference is for marriage between children of high-class parents. Through intermarriage comes relationship, so a tendency does develop for high-class status to be reinforced by kinship ties, and for the stratum to become thereby less open-ended. Miss Ray's plans for the marriage of her son Vidi to the alcalde's daughter were complemented by her husband's appreciation of the political advantage of being allied to such an administrator, by Miss Ethel's desire for the good marriage of her daughter, and by the alcalde's appreciation of a closer relationship with wealthy Mr. John. Such alliances are not unusual, but they should not be regarded as an imperative either. Endogamy is not an article of faith on the part of high class people, for they marry outsiders, a situation also necessitated by the small population. In any case, the reputation and responsibility of a person, so necessary for his status, must be proved independently by each individual. One born into a high-class family naturally starts off with great advantages in this process, but these are not sufficient. High-class exclusiveness, then, is in part reinforced by kinship, which in turn establishes a recognition of the fact that to be kin means primarily to be a social equal.

7 Sentiment and Structure: Friendship

In the previous chapter it became apparent that a major dimension in the structuring of social relations rests upon the separation of the sexes. A woman's social life centers on the household, the family, and kinship, and she in turn retains effective control in these domains. We may view this concentration as being not only structurally complete but existentially satisfying, for unless it can be seen that structured relations fulfill the individual's sense of being, neither our description nor our understanding is adequate. Although men are not excluded from the domestic domain but are incorporated in a more formal sense with certain legal responsibilities, it cannot be said that they achieve or are granted existential fulfillment or that their sense of emotional well-being is satisfied in the domestic domain.

If, however, social relations are premised on a separation of the sexes, and if males are peripheral to domestic relations, then clearly we cannot complete our study until we have discerned and analyzed the complementary domain of male social relations. Speaking in a purely formal sense it would appear that such structurally institutionalized domains as the political, economic, and legal are where males are preeminent. But in Providencia, with its quasi-colonial status, and throughout the Caribbean in general, the ultimate control, standards, and terms of these domains come from outside the society and cannot provide the existential meaning to life which is so vital for the integrity of any structural principle. At best these domains provide certain statuses that give form to the structure, but the occupants of these statuses never feel at one with them.

This is such an important consideration that it bears some further elaboration, especially as it has been almost totally overlooked in anthropological studies of the Caribbean.

Parts of this chapter are adapted from "Caribbean Crews: Peer Groups and Male Society," *Caribbean Studies* 10, no. 4 (January 1971): 18-34, The Institute of Caribbean Studies.

It may be said of most societies studied by anthropologists that

> from whatever side we approach the culture, whatever institutions we study, we find the same sort of contrast between the life of the men and that of the women. Broadly we may say that the men are occupied with the spectacular, dramatic and violent activities which have their centre in the ceremonial house, while the women are occupied with the useful and necessary routines of food getting, cooking and rearing children—activities which centre around the dwelling house and the gardens. [Bateson 1958 : 123]

We have seen this to be the case for women, but what of men on Providencia? Such concerns receive their ultimate sanctions from *within* the culture in the case of a society such as the Iatmul. But not so in the Caribbean. To become mayor (cf. chief), for example, is to assume an office whose standards and terms of reference lie *outside* of the society and whose function, in the colonial situation, is often opposed to the norms of the society. Furthermore, in the eyes of the people of that society, one who achieves politico-legal office does not thereby gain respect or obedience, and so he does not achieve personal recognition and fulfillment. This can only happen if he succeeds in terms of the society itself. If this is possible in a society such as Providencia, as indeed it is, then it clearly indicates the presence of an ethos integral and harmonious with the autonomy of social life and different from, if not opposed to, the imposed, alien culture.

I therefore suggest of Providencia, and by implication of other Caribbean societies, that there exists an existentially valid structure of relations by which men secure their identity more or less separately from women and which is both congruent with their culture and independent of the outside.

REPUTATION

A man takes great pride in his children, particularly, as I have already noted, when they are very young. Through his children, of course, a man is most positively aligned with a sphere of domestic relations, for where a man's children, there he has right to be—providing he does right by them. A man also has genuine affection for his children, men in the Caribbean being no different in this respect from men anywhere else. But what is also important about a man's relation to his children is that they are the evidence and embodiment of his maturity and manhood, and through them he earns respect in the society at large, especially among his peers. Fathering children is a sign of strength, not necessarily in the muscular sense but in the sense of character and spirit. It is said of a man who fathers many children that he has "strong blood"—and it is the blood that contributes the spiritual and vital part of the person in his conception. Such a man also has charisma to attract women and make them want him to father their children. If after they are born a man continues to show an interest in his children, he is recognized as being even stronger and more of a man. Virility is far more than sexual potency.

This sense of a man's strength is the foundation of his reputation, that constellation of qualities by which he achieves a place in the world of others where he is both an equal and a unique person (Wilson 1969). A man's reputation is the stimulus of other people's respect for him, and a concern for respect, for one's good name, is always smoldering. As an oft-cited island adage puts it: "He who steals my purse steals trash, but he who steals my good name steals everything." [14]

Reputation stipulates the minimum requirements for adult manhood and respect. With a good reputation a man can take his place in society, and thereafter he may build it up to create his own distinctive position. If there is a minimum requirement it is that a man should father children, just as, for a woman to be recognized as a truly mature female, she must begin to have the "children that are in her belly." A man who has no children must wait until old age before enjoying the full respect of his society, though he is never a non-person, and he may achieve status through other activities. But even if he becomes the richest, toughest man around, yet has no children, he can still be sneered at and be the butt of jokes that even the humblest can crack at his expense. Nor is there any excuse for a man to have no children, since only women are thought to be infertile. Homosexuals or *marecas,* as they are called, are among the most despised of men, even though homosexual activities are widely indulged in.

Beyond the minimum of fulfillment, there is great scope for differences in reputation. A man who fathers many children by many women is "stronger" than one who has only a few. And such increments in reputation are often marked by such devices as titles like king, duke, or *cacique*. There is some lightheartedness associated with the bestowing of these titles, but as a man grows older they become a part of his identity and a signal of the respect which is his due. In Bottom House, for instance, lived Captain Hector Henry, known as King Hector. Now in his seventies, he sat day after day in his rocking chair with his memories for comfort and company. But he was the first man from Bottom House ever to own and skipper his own boat; he had constantly and successfully fooled police and customs officers during his career as trader and smuggler; he had fathered at least twenty children, though there were probably many more scattered through many lands of all colors and nationalities. His word was heeded, his advice was sought. He was greatly respected.

If the foundation of a man's reputation and respect is his virility, this is also likely to be where he is socially most vulnerable, especially in his early manhood years. Mothers and fathers show great concern that their sons give early signs of great potential. From the time a toddler starts to walk, parents are on the look-out for any signs of manliness. A boy's penis is fondled and often some sort of supernatural aid is enlisted to make sure of his virility. The most common practice is to bury a piece of manioc treated with special medicines from the *obeah* man, and as the root grows, so does the boy's penis. All evidence of boyish behavior is encouraged and rewarded: a proclivity to fight, to argue, to shout, to tease and tweak girls all receive due measure of applause and admiration.

This is only to give the boy a good start, though. A reputation must be earned and cannot be inherited. Girls are not uncontrollably ready to fall into a boy's arms, and although sexual intercourse is an accepted part of the relation between a boy and a girl, "you can't get it just because you want it." Love magic is constantly employed by both boys and girls, but more importantly the boy must convince the girl he is worth her while. Sweet talk is what he must give her, telling her how good he is and how he is prepared to prove it, as well as telling her how exceptional she is. Sweet talk is the effort to convince a girl at the same time of one's sincerity and sophistication. Hyperbole and superlative, sweet phrases (usually quoted from songs), devout protestations, and a somewhat immodest recitation of one's worldliness are the ingredients of sweet talk. In addition, notes couched in flowery language promising undying devotion, everlasting love, and impeccable sincerity are constantly passed from boy to girl.[15]

Mere words are not enough, however. A boy is expected to give gifts to a girl, usually money, especially if he has "privileges" from her; and this money has to be earned somewhere, somehow. A man must appear "presentable" if he is to impress a girl, not just smart but with worldly items about his person such as a good wristwatch, several pens in his pocket, a good knife, sunglasses, and a distinctive hat. These too cost money, so to look good and to be able to give presents are signs of a young man's ability, maturity, and manhood in the sense of responsibility and generosity. It is no good simply earning money, one must be generous with it, so being able to both earn and give (and lend) are proofs of manliness. Money is a means, not an end.

Reputation is not just manliness but is also a constellation of skills. Variations in reputation are a function of the number and worth of these skills and the varying degrees of proficiency in them. Nor need these skills necessarily be economic, for among the most important of them are sexual skills and closely allied verbal or expressive skills. Sweet talk is part of a wider spectrum of expressive skills that takes in musical ability and numerous forms of verbal activity. All men like to sing, and most of them on Providencia play the guitar. Only a few can sing or play really well, and to the extent that they can they enjoy a higher reputation. Some men who have been able to perfect their skills enjoy respect throughout the island. Their level of achievement in such musical skills is often taken as evidence of their ability in certain other realms of reputation, particularly the sexual. If a man is a sweet singer, it is thought, as likely as not he is a great lover, even though real evidence of such may be missing.

Since a good reputation based on musical skill is not a political reputation but a social one, it is worth examining in more detail how men with such reputations take their place.

Cassio is in his middle fifties, married with grown-up children. A clear-skinned man, he is also quite well-off since he receives a pension from the navy, has his savings, and gets a small income from selling coconuts and cattle.

Cassio is rarely sober. When he is, he is soft-spoken and always well-mannered. When drunk he wobbles precariously and slobbers sentimentally. People often laugh at him when he is in this state, and he frequently has to be taken home and put to bed. It is all right to be so helpless occasionally, but usually a man who is helpless so often is openly derided. Not so Cassio. It is commonly agreed that he has the sweetest singing voice on the island—a truly fine baritone. He also has a large repertoire of love songs in English and Spanish, and he is ready to sing at the slightest sign of encouragement. When drunk, he sings very slowly, exaggerating every word, dragging it out in slurred incoherence. On the rare occasion when I have heard him sing soberly, he showed a sense of style and soul. But drunk or sober his performance is always greatly admired by everyone, and people, high or low class, are prepared to overlook all his failings on these occasions. In keeping with his troubadour image, he always sweet-talks the ladies, reminding them of his prowess as a great lover, reminiscing on his past exploits and playfully hinting that he is available should he be needed. Coming from him such freshness is enjoyed and he is considered a great joke. Coming from anyone else such behavior would not be tolerated.

Cassio is a high-class man whose wife keeps a most respectable household. His drunkenness does indeed cast a slur on their respectability, but this is more than compensated for by his reputation, which in a sense transcends class. Reputation is a matter of culture in its expression and of *communitas* in its function. It is one's identity as a man, not as one of a class of men, that is defined by reputation, so all men are individually subject to its terms of reference.

Another example is Sludge, who is actually from San Andrés, but who loves Providence so much that he decided many years ago to live there permanently. He has come to be more or less completely accepted as an islander. Sludge is very black and decidedly "other class." Probably in his late fifties, he is tall and gangling, toothless and smiling—and rarely sober. By common consent he is the finest guitarist on the island. When sober he tends a small garden and keeps house with his deceased wife's brother. Somehow or other he manages to secure a sufficient income, though how I was never able to determine, for as often as not he would refuse payment whenever he played the guitar, though this was the main way he could make money. Actually he is paid indirectly, since he is an inveterate borrower and most people probably waive his debts. When not immobilized by rum, it is his habit to wander the island playing his guitar to whoever will listen, sitting beneath palm trees, or in someone's house, or in a rum shop. He is always assured of hospitality and is usually welcome to stay as long as he likes.

Like Cassio, Sludge sang all his songs in the first person, what Abrahams calls the "intrusive I" (1970a : 58), implying that he had actually gone through the experiences he was singing about. Like Cassio, again, he would follow up the songs with stories, couched as reminiscences of his exploits, all of them vouching for the hero's prowess.

The reputations of both Cassio and Sludge as musicians gave both of them standing as men and allowed them to associate freely and intimately with other people, quite independently of their class position. Even Miss Ray, a tartar for manners if ever there was one, would welcome Sludge into her home if he came to play a tune. In fact she was flattered—and it was admittedly a rare occurrence. On the other hand, the authority of these men did not go far beyond their specialties. Had Cassio been sober more of the time, it is possible that he might have enjoyed greater authority in political and social affairs; but as it was, both men enjoyed good reputations in that they exemplified possibilities of attainment in activities admired throughout the island by everybody.

Music and singing are artistic counterparts of sweet talk. They are closely related to certain other more or less stylized modes of verbal skill. Thus it is common for men to brag of their prowess and exploits, and it is necessary for their reputations that they do so. Boasts are not set texts or forms like poems or tales, but they represent a common manner and style of discourse which is deployed in certain social contexts.

Exaggerated claims of potency and prowess are all part and parcel of seeking to establish one's reputation. Some of this is made necessary because most men leave the island during early manhood, a crucial period, and so the children they father may not be evident on the island, and the deeds they perform cannot be seen. So when men gather together in rum shops or beneath the palm trees on the beach much of their conversation is taken up with stories of their exploits—mostly those that occurred abroad. These stories are almost exclusively concerned with sex, fighting, drinking, and other forms of competition. The teller is always the central figure, and to one from a European background the tale and the teller seem quite immodest. It helps the teller to have someone in the capacity of witness to confirm the story. These witnesses are usually a man's best friend, and witnessing may be thought of as part of the role of being best friend. Best friends are those who stick by each other through thick or thin, who help each other confirm their identity. Above all, a best friend is someone you can "confidence" or trust.

Let me give an illustration of one of these stories, which I have reconstructed from my notes as I could not record it verbatim. About half a dozen of us were sitting on the beach at Old Town drinking rum, and talking mainly about the cunning of *panyas* or mainland Colombians. Ellsworth came up with this story.

Ellsworth was mate on the Simco, *and the boat was tied up in Cartagena, waiting to unload a cargo of copra. The crew had gone ashore, and only Ellsworth was left behind to mind the boat. At that time, he said, he always carried a gun, but just at that moment he had left it in his bunk. There he was sitting on the deck, having a peaceful smoke, when he sees a bunch of 5 or 6 panyas nosing around the dock, looking like they were up to no good and coming closer to the* Simco. *He could hear them jabbering away and, though he did not understand Span-*

*ish too well, he thought he heard one of them say the boat was
empty. Anyway, he decided to hide behind the capstan and wait
and see what happened. Sure enough, the six of them came
on board, and he noticed they were all carrying knives and cut-
lasses (machetes). It did not look so good, especially as he did
not have a gun or a knife. So he picked up a piece of pipe lying nearby and waited till they were all aboard and standing
in a group near the bridge. Then he stood up, making himself
look as big as possible (he weighed nearly three hundred
pounds and was well over six feet tall).*

"What de goddam you fuckers doin' on my boat?" he yelled.

*They turned around and stood motionless at the sight of him
—a big, black NIGGER man, and them so small. Before they
could move he charged at them, and he had thrown all six of
them into the water before they could raise an arm in defense,
saying they should think twice before they came on board his
boat again without his invite. Next time, he said, he would
make sure they were unconscious before they hit the water so
they would not be able to swim away.*

*When the captain and the crew returned, Ellsworth told
them what had happened, and they said they should unload
and move off quickly in case the gang came back. But Ellsworth needed a drink, and after assuring them they had nothing
to fear, he and some of the crew went off to town.*

The story was told rather more ornately than I have been
able to convey and with great feeling. Those sitting around
responded in the accepted way by asking what happened next,
acclaiming, and saying " 'ats right" in the correct place, and
then finally offering their congratulations.

Fighting, drinking, and performing great feats are all taken
as evidence of masculine strength in the physical sense, the
complement of the spiritual strength evidenced in virility and
verbal skill. These physical activities are far more competitive
and lead to an informal ranking of men on the basis of reputation. Men who are renowned as fearless fighters or sailors enjoy
a greater measure of prestige and authority in manly affairs.
Sometimes this is recognized by the bestowal of a title or a
nickname, as I have noted above. Ellsworth, for instance, was
known as Cap'n Nigger.

Although there is some fighting on the island, it is by no means as frequent or as pervasive as the talk about it. Islanders apparently fight less with each other than they do with outsiders —especially San Andrésanos or mainland Colombians. Their reputation, then, is largely built up on the conquest of outsiders, though it rests on verbal competition when only islanders are involved. The most typical of these verbal contests is the more or less stylized slanging match in which insults are traded.

This may begin slowly as a rational argument, but it soon gives way to irrationality and continuous affirmation that the other is wrong. When sheer voice power and reiteration fail to win the argument, insults are traded. By this time a crowd has usually gathered around, so the argument becomes public and subject to refereeing and judgment. The winner is informally agreed to be the man who has succeeded in cursing continuously without repeating himself and outlasting his opponent. The combatants always threaten violence but are willingly held back by bystanders.

Less dramatic and less emotional is the argument. It is generally expected that when a group of men gets together, they will engage in an argument. The most prominent and inevitable occasions are at horse races and boat races, but even when gathered at the rum shop to be sociable, men argue. An argument can arise over anything, but it is rarely personal and generally concerns matters of fact or interpretation. Here are a few topics taken at random from my notes: Joe Louis held the heavyweight boxing championship of the world longer than anybody else; Francis Drake discovered America; Fred Robinson had fifty-six children; New York is the biggest city in the world; Fenton's horse is faster than Radley's; rum is stronger than whisky; 'Reste is a better navigator than Jamesie; the next lucky number in the lottery will be 543; sugar cane from Lazy Hill is sweeter than that from Rocky Point; Protestants came before Catholics; Providence was better off when Rojas Pinilla was president and Max Rodriguez was intendente; there is gold buried in Bowden; the Magdalena is the biggest river in Colombia—and so forth.

One thing these topics have in common is that they give scope for "learning" and "erudition." It is important among

men not only to be articulate but to have learning, for these
two qualities contribute immensely to a man's reputation. Thus
those who have a higher education enjoy great prestige, and
schoolteachers, doctors, and other professionals are greatly respected. Learning, however, is not just a matter of books. A
man learns from experience, and for a man to be able to give
an account of his experiences in different parts of the world, to
be able to speak intimately of such great cities as New York,
Tokyo, or London, is to be able to establish a claim to being
learned, and hence respected. Traveling abroad is almost in
itself an act of manly aspiration bringing its own rewards (cf.
Gonzalez 1969, Midgett 1968). Similarly, skill in navigation,
in the lore of the sea, or in fishing are marks of learning greatly
respected by all islanders.

The argument, then, is a form of expression in which various
aspects of reputation are asserted and affirmed in a rather competitive manner. In many instances the apparently informal
nature of the argument is made more meaningful and structured
by the placing of bets. Protagonists are willing to place their
reputations on the line in a tangible way through betting they
are right. When this happens, an argument is not simply resolved, but there is a winner and a loser—a man who improves
his reputation at the expense of another.

It is perhaps surprising that storytelling does not seem to be
much of a pastime on Providencia, given the importance of
verbal skills. I must allow for a deficiency in fieldwork in making such a statement, but, though people mentioned Anancy
stories, and stories of duppies or ghosts, I never heard one
told. There are a few old men with reputations for storytelling,
but the most famous of these, Uncle Bug, was too old and
infirm for me to talk with him. On the other hand there are
a number of anecdotes about individuals that crop up again and
again. Many of these concern the "history" of the island, but
others are contemporary, have a moral twist and are humorous,
being told for purposes of entertainment. One such anecdote,
which I heard a number of times, goes as follows:

*'Reste was getting sore vex 'cause someone is teefin' his
coconuts. Him a know it is Pio, but him never able to catch
the teef. One day, him a put on his gun an' say him a gwan'*

scare Pio so him never able to shit the rest of his life. He put a stop to his teefin'.

But all 'Reste say was him gwan fe shoot pigeon.

When him get to Cocopiece, him a shout to Bert as him gwan fe get plenty fat pigeon. Them both laugh 'cos they knows is Pio up in the tree, listenin'. Then 'Reste say:

"There, there is pigeon!"

An he shoot up the tree.

Pio, him a start to scream an' shout, an' say to stop the shootin'. Bert say that is a noisy pigeon, so him bes' shoot some more to make him quiet. Pio come a slidin' down the tree like him a cover in pig fat and shoutin' all the time:

"Mercy! Mercy! Don' shoot, else I is dead." 'Reste say him is gwan shoot dem teefin' pigeon, 'cos now him a have no coconut left.

Pio shaking like a banana leaf and tell 'Reste him a mak' a mistake—him a not know as 'Reste trees. An' if he know it is 'Reste trees him a no climb them. But 'Reste, him is most angry—'cept as him is laughing all the time. He tell Bert how he gwan roll on that pigeon when it land so it don' teef no more. ['Reste was about 6'6" tall and weighed about 330 pounds.]

Pio tell him no, no, no, no, an' he run—oosh him a run, man. Him run so fast through the bushes that him a lose his pants an' all you can see is his teefin' bare arse scratchin' on the cockspur.[16]

'Reste and Bert just stand there to laugh.

When this tale and others like it are told everyone laughs heartily and frequently, interspersing comments, some of which will be elicited by the teller who will stop and say "A'nt so?" or "Tis as I say?" A number of such stories appear to be part of a repertoire, even though they are told spontaneously. They make up what might be considered a local folklore that would also include the innumerable stories about buried treasure and pirate exploits, especially those of Henry Morgan. Being able to tell these stories, or being made the hero of such a story, makes a great contribution to a man's reputation.

The heart of a man's reputation is that which proves him to be a man, his spiritual and physical strength. By fulfilling the minimum requirements, as it were, each individual enjoys the respect and recognition of his fellows. Thus all men are equal and possessed of a common measure of dignity. But over and above this basic reputation, there are certain occupational roles which embody and elaborate to a high degree the skills of strength and knowledge that are ingredients in reputation. By assuming such a role a man comes to acquire greater prestige and standing among the majority. Above all these occupations stands that of sea captain, but in addition are such occupations as doctor, schoolteacher, clergyman, and lawyer. Learning and knowledge are the key acquisitions in these occupations, and they have come to be among the most highly esteemed qualities that a man can possess, after his basic reputation. It is also because of this that the elderly enjoy great respect, for they have come to know so much that others do not. Their knowledge is born of experience rather than books, but it amounts to the same thing: knowledge translates to power. To know recipes for medicines and spells for *obeah,* to have known in person those who are but names on a genealogy or wandering duppies, to have lived through what others can know only as history, to be able to see the outcome of behavior hardly begun—all this is to have power and thence respect. For younger people the avenue to such power lies through education, which is partly why education is so highly valued. It is also seen as a possible entry into the outside world of respectability signified in the ability of the educated to live a better style of life.

It is important to emphasize, however, that even those having such prestigious occupations must prove themselves according to the basic standards of reputation. They cannot automatically enjoy respect. Thus a schoolteacher, however learned he may be, will carry little authority unless he fathers children, mixes freely with other men in the rum shop, and can compete with them when challenged. This factor is particularly important in politics. The mayor who fails to achieve a manly reputation simply has no credibility or authority. The official who is also a "man" is able to complement the power of his office with a real authority. Respect comes to the man who secures his reputation and who carries out his role activities skillfully.

Certain of the values of reputation may conflict with the demands made by certain statuses. It is also clear that, in simple terms, there is a contradiction between the qualities of manliness and the qualities of respectability. In actual fact some sense of balance is maintained, primarily through discretion. A man must drink with his peers, but by not overdoing it, he does not tarnish the respectability of his household if it is high class. The matter of conflict between reputation and status is not always so easily managed. Take, for instance, the status of storekeeper. It is part of the manly ethos to be generous, and generosity is taken very seriously on Providencia. But for a storekeeper to be overly generous is certainly not conducive to good business. He is under constant pressure to extend credit by virtue of claims against his reputation by his kinship connections. To deny requests is to be mean and therefore not a man. To comply can be ruin. Those storekeepers who succeed are those who remain quite firm to their business interests and who are very selective in their choice of debtor. Stories of storekeepers' stinginess are among the most frequently recited, matched only by the stories told of storekeepers who have gone broke. It may well be that one reason why women are, on the whole, more successful at small-scale trading is that they do not have to comply with the obligations of reputation.

GOSSIP

As we have seen, much of a man's reputation is dependent in one way or another on words. Words as well as deeds must be relied on to build up a reputation and to sustain it. By the same token words are the principal weapon that threatens the integrity of a reputation, that can be used to erode and nibble it away. A critical aspect of speech behavior which bears directly on reputation, then, is gossip, which for present purposes alone I define as talk about reputation and respectability (but cf. Gluckman 1963, Paine 1967).

There is always some possibility of doubt attending the recitation of claims and deeds performed in support of a reputation. So often, as in the case of Ellsworth's story quoted above, the deed took place abroad and in the absence of witnesses— there was no member of the crew present during Ellsworth's exploit. So it is almost inevitable that when a man sends himself up, someone will try to bring him down. Not long after Ellsworth had told us his story I was present at a discussion among some of those who had heard Ellsworth, and the subject of the talk was the putting-down of Ellsworth. It was suggested that he had made his money by killing certain people, and further that he was nowhere near the great drinker he claimed to be. One man told of how a friend of his had seen Ellsworth outdrunk by a San Andrésano. On another occasion, after Sludge had given a "free" concert, one or two men asserted that he was not playing as well as he used to—this after everyone had been praising him to the skies while he was playing. Storekeepers and those in prominent positions are always being maligned privately, usually by making insinuations about their reputations, or contradicting the storekeepers' own claims. Mr. John, who always took every opportunity to assert how generous he was, was a constant target of gossip. Hamwell told those of us sitting in his rum shop how Mr. John, having promised to pay for the wood for Hamwell's mother's coffin, then sent Hamwell the bill. And the wood turned out to be rotten. Mr. John, at dinner one night, recounted the story of how Hamwell had contrived with his store assistant to steal from Mr. John, and that was how Hamwell had been able to go into business in the first place—that plus a loan from Mr. John.

Gossip may also take the form of speculation about what a person who has not been around for some time is "up to." Everyone's movements are closely watched, and the moment one sets foot outside the house, the question arises as to what you are up to.

Women's gossip is, for the most part, aimed at that vulnerable part of her social personality, her pretense to respectability. I once overheard Miss Ray and Miss Bercita chattering away about how Miss Bernie seemed unable to keep her granddaughters under control, "them being so flighty," and she who should know better. Later Miss Bernie held forth about Miss Ray's son-in-law who was misbehaving himself. The irony of this was that he was having an affair with Miss Bernie's granddaughter! Miss Bernie also went on about Miss Ray who was "so high and mighty, yet she got a son who is black as a Bottom House baboon, and him got a daughter blacker 'an he."

But the major subject of gossip is men talking about women and women talking about men, and it is here that some of the key features of reputation and respectability are thrown into relief, and where we can see some of the interdependence of men and women for the preservation of their social personalities.

Men, especially young men, often discuss the characters of young women, and the focus, not surprisingly, is usually the latter's sexual availability, willingness, and technique. These conversations are not only pursued for their intrinsic interest but also have some bearing on the way in which young men arrange partners for each other. In some cases a man, having seen a girl to whom he has taken a fancy, tries to find a man who knows her and who can introduce him. Often such a go-between is a kinsman. In other instances young men recommend girls to each other and make the introductions. Equally, of course, girls take the initiative in seeking an introduction to a boy to whom they feel attracted.

These conversations among men about women are spiced with ribald humor; and the opportunity is taken at the same time to enhance one's own reputation by implying one's own outstanding performance as a conqueror, giving details about a particular girl, or being able to refer to many girls in such a way that it is supposed to be evident that one has enjoyed many privileges.

Interestingly, this gossip and these introductions are not without certain risks and contradictions. Every man is kin to at least one woman in his life, though actually in the vast majority of cases he has many kinswomen. Depending on the specific relationship between a man and woman, the former has a certain degree of commitment to her respectability, especially if they are members of the same household. His most intense commitment is to his mother, but he is bound in some sense to other women, in that his own reputation depends in part on the control he can exercise over the respectability of his kinswomen. To some extent his own respect hinges on the overall respectability of the household with which he is affiliated. And yet, kinswomen are the easiest to contact and introduce to a friend. To some extent this dilemma is circumvented by effecting an indirect introduction. I ask my best friend (i.e. the one

I can trust) who knows a cousin of the brother of the girl I like to pass the world along. With sufficient intermediaries the eventual meeting can be made to look almost accidental.

Conversely, by talking about a girl known to be related to a certain man, one can chip away at his reputation by making all sorts of insinuations about her. If I boast of how willing she was, how completely I had her under my spell, my own reputation is advanced and that of her relatives diminished. By the same token, if erosion of another's reputation is not actually intended, then boasting of one's prowess must be done with discretion, taking good care not to mention the lady in the presence of her kin.

Women, in their turn, talk about men. Most often, it seems, they gossip to undermine or criticize the claims of other women to respectability by referring to the disreputable behavior of their menfolk. Far and away the most common content of such gossip is the "foolish" or "ignorant" behavior of men, often of young men, who when drunk betray those with whom they live, especially since the women were supposed to have taught them to know better.

Just outside the store one day Gussie and Bertha met while shopping. They were chatting with Milda, the shop girl, through the open window, and since I was in the store, I was able to hear, whether I wanted to or not, all that was said. One part of the conversation went something like this:

Bertha, who is from Rocky Point asked what it is she heard about Rexford, and is it true?

Gussie: *Aw! You'm shoulda seed him las' night...*

Milda: *See him! Haw! Me na see him, but me hear him. An' man, him a so drunk him na walk. Him a crash the tank [water cistern] an' me hear crash. Me think him a drown, but it the iron he knock off [i.e. the zinc cover].*

Gussie: *An' him a curse and swear so foul I afeared for the children wake up an' hear him, man. 'Poldo [her husband] go out with his gun, but when him a see 'tis Rexford he try fe put him a bed. But him so drunk and foolish, man, him a jus' fall sleep in the mud and no move like him a dead.*

Bertha: *[who has been tut-tutting and shaking her head as*

if she had never heard of such behavior before]:
*I'don' know what as Miss Tilly [Rexford's mother]
done wi' they children.*

Gussie: *Tscha! It is not they fault. Them is so ignorant 'cos
they is not raised right.*

Bertha: *An' she is so God fearin' an it mus' be a vexation
to her.*

Gussie: *Haw! She'm a God fearin'—but she no a God
doin'!*

Milda: *An that is right too.*

It only needs to be added that Miss Tilly and her husband
lived in Lazy Hill, that they were Seventh-day Adventists, and
that they claimed a high degree of respectability.

You can see how Bertha, Gussie, and Milda seek to impugn
Miss Tilly's respectability through her son's manly but disreputable behavior. The story of Rexford's night on the town
would be relayed throughout the island to be savored by all
those concerned about Miss Tilly's respectability.

Through gossip the primary values of island ethos, the male
value of reputation and the female value of respectability,
can be eroded or kept in bounds. Each sex is susceptible to
challenge through the real but often attenuated attachment of
the opposite sex to its primary domain: men are marginally
attached to the household, the woman's domain, women play
a subordinate role in the male's politico-jural domain. A man's
reputation is vulnerable to a woman's conduct; a woman's respectability is vulnerable to a man's conduct. This mutual vulnerability and interdependence is made obvious in gossip.

CREWS: THE SETTING

In discussing the values, premises, and ideals that underlie
the conduct of social relations, the standards by which people
evaluate each other, I have specified that it is in the domestic
domain, the household and the family, that the female achieves
both existential and structural eminence. It remains to identify
the complementary primary social context in which male social
relations are enacted, and where the dominant male value of
reputation receives its principal expression and support.

As already suggested, the deeds and performances considered

manly are not so much ends as means. The end is to gain the respect of one's fellows. Rabelaisian figures and exotic orgies are no more the order of the day on Providencia than they are anywhere else, and it is only the rare individual who becomes a hero or "big man" by achievements that others can only dream of. What is important is that a man successfully conveys the *promise* of performance, that he gives an *impression* of what he might be capable. Potentiality is shown by signs: by being able to drink as much rum as anyone else a man indicates that he may be thought as much a man as anyone else. But to drink too much more, or not as much, begins to raise questions and threatens to upset that sense of equality and stability which is the ideal state of social relations. Likewise one must indicate that one is willing to fight, though to actually be called upon to fight is rare. Boasting is yet another sign by which a man indicates that he deserves respect.

What is clear is that reputation and its corollary respect are specifically social matters. They depend entirely on the reciprocal evaluations of persons related to each other by commonly held standards. But Providencia, unlike so many culturally homogeneous societies, has no institutions integrated into its daily life by which the total society confers recognition upon its members and on their achievement of adult status—no initiation ceremonies, no organized competitions or tests of skill like hunting expeditions. Nor are there institutions such as men's ceremonial houses or even club houses where, in societies such as Iatmul, mentioned above, men's life is concentrated. There are, however, places in each community where only men gather and that women enter only in cases of emergency and at risk of embarrassment to themselves. These are the rum shops.

Usually a rum shop is no more than a room in a private house, or perhaps a special addition to the house. In a few instances it is a separate small hut. It is crudely furnished with a few rough-hewn wooden tables and chairs or benches, a dirt floor if it is a separate hut, walls hung with ancient calendars and Coca-Cola advertisements, and usually one glaring Petromax lantern suspended from the ceiling. This may often remain unlit and small kerosene lamps take its place. In some shops there is a crude bar from behind which the proprietor serves the drinks, and one or two shops have a kerosene refrigerator in which are stored beer and soft drinks and perhaps homemade fruit ices for children. In St. Isabel Hamwell's rum shop recently acquired a radio, otherwise no entertainment is provided.

Men sit at the tables talking, playing cards or dominoes and, naturally, drinking. The rum is made on the island, where it is known variously as Jump Steady, Jom's Toddy or Cumfia. In my own rather amateur opinion it is pretty poor stuff, very rough and more like gasoline than alcohol, though there is no doubt of its being alcohol! Whenever it is drunk it is the habit to grimace and shudder after the swallow. I believe that in most instances the habit is genuine. It is sold in liter bottles or in soft drink bottles at three pesos a liter. It is made by fourteen distillers who work independently and secretly, using crude homemade stills except in two instances where the distillers imported parts and assembled a respectable and reasonably sanitary contraption.

Rum is drunk by the shot with each man taking his turn, swallowing in one gulp and quickly following up with a chaser. Occasionally the rum and soft drink are mixed. In most instances a small libation is poured on the ground before the drinking begins, and usually before each man drinks he offers a toast. Sometimes toasting can be competitive as each man tries to outdo the other and to outlast him. These toasts are not usually original and there is a common repertoire on the island. Here are a couple of examples:

> Here's to the man who takes a wife,
>   May he make no mistake,
> For it makes a lot of difference
>   Whose wife it is you take.

> Here's to the only ship you can't sink—
> Friendship.

Drinking is mostly social, but whenever a man goes to the gardens, goes fishing, or does any other job, he is likely to have a bottle with him. There is a tendency for a man to patronize one rum shop in particular, and for the same men to sit at the same table. Only special regular customers are allowed into the back room, a private part of the shop, where they will not be disturbed and where they can enjoy long, uninterrupted, and very serious games of poker. The idea of regular patronage is not so much deliberate as a simple outcome of association and convenience, encouraged somewhat by advantageous credit arrangements which can be established. Proprietors have to steer a delicate course in the matter of credit because they must pay distillers in cash (their trade being illegal they can have no recourse to recover debts). Rum shops can count on very little passing trade and so are dependent on regulars, who expect credit. The proprietor must go carefully.

In addition to the rum shops themselves there are many spots all over the island where men gather to drink, talk, and play. In Lazy Hill, for example, there is a boat shed and a huge cotton tree; in Old Town a clump of coconut palms on the beach provides a welcome shade, or there is the yard at Miss Crissy's house. In addition to the rum shops, beer is sold at one or two stores, and soft drinks are available at all stores. Mr. John's store, which sells beer, also provides electric light and music through a loudspeaker, all of which encourages sociability.

These informal, almost makeshift locales provide the settings for male fellowship. In them the men of a community gather: here male concerns, interests, and cares are discussed and worked through; here males earn recognition in an environment that is their own.

CREWS: THE GROUP

In an almost spontaneous, accidental way the men of a community divide up into small groups of approximately four to seven members. They are essentially groups of equals—of the same generation if not the same age, of the same life situation, and with a mutual compatibility. In that the men are of similar ages such groups are akin to peer groups; but their sentimental compatibility is just as important as their similar age in making a group. Though they may enjoy equal life circumstances, there is some scope for different members enjoying different life styles.

The nautical term *crew* is an apt term for these groups on Providencia because in many instances the members have sailed together in a boat's crew or fished together as a crew. In addition these men may work together in a laboring gang or in an office. Younger men especially hang around together and pursue their pleasures together, often getting up to no good together—thus fulfilling the image of the term when it is used pejoratively. These crews may come to play a sort of political role, and in so doing they may conjure up the idea of a clique or a cell. Terms such as *gang, peer group, clique,* or *cell* have a rather too specific and often unsavory connotation, whereas the term *crew* seems a little broader and has certain shades of meaning most suitable to the Caribbean or at least the Providencian situation. There is also a crucial difference between the crews that I am about to describe and the gangs or peer groups which have received such wide attention in sociological literature. In the latter, such groups are normally comprised of adolescents, but in Providencia they are usually adult and rarely if ever adolescent. There is some reason to think that this phenomenon is widespread throughout Caribbean societies, though as yet there exists no explicit report of them other than the one I have published (Wilson 1971).

One further preliminary word. My information about Providencia crews is incomplete simply because at the time of fieldwork I did not fully appreciate their importance.

Since boys and young adolescents are in the process of forming attachments, their actual relations do not coalesce until they are of an age to seek proper employment, when they can consider themselves big enough to become independent of the household. It is then that they find, through their work experiences, the companions and shared situations which cement friendships and lead to coalitions. It is therefore with the adult segment of a community's male population that we are most concerned, for this is where such groupings become socially relevant (cf. Kaiser 1970).

Table 6 breaks down the population of St. Isabel in terms of age and sex. The most important age category for our purposes is that between sixteen and fifty years, and there are twenty-nine men in St. Isabel in that category. Within this population there were three crews, some of whose members were in fact over fifty years old. Those who were not crew members included four storekeepers, the Baptist pastor and his assistant, three Seventh-day Adventists and one "madman."

The first crew I shall describe includes a core of five regular members between the ages of twenty-five and thirty-five years. In addition to these are two other men who join in with this crew on an irregular basis and so remain largely peripheral in the total relationship configuration. Two of the men were recently married and a third is engaged to another member's sister. None of the crew are consaguineally related to each other, though there may be distant kinship ties between them.

TABLE 6. Population of St. Isabel

Age	Male	Female	
0–15 years	54	39	
16–50 years	31*	59*	
51 years and over	17	8	
TOTALS	102	106	208

* Includes 2 foreign priests and 2 foreign nuns.

Vidi is their acknowledged leader. At twenty-eight years of age he is the father of three children, all by different women, and he is engaged to Roberto's sister. He has already taken over many of the tasks of running his father's business, which he will eventually inherit. He has had a mainland high school education, is bilingual in English and Spanish, and in many ways has demonstrated qualities of initiative and leadership. He introduced the first battery-powered phonograph, he taught himself photography, setting up his own darkroom and earning money and prestige by taking people's photographs. He was instrumental in helping to form an island-wide baseball league, was president of the newly formed Island Sports Club, and later won election to the Island Council.

Roberto, twenty-seven years old, is the alcalde's son and a schoolteacher. He and Vidi were in Cartagena together, went to the same school, and spent their vacations working together.

They call each other *primo,* which means literally first cousin, but is commonly used on Providencia to mean best friend.

James is thirty years old and is also a schoolteacher. Unlike the other two, he grew up in Rocky Point, but he has lived in St. Isabel for some time and has taught there for four years. Quiet-spoken and a little shy at first, he turns out to be the crew's practical joker and wit. He is married with two small children.

Juan, at thirty-two years, is the oldest member, and he has been married for some time. He is originally from San Andrés, but being married to a St. Isabel girl and preferring life on Providencia, he thinks of himself as an islander. He works as the judge's clerk and, like the others, has had a high school education, speaks both English and Spanish fluently, and is considered very intelligent—though many people think him a little too clever and rather cocky.

Septimus, about twenty-nine years old, is the principal assistant in Mr. John's store. He went to school with Vidi in Cartagena but did not finish. He plans to marry a girl from St. Isabel, though he and his family are from Old Town. He lives in a rented room in St. Isabel and goes to Old Town once in a while.

These are the core members. In addition there is Sherry, who has been deaf from birth and so has never been able to speak properly (not because he cannot learn, but because no one knew how to teach him). He is very intelligent and worked out his own sign language which he taught to others, thus permitting him to lead a near normal social life. He works as a mason and carpenter.

Finally there is Ulisse, Vidi's brother-in-law, who, at thirty years of age is one of the youngest licensed sea captains in Colombia. Whenever he is at home on the island he joins in with the crew, with great gusto, it might be added.

This is a crew of equals. With the exception of Juan, they have known each other for many years, they are all well educated to approximately the same level and are all proficient in Spanish and English; all earn a cash income (though they are not all as well-off as Vidi), and they are all recently married or about to be married. The only discernible "structure" to the group is the slight deference accorded to Vidi as an informal leader.

During the day, most days of the week, these men work separately at their jobs, though Vidi and Septimus are often in the store together and Roberto and James teach at the same school. They all come together at Hamwell's rum shop some time in the afternoon when work is over. There they drink a little *tinto* (thick black coffee) or have a beer. They sit at "their" table but may engage in conversation with the other crew which regularly patronizes Hamwell's shop. Sometimes one or two of them may eat an evening meal at the rum shop— prepared by Hammy's new wife—but this is not a regular thing. Otherwise, after supper on most weekdays, and always on week-ends, Vidi and his crew share bottles of rum, play cards or dominoes, and talk. Sometimes they spend less than half an hour before moving off to a dance, a party, or to see some friends, but on most evenings they gather for several hours.

Apart from spending their leisure time in each other's company, members of this crew pursue most of their outside social activities together. They go to dances, not necessarily all together, but usually in groups of two or three. If it is an invitation party they go with their wives or fiancées, usually deserting them soon after arrival for the company of other males and only periodically having a dance. If it is a paid party they go without their womenfolk because there they will have a "spree" with some girls. It is at such affairs that they may get involved in fights with men from other communities. Quarrels usually arise between individuals, but crew mates stand by ready to render assistance when needed, or to make sure a fight is fairly fought, or, as often as not, to prevent anyone from actually coming to blows.

Vidi's crew was noted throughout the island for doing things in style, for being the pacemakers and the tastemakers. They organized picnics to be held on Crab Cay, a small, very pretty off-shore islet, and as a group they provided the impetus and organization for the revival of the island Sports Club, headed up by Vidi. They were also politically ambitious and were instrumental in organizing an election campaign which resulted in Vidi's being elected to the Island Council. In that they involved themselves in politics primarily for their own interests but nevertheless within the framework of party political organization, they could very well be considered a clique. Not only were they active in getting Vidi elected, they later succeeded in getting another man whom they favored elected to the council, thereby upsetting his opponent and the other political party. Given their social positions, the individual members of this crew enjoy a large amount of prestige and influence which through their crew membership was enhanced and turned to political advantage.

Each member of this crew has many friends and acquaintances on and off the island, so that through their individual ties they can, as a group, mobilize a lot of support or lay their hands on a lot of information if and when necessary. Since a man can be a member of more than one crew at the same time, this makes for the possibility of alliance. Usually the different crews of which a man is a member are not in the same place: Vidi had crews that he joined whenever he went to San Andrés or Cartagena, for instance, and while he was on Providencia he was in only one crew. But with these close ties with other crews, connections can be exploited. Other members of Vidi's Providencia crew would be on good terms with his San Andrés crew, even though they may actually be members of other crews there. Socially, then, membership in a crew also implies an entrée into a ramifying network of ties which, if the circumstances called for it, could be politically advantageous too.

If Vidi's crew is in some ways a clique, it is not exclusively political in its interests and activities. The alcalde's crew on the other hand, is dominated by political concerns because of the occupation and interests of most of its members. This crew also meets in Hamwell's rum shop but occasionally moves to a back room in Shenstone's house as an alternative.

Richie, the alcalde, is about forty-eight years old, married, and has been an administrator and civil servant for most of his working life—quite an exception for an islander. He is bilingual and has had a high school education. He depends almost entirely on his salary for an income, although he has a few acres of land which he uses to pasture his horses, his pride and joy.

Ashton, about fifty years old, is the tax collector. He lives with his common-law wife, whom he says he will marry "when he is ready and she is willing." Though without a formal education, Ashton speaks Spanish well, has a good mind, especially for figures, and has gained considerable experience working as a sailor and at various jobs in Cartagena, Barranquilla, and Panama. As he says, he is as good as any of the others who have had to spend a lot of money to find out what he learned for nothing. He enjoys the distinction of being able to curse longer than anyone else on the island without repeating himself—going on for forty-five minutes, which is no mean feat. He owns about eight acres of land, which he cultivates and on which his household depends for most of its food. He keeps a few pigs and two cows and occasionally "acquires" a case or two of American cigarettes or Scotch whiskey which he wholesales.

Fenton and Shenstone are brothers, in their late forties, and sons of the island's only Chinese inhabitant, who is married to an island woman. They have worked together as sailors, in a joint business venture as agents both in Cartagena and in San Andrés, and they have both had some clerical experience. Fenton invested his money in business shares and in part ownership of two boats. This brings him in a good and regular income. Shenstone was never able to hang on to his money and so works as a cleaner, caretaker, and dispenser at the island clinic. Both men are literate, bilingual, and highly competent.

Fenton owns about twenty acres of land, on which he grows coconuts and sugar cane, grazes a herd of cows, and pastures his horses. He is Richie's greatest rival when it comes to horse racing. He lives in a newly built Spanish-style villa with his common-law wife and their six children. His legal wife, a mainland Colombian, is quite out of the picture, but since Colombian law does not permit a divorce, he cannot remarry. Shenstone lives in a large house with his wife and nine children, and he uses some of the rooms to make a little extra money by serving drinks and light refreshments.

Fenton and Shenstone are the nucleus of a third crew which meets regularly at Shenstone's house, but since I was rarely a guest of this crew, I can say no more about it.

José is the head teacher of the main government school in St.

Isabel. He is subordinate only to the priest, who acts as the superintendent of island schools. José is married, has had a high school education, has spent some time working on the mainland, owns about nine acres of land, most of which he rents out, and makes a little extra income "wholesaling" goods.

Oswald, in his mid-forties, is secretary of the alcaldía, second only to the alcalde in the administrative hierarchy. His home and family are actually in Freshwater Bay, but for most of the time he lives with his common-law wife and six children in St. Isabel. Many people on the island consider him the most intellectual and capable person on the island—he knows more, has read more, thinks more, and talks better than all the others. He is entirely dependent on his salary for subsistence, even though he owns almost twenty acres of land. He leaves it fallow.

Dr. Valdes is the island's private doctor. He is about sixty years old but is not in good health. Nevertheless he enjoys being sociable; and though he drinks no alcohol, he is a fine poker player and spends whatever time he can with the crew. He lives with his daughter, who cares for him, while his wife, from whom he is estranged, lives alone immediately opposite him. He owns a lot of land, some of which is rented out and some of which is used to graze a sizable herd of cattle. He also owns two small stores, one in Bottom House and the other in Southwest Bay. He is part-owner of a number of boats and has an interest in a number of Colombian companies, most of which operate in San Andrés. Altogether he is a wealthy man. He has for a long time been active in island politics, and though he has never sought office for himself, his influence is considerable.

Finally there are two marginal or guest members: Cassio, the singer whom we met before; and the judge, a Lebanese by birth but now a naturalized Colombian citizen, known as the Turk. The judge has been on the island for five years but is now permanently resident there.

Sometimes at midday and invariably after work these men gather at Hamwell's for a *tinto* and a chat. Occasionally they take their coffee into the little square opposite the alcaldía. Here they may well be joined by other men to discuss odd, trivial matters such as the weather, the latest news of boats, or just how they feel. But the single most important activity, exclusive to the crew, is their weekend game of poker. It begins at about midday on Saturday and breaks up some time around dusk on Sunday. It takes place on the average of about once a month, while at other times in between they play such shorter games as blackjack, twenty-one, or dominoes. All these games are played for small stakes, except the monthly set-to, at which comparatively large sums of money change hands (as much as a thousand pesos). Every session is accompanied by the rum bottle, but the drinking is less stylized and more for refreshment than among the younger men. There is no need for these men to prove themselves to each other or to outsiders as far as drinking capacity is concerned.

Cards is not the only pastime. Conversation and a good joke are enjoyed just as much. Island affairs and island people are discussed and dissected without restraint, for in Hammy's rum shop the men are no longer public officials, and the walls no longer have ears. Richie comments satirically on a case he dealt with, giving an impersonation of the plaintiff and snidely, but with wit, commenting on how "some people" manage to live. Ashton brings up the subject of the latest directives from San Andrés, which leads them into a discussion of the incompetence of people there, and this brings up the question of the disadvantages suffered by Providencia: everything destined for the island is intercepted in San Andrés and Providencia is left backward while San Andrés has its electricity, its tourists, and the money. "Just as well," murmurs Dr. Valdes.

Yet, while they relax from their public duties, the rum shop is the scene of much decision-making. The alcalde and his crew talk over unofficially such matters as raising taxes, how to disperse the island budget, how to get so-and-so a job (at least one member of this crew will be appointed to any committee that might be formed by the administration).

Both of the crews mentioned so far meet in Hamwell's shop. They belong to different generations, but they are linked together by ties of close kinship between members as well as by certain common political interests. Roberto, in the first crew, is Richie's son, and Vidi is to become Richie's son-in-law. Vidi secured election to the Island Council, which decides on policy for internal matters, so that the political interests of Richie and Vidi overlap considerably.

Together, these two crews comprise the major part of Hamwell's clientele, and Hamwell is in a sense dependent on them for his living. At one time Vidi and Hamwell quarreled and Vidi, with his crew, built a "night club" which they called the *Kiosko*. It was constructed of palm fronds and thatch and was to be open to the public. Had it stayed in operation Hamwell would undoubtedly have gone out of business. First he tried to get the Island Council to stop the *Kiosko* by claiming it was less than one hundred meters from the Baptist church, which was against the law. But when it turned out that Hamwell's rum shop was even closer to the church the objection was quickly withdrawn. Fortunately for Hamwell, soon after the grand opening of the *Kiosko* it was blown down in a storm.

While they have much in common, the two crews have important differences: they are in different life situations, with Vidi's crew starting out on their careers and Richie's at their height; they have different physical capacities and needs, so that Vidi's crew drinks more seriously, goes to more parties, and in general expends more energy gallivanting, while Richie's crew enjoys its sedentary games, drinks just for fortification, and is far more intent on relaxing. Lastly, the men in the first crew spend very little time in their respective households and have minimal responsibilities there. The men of the second crew are rather more permanent and active members of their households, though they still spend most of their leisure time, as well as their working hours, away from home.

Most of the members of both these crews are of "high class" status, and they enjoy relatively well-off life styles, even though there are individual differences. But though occupations, marital status, income, and other markers of status may differ, by and large the crews are homogeneous. By virtue of their social standing, their occupations, and their interests, these crews are influential on an island-wide basis. Other crews located in other communities enjoy a sphere of influence confined far more strictly to their particular communities. Such crews are, in effect, the local group as far as the men are concerned.

Crews are characteristic of all male social life and they are not limited to specific social strata. Thought of as a social form, crews are part of the culture, and I will turn now to a description of a lower status crew from Free Town.

There are five men from Free Town in this crew and one from Santa Catalina, across the bay. Their ages range from twenty-five to thirty-five years and most of them are related to each other. Larwell and Archilus are twins, Garston is their cousin, Sixto his cousin, and Stew and Black are unrelated. This crew includes five of the twelve adult men of Free Town, but in addition there are two other men who join the crew occasionally when they go on a spree but are not reckoned as full members. One of these is a lad of seventeen years, Larwell's younger brother. He is just starting to go around with a crew and thus

TABLE 7. Population of Free Town

Age	Male	Female	
0–15 years	20	15	
16–50 years	12	24	
51 years and over	6	3	
TOTALS	38	42	80

beginning the process of transformation into an adult. He will either join the crew permanently or join another of his own age group when he is a little older. The other men in the community tend to assort themselves according to age, and though they sometimes chat and drink with this crew, they join them neither often enough nor in enough activities to be considered members. The age and sex composition of Free Town is given in table 7.

No member of this crew was married or living with a common-law wife. Sixto and Larwell regularly visited their girl-friends, and all of them except Black had children. Sixto was the acknowledged leader, for he had a reputation for cunning and ruthlessness inspired by his ability to keep cool in all situations and his apparent readiness to use a knife. Like other members of this crew, he was reputed to be skilled in the use of *obeah* and *science* (i.e. black magic), though it was Larwell who was thought to be the most skilled. As with Vidi, Sixto's apparent leadership was not a formal feature, but stemmed from his competence and confidence, which gave him an authority. He had no means of coercing the others and there were no rules accepted by all that gave him any prerogative.

No member of this crew had a regular occupation, although they all worked periodically as sailors or laborers. When they left the island for a voyage or to seek work they never went alone but always in pairs, or if possible, as a crew. On the island their main source of income was performing odd jobs for Jenkins, the trader. In fact, as time went on they came more and more to assume a regular relationship with him, taking on a status resembling that of retainers. They placed themselves at Jenkins's beck and call, and he occasionally advanced them money which ensured that they would always be available when he needed them. Though he never paid them a wage he always saw that they had access to cash. They became involved in Jenkins's political activities (he was leader of one of the two political parties), acting as his strong men to make sure of votes, or visiting some of his debtors to remind them it was time to repay. Whenever one of Jenkins's boats came in, this crew would be on hand to unload and deliver the supplies. The relationship stopped just sort of the classic patron-client arrangement, though something of this kind was clearly developing.

Like most island men who sail, members of this crew had, in the course of their travels, established friendships with other men whom they met on board or on shore in different ports. A loose network of ties had thus developed between individuals which was, in essence, transferable to other members of the crew. Thus a crew member could be assured of hospitality in Cartagena, for instance, by establishing his connection with that member of his own crew who had a friend in the port. Men in Free Town had close connections with men in Free House, Southwest Bay, Cartagena, San Andrés, and Panama all built up in this way. Whenever a boat came into Providencia it was likely that the sailors would have such a contact on the island, and they were thereby assured of hospitality and reciprocity.

Unlike the other two crews I have described, relations within Sixto's crew were not always harmonious. These were men who were always getting blind drunk, and when they were drunk they were as often as not hostile toward each other, and quite vicious at times. They were not card players, though they did enjoy a game of dominoes, and their socializing turned almost exclusively on drinking, conversation, and some singing and guitar playing. They had a reputation throughout the island as being rather "evil" and it was only where they had sure contacts that they were in any way welcomed or even tolerated.

Most of the men of Providencia are, or have been, members of crews such as these. These crews have no formal status in the institutional structure of the island's society, but since the institutions are of alien origin, this is not surprising. This does not, however, diminish the importance of these crews to the social and political life of the island, or to its public as contrasted with its domestic life. It is this public life that centers on men, and it is through crews that much of the public life is activated. These are also the only "social groupings" that arise out of the very nature of social relations among men rather than being imposed from the outside.

These crews must not be thought of as "building blocks" out of which a social structure may be erected. This conception of social structure is basically a mechanical and political one, and on Providencia, as in most of the Caribbean, where political structure is a framework imposed from the outside, crews do not coalesce or transform into larger groupings. But they are, in a *coincidental* sense, incorporated or involved in *networks* of relationships based not on the crews but on the crew, and extra-crew ties of individual members. Such ties and hence such networks are extensive and far-ranging—in fact they are international. They mark out the routes of various aspects of social communication, notably those based on migration. But they are the expression rather than the basis of the relationships concerned, and as Manners (1965) has pointed out, they lead us, if anywhere, to matters transcending island and society boundaries. We must be careful not to impose upon Caribbean social structure a reality—the social network—that is in fact derived solely from and for our own analytical convenience.

Yet crews and their network linkups may indeed be considered as the foundation of a noninstitutionalized, grass-roots structure of information dissemination and, possibly, mobilization. If anything, in their ideology, which is certainly not formalized in any sense, this is a counterpolitical structure. It is used to avoid, criticize, or even break the law (e.g. through smuggling and illegal immigration). It is used to subvert the law by mobilizing opinion to agree on overlooking an official edict, for example, allowing illegal rum distilling. Officials also make fun of themselves and the law: Richie and his crew talk against their offices, their superiors, and regulations; Vidi's campaign was carried on surreptitiously by seeking to influence voters quietly and individually rather than in public meetings. Sixto's crew was employed explicitly as underground men for Jenkins.

There is no evidence that these crews are necessarily permanent or that all members will remain together as a group for the rest of their lives. Though the present study is confined to a very short period of time, I suspect that men change their affiliations and alliance, just as they may consider themselves members of more than one crew at a time, though there is usually only one crew in which they may be considered primary members.

What seems to me to be the crucial importance of these crews is that they are expressions of a total situation, and that as such they provide a means whereby males achieve existential satisfaction, confirming their own identity in a common culture and thereby building up a sense of *communitas* based on common values and sentiment. Perhaps one could regard them as manifestations of the male bonding phenomenon described recently by Lionel Tiger (1969).

When men pursue their social relationships with each other they do so in a common style—they are able to act and talk by taking certain things for granted. Some of this style is formalized or certainly regularized. Take rum-drinking for example. Everyone drinks from the same bottle and out of the same glass, which is passed around. Not to share a glass or a bottle is symbolic of difference; sharing means equality, and equality is the prime assumption of all crew members about each other. Drinking is solemn and serious, and is always social —the lone drinker is looked on with disdain and pity. Games are played according to a set manner: the cards or dominoes are banged down hard on the table, usually accompanied by an expletive or a challenging cry of triumph—"beat *that.*" Each game, when finished, is reconstructed move by move with no criticism withheld, particularly between partners. Conversations are uninhibited, animated and intimate, full of banter, joshing, and confidence, quite unlike the style of conversation in the home or in public places. Members call each other by nickname and speak of each other in complimentary terms while at the same time feeling free to insult and playfully derogate each other. They listen closely to each other and get wholly caught up in arguments. But more important than anything else is the fact that these men "confidence" each other, that is, they place the utmost trust.

Confidence and loyalty are the cornerstones of the crew and of best-friend relations. One's best friend is *primo* or *compadre,* the man one has chosen as a brother, unlike real brothers, who usually quarrel. When the idea of confidence is invoked it means that a man can be trusted not just to help but to confirm and aid in any way possible another man's image through enhancing and polishing his reputation. If a primo says he did a great deed, one must confirm it; if he denies an accusation, one must back him up. If he wants help, one must give it to him, if he has a secret, one must keep it. Time after time it was explained to me that a man would die for his best friend, that he cared more for his best friend than for his father, his brother, his sister, and even his mother. Crew mates are one's equals, almost one's other being, and they make up that small part of the world at large which believes in one, and in which one can believe.

This intense and authentic friendship should be distinguished from the theatrical protestations often made by young men in particular about their reliability and trustworthiness, of their inexhaustible resources for friendship. Such expostulations usually precede a request for a loan or a favor (not least to visiting anthropologists and other outsiders). Or they are made in a context where the intention is to put another down. Such protestations are also part of more general boasting behavior.

Crews are common to all male life on the island irrespective of socioeconomic differences. But while they retain their status identification to a large extent, they really serve to affirm the ethic of equality. For crews in more or less the same generation, and irrespective of the social status of their individual members, have occasion to interact in work and at events such as paid parties. Crews of different generations have less to do with each other, and their social status differences may become more apparent. In their exemplification of the idea of equality, crews play a notable part in the general dialectic of values which dominates island life as a whole.

Crews and the male life cycle are also related. There is a certain progression in the order and character of crews, which changes as their members grow older. Young adolescents, breaking free from the household, females, and to some extent from school, begin to form ever more meaningful friendships among themselves and with older men. But it is not until they leave the island and begin their first work experience that these friendships become functional and start to take on an existential meaning as well as begin to coalesce into a group relationship. Crews emerge when young men come to share common life situations and life experiences, when they find the need of mutual support, particularly among their own kind. For as soon as they leave Providencia they are among foreigners, and they become foreigners in their turn. This should also be true of other parts of the Caribbean when young men leave the countryside to seek work in towns. As young men move into biological manhood, they must become men in a social sense. In his quest for recognition a young man must depend not only on his own resources but on the backing of his peers, who will by their support and reaction identify him.

The actions and settings of the crew are independent of the household, but as a man comes closer to forming his own household, he becomes much less dependent on his crew. Relations become less intense as his reputation becomes more and more confirmed publicly. And for many, their reputations confirmed, the next move, so to speak, is to achieve respect, much of which stems from the respectability of the household and family. With marriage, a household, and increasing age, accompanied, one hopes, by a degree of economic maturity and security and by a less welcome decline in health and strength, a man and his crew move into another phase. Gathering in rum shops becomes less frequent and old men sit around yarning on the home porch. Indulgence in parties, sprees, and sports becomes less feasible and less enjoyable, so that meeting with one's crew is a quiet time for passing the day. In any case, by this time a man's reputation is firmly fixed, and his image rests on his history, not his potential.

Through crews, their interrelations, their codes, and their activities a man gains genuine respect in the world of men—a respect that he needs if he is to succeed in the public domains of social life. To back up the power of office, for example, one must have the authority born of respect. This was shown up rather nicely in the comparison between Mr. John when he was alcalde, and Richie, the present alcalde. Everyone agreed that Mr. John was a terrible alcalde. He simply was unable to get anything accomplished because no one took much notice of what he said or did. People did not pay their taxes, did not volunteer for jobs, did not obey ordinances, and in a hundred and one subtle ways withheld their support. Mr. Richie, on the other hand, was outstandingly successful and enjoyed the respect of everyone, even his political opponents.

Mr. John had power—this came from his office. But he had no respect. Mr. John had never satisfied anyone that he was truly a man—not that he was not virile (he was) but he had never proved that he could really be trusted, that he had been loyal, that he was prepared to forgo status differences to be a man like everyone else. Richie through his membership in a crew obviously subscribed to basic island values of equality (however romantic or idealistic they may seem); he could be seen drinking and talking in the rum shop, he argued in public, especially at horse races, and it was well known that he had stood by his friends in their times of need. In short, he had a manly reputation and he was respected for it. He was also respectable, and all this conferred on him a certain authority which gave sanction to his word, which gave people a sense of confidence in the rightness of his decisions and actions. He rarely had to call upon the island police force.

If a man cannot get himself respected, he cannot enjoy much authority. Outsiders, unless they are able to "get in" with a crew, forever remain outside the pale. Certain islanders, too, because they do not join crews and because they do not subscribe to the system of values on which crews are based, find themselves socially ineffective. This is particularly true of Seventh-day Adventists and of other young men who seek careers in the church. They, in effect, forswear the principles of reputation, and they often have to condemn the behavior it entails. In the process of doing so they discount themselves from ever achieving the respect of their peers. They become respectable before their time. This was true, for instance, of young Lleras, an Adventist and college-educated man who came back to the island determined to help the people improve themselves and modernize. He came up with all sorts of ideas—for a new wharf, for improving medical facilities, for selectively breeding pigs, for a fish cannery, and so on. Some of these ideas were quite workable, and they all appealed to the islanders. But they laughed at him to his face and all his attempts at leadership and initiative fizzled because he lacked authority—not as an individual but as a social person.

The ideal is somewhat the reverse. A man lives to acquire a reputation, and having done so he can preach reform and improvement. In his personal life, with his reputation secure, a man seeks to establish his respectability—by marrying, by regularly attending church, by becoming a true believer, by giving up alcohol (often medically advisable anyway), and by living properly.

CREWS IN THE CARIBBEAN

The male in the Caribbean is frequently described as being marginal to the household, yet the studies that make this assertion offer no suggestion as to the ways and groups in which males might be central (cf. Gonzalez 1969). If we leave aside questions of structure and simply ask how a man can achieve a sense of identity and social fulfillment, we quickly realize that

there must be a pattern of social relations existentially fundamental for men, with possibly considerable structural importance. The discussion of crews points to a possible answer,
with some of the implications drawn out. Now the question is,
how far does our Providence material apply to the rest of
the Caribbean? The evidence, to say the least, is scanty. But
one hopes that current research being conducted in a number
of societies will confirm, modify, or possibly refute the present
hypothesis that groups comparable to crews are the foundation
of male social relations.

The following quotation, which is about Barbados, is fairly
typical of the comments made about the social life of males in
various Caribbean societies:

> The man is away all day and has very little contact with
> other members of the household. Normally he will not see
> them until dinner time. On his way home he may stop at
> the "shop" and spend several hours drinking and talking
> with other men. If he has work to do on the land, or re-
> pairs to do around the house, he will go out again after
> eating. Often he will go back to the "shop" after dinner,
> not returning home until after 11 P.M., when the local
> radio station signs off. The shop provides the only place
> for men to come together and drink, talk and relax. It
> might be said to function more as a social center than as
> a center for the distribution of alcoholic beverages. [Green-
> field 1966 : 85]

Given a situation such as this, one must surely attempt to
inquire into the organization of social relations focusing on
the rum shop and perhaps men's work. Fortunately Anselme
Remy in an unpublished report of fieldwork in Barbados has
described the preliminary results of just such an inquiry, showing
such relations to be patterned, distinctive, and often of a political nature (Remy 1970).

Slight hints occur in the literature about other societies: in
Trinidad male peer groups, known as *limeys,* are mentioned
(Cloak 1966, Saxe 1969), and again current research promises
to make more explicit the patterning of male social relations.

Hyman Rodman also mentions such peer groups in his recent book, though he does not recognize their significance:

> In interaction with these male peers he [the male] develops a group structure in which gratification is less contingent upon his performance in the worker-earner role. This group structure may take the form of a delinquent gang or a street corner group; in Coconut Village it was a group of talking and occasionally drinking or draughts playing men. [Rodman 1971 : 180]

Such a description would fit crews in Providencia, but as we have seen there is far more to it than drink, draughts, and chat. There are other, briefer references to such groups in Jamaica, where, for example, Davenport refers to "loafing groups" (1956); and in Honduras, where Kaplan makes explicit note of the importance of these male peer groups (1966). She also points out that these peer groups may be associated with fundamental social values in that within each peer group operates a principle of equality.

Clearly there does exist in these and other scraps of evidence a pattern that we are here trying to describe more fully. Whether or not the picture is the same as that shown for Providencia must wait upon reports of further research. I suspect the differences are not too great.

8 Caribbean Cruise: Some Comparisons

Thus far my references to other Caribbean societies have been piecemeal, singled out for comparing particular aspects. Now the question is, does the overall pattern described and analyzed for Providencia coincide with the overall pattern of other societies? After all, Providencia is isolated from other Caribbean societies and has a unique political status. There might be every reason to think, therefore, that the social pattern of Providencia is an anomaly. However, as I argued earlier, the island's singular status gives it the peculiar distinction of being in some sense an amalgamation of much that is typical in the Caribbean, and I would prefer to think that the present findings are widely applicable.

The approach to the analysis of social behavior and structure which is explicit in the organization of this book and in the emphases placed on forms and values constitutes, I believe, a considerable departure from previous anthropological work in the Caribbean. But while the approach may be revealing for the society of Providencia, its wider pretensions can only be sustained if it can reveal more about other societies and make more sense out of existing ethnography. Ideally one should attempt a comparison of total societies; but this is simply not possible at this stage of Caribbean studies. Alternatively, if one considers the present analysis as a paradigm for Caribbean social structure, one may ask if there is evidence from these other societies which fits the essentials of the paradigm. If there is such evidence, then one may hypothesize that the total social structure does indeed correspond to the structure here presented, but that further research is needed to substantiate, elaborate, or refute the present argument.

The present chapter, then, is not an attempt to prove the rightness of my argument; it is rather an effort to indicate that there is a case. Since other anthropologists placed the emphases of their analysis on different social phenomena, it would be ridiculous to expect that they would provide anything like substantial ethnographic data sufficient to enable me to reanalyze these societies entirely within the terms of the present approach. It is the facts whose importance was not evident to the observers, the behavior they recorded in passing and either did not understand or simply did not recognize as being socially and culturally significant that constitutes our evidence.

HISTORY

The outlines of the history of British colonization in the Caribbean are well enough known to need no repetition here. What concerns us are certain of the sociological consequences of this colonization, some of which have persisted despite the changes from slavery through emancipation to political independence.

At all times, the African population has been in the great majority. But they were kept socially separate and subordinate to the small British populations whose ideas, values, and institutions ran the country and the economy and were imposed as the "morally" correct and superior ones. In some contrast to Spanish and French planters, British colonizers in the Caribbean thought of themselves as living in a temporary self-imposed exile from England, whither they would return as soon as their fortunes had been banked. Thus there was little attempt at institutional integration of the colonies. Sidney Mintz has succinctly summarized this effect of colonial plantation systems on societal integration:

> The plantation system partially interdicted societal coherence at two levels of local group formation: the community level on the one hand, and the familial level on the other. It also implies that these effects in turn limited modes of integration of family groups and of communities with larger social groupings—the total insular society or "nation," and with national institutional frameworks such as the educational system, the political system, national religions and the like.
>
> The workings of these negative effects are perhaps most clearly revealed by the extent to which the *bipolar structures of traditional plantation societies have persisted into the present,* expressed today in the highly differentiated

modes of mating and domestic organization, the relative paucity of local community organization, the limited
participation of citizen masses in national decision making, the strong division into rural and urban sectors, and
the lack of effective communications among different strata
of the social order. [Mintz 1967 : 150–51]

An evident duality has continued to exist in the social systems
of Caribbean societies: one is premised on the British institutional structure with its attendant canons of morality; the other,
which is that of the majority (the citizen masses), reflects a
sense of adaptation to total environment, in which there occurs
a set of values which gains its definition by *contrast* with the
superimposed structure. A major consequence of this is the
frequent manifestation of ambiguity toward *all* possibilities for
social life (cf. Fanon 1967, Reisman 1970).

The social system which I have sought to analyze in the
present work is that which arises out of adaptation and appro-
priation—that which is neither African or European. In a way,
what I have described here might be considered the secular
counterpart to the adaptive or "creole" religious systems analyzed by Bastide (1967) in his fascinating work.

SLAVE SOCIETY IN THE LEEWARD ISLANDS AND JAMAICA

Our Caribbean cruise begins with the British Leeward Islands and the fine detailed study of slave society at the end of
the eighteenth century by Dr. Elsa Goveia, whose work suggests that there is a basis in the historical situation for the present findings and analysis. In many ways this study, though restricted in locale, appears to describe a situation typical of
many Caribbean societies at this time. Justifiably this is the
author's claim (Goveia 1965 : vii), and so for present purposes
we may well consider it in its broader provenience.

From the very beginning, although they were placed in the
same colonial situation, the neighboring islands of the Leewards
never cooperated, but "each island preferred to go its own
way, concentrating its attention upon its own separate existence
and its own separate institutions (ibid., pp. 71, 81). This refers

initially to the white planters, but clearly if the whites of neighboring islands never got together, it is doubtful that they would allow their slaves to do so. Thus from earliest times there developed a sense of insularity, a sense of island identity, a trait which most observers and present events constantly confirm (cf. G. Lewis 1968 : 15).

The proportion of whites to blacks was approximately one to ten (Goveia 1965 : 203), but since most whites lived in "urban" areas and blacks in rural areas, the races were virtually separate and formed their own society. In spite of these proportions, blacks were given no political rights (ibid., p. 82), while eventually all whites whether propertied or not received political franchise, and only the exclusion of women from politics continued to be accepted without question (p. 93).

Any formal organization among the slaves was regarded with suspicion, for the policy of the whites was to keep them divided and weak by depriving them of all appropriate occasion to associate. This was considered dangerous, for it could provide blacks with the means of challenging the system of white control (pp. 94–95).

Slaves were prevented from publicly imitating whites, for example, in their funeral practices (p. 167), and every effort was made to maintain "the social and cultural distance separating slave from master."

> The marked cultural difference of field slaves from their masters was regarded as a fitting symbol of their subjection to the slave society, and it helped to confirm the whites in their belief that Negroes were really a separate and inferior species of man. [p. 242]

In other words, slaves were left to adapt to their environment in their own way and as best they could.

While they were not allowed to imitate whites in formal organization, the individual African characteristics that initially assorted slaves were quickly lost and the

> pressures of slavery and the emergence of a Creole population had largely effaced the original differences among

them and had produced instead a certain homogeneity of
culture common to the majority of slaves, and shared by
the long resident Africans as well as by the slaves born in
the islands. [pp. 244–45]

Slaves were developing a pattern of social life which was
neither African nor European but their own. Some of it may
well have been a mockery of European ways, though this is
only speculation. That it may not be too far out, however, is
suggested by this account, quoted from an official document.
Mockery and satire could well have been the name of the game:

> In 1770 St. Kitts was alarmed by the fear of a slave revolt.
> When the matter was investigated Governor Woodley re-
> ported: It proved to be nothing more than a meeting every
> Saturday night of the Principle Negroes belonging to
> several Estates in one Quarter of the Island called Palmetto
> Point, at which they affected to imitate their masters and
> had appointed a General, Lieutenant General, a Council
> and Assembly and the other officers of the Government,
> and after holding Council and Assembly, they concluded
> the Night with a Dance. [p. 95]

A contemporary observer notes that the Negroes' vivacity
and verbal agility were well demonstrated in their songs, and
that these were well adapted to raillery and sarcasm (p. 140).
Then, as now, verbal skill was apparent and was probably
highly valued; and satire seems certainly not to have been beyond them.

Within the slave population, domestic and artisan slaves
were ranked above the vast majority, the field slaves. They
enjoyed a higher standard of living, and they were enabled to
enjoy greater mobility, often being hired out to work for
others by their owners. Hence on the basis of occupation slaves
were ranked among themselves and enjoyed different life styles.
Since domestic slaves were usually women, women from early
on were enabled to gain a certain independence and status.
Eventually the artisan slaves achieved a position whereby some
of them could purchase their own freedom and compete successfully against the poor whites (p. 147). Slaves were also

able to gain control of subsistence farming and the internal marketing of produce, so that this, and basically land, was the chief source of a cash income for them (pp. 226–27), providing the basis for achieving a degree of economic and social status within the Negro population, and, to some extent, beating out the free colored.

In spite of their apparent confinement to plantations and their own developing autonomous culture, slaves, through subsistence farming and marketing as well as deployment of their artisan skills, were able to penetrate the society at large. Though forbidden to imitate whites, they apparently did so to some extent. And although being a slave meant, nominally, that all were the same, there were clearly marked differences in social emphasis, based primarily on skills and occupation. Once again we see the beginnings of a contemporary pattern. Furthermore, it is suggested that old people enjoyed great respect, and, since singing and talking were developed pastimes, we might also conclude that those who sang or talked better enjoyed some sort of reputation.

The total society was marked by a complete separation of the races, with one major exception: white men and black slave women mated, though they did not marry (p. 215). Instead there was a well-developed system of concubinage, which implies a set of continuously maintained, regular relationships. So widespread was this pattern of white male, black female union that it cannot be an exaggeration to claim that, from the beginning, this must have been an important factor in the social separation of the sexes among the black slave population. From these unions, of course, issued the majority of the free colored who became an increasingly numerous segment of the population, intermediary between the white and the black but regarded by each with equal ambivalence. What I wish to stress for purposes of the present argument is that, from early on, black women were treated differently from black men and were more readily and firmly attached to the alien society of the whites. To black women concubinage offered the opportunity to "improve the color" and, through their children, improve their social standing—*but according to white values*. For the woman herself, association with a white man was likely to bring increased privileges and possibly even manumission for her and her children (p. 217).

Within the slave family the husband was not essential, since the children, who took the status of the mother, and the mother herself were the property of the slaveowner. The relationship between the slave mother and her children was fundamental (p. 235). Marriage, which is after all only a politically legalizing institution, could serve neither the purposes of the state nor its administering bureaucracy in the colonial situation. Hence the relationship of males and females in the domestic domain was quite different, males being legally superfluous. One might also surmise from this situation that kinship was far less significant to males than females in the structuring of their social relations.

The concern of missionaries for work in the Caribbean became effective toward the end of the eighteenth century. Before then, they had met with considerable opposition from whites and had been prevented from working in the colonies. Their efforts were directed almost entirely at the black slave population (p. 302), and their concern was a purely religious one—though this was sometimes doubted by white planters fearful for their own security (pp. 294–95). Missionary teaching was concerned to remove all traces of heathenism (i.e. Africanism) and to adhere rigidly to the precepts of Christian (i.e. European) virtue and morality (cf. p. 302). Much of this teaching was directed against "promiscuity," which was thought to be based on the slave custom of polygyny (p. 299). Theological teaching was of little concern.

What must be emphasized about the establishment of missionary churches in the Caribbean is that the church became the first and major institution from the distant, alien colonizing power to root itself in the colony. It was the first and only white institution that Negroes were allowed, let alone encouraged, to join. As Goveia writes, "The Christian missions gave the slaves, for the first time, a "respectable" form of social organization, to which they could devote their individual talents and through which their yearnings for social recognition and self-expression could be, to some extent, satisfied (p. 303).

Nevertheless the church was bound to support the institution of slavery as a condition of its being allowed to missionize. Its teaching of brotherhood, however, directly contradicted its stance on the sanctity of authority. Nor is it only that "the social ambiguities of the religious policy" prepared Negroes to accept the ambivalence of the society following emancipation, but that such blatant contradictions would sooner or later lead Negroes to place the church in their own framework and to use it for their own social ends. Be that as it may, the church became the major institutional inspiration for the social canon of respectability, of a way of life white in origin and in reference. Becoming Christian did not mean becoming white, but it meant joining an institution recognized, even respected, by whites— and thus there was the apparent basis for establishing a sense of moral continuity between black and white. There was even the possibility that, if blacks followed the teachings of the church more conscientiously, they could become "better" than the whites, who for the most part so blatantly disregarded the moral teaching of the church.

Goveia's delineation of slave society in the Leewards probably applies, with some modification, to other societies of the formerly British Caribbean. Turning to Jamaican slave society for a historical comparison, we find a situation similar in its broader dimensions to that of the Leewards.

There was considerable social differentiation within slave society, particularly on the basis of occupation. Patterson suggests a threefold vertical division between domestics, skilled workers, and field Negroes, and a horizontal division within each of these groups such that, for example, each occupation had its own headman and field slaves were headed by drivers (Patterson 1967 : 54, 58–63, M. G. Smith 1965a : 101–02, Curtin 1970 : 19). Great emphasis was placed on authority as the attribute of status, leading in some instances to the quasi-political organization of slaves on an estate (Smith 1965a : 103, 105). Slaves were given plots of land on which they raised crops not only for their own subsistence but for a marketable surplus. In effect slaves came to supply the island (including planters) with food (cf. Patterson 1967 : 220–21). Slaves were "extremely tenacious" of their rights to land (Smith 1965a : 104), and it was primarily through land and marketing that they

were able to better their economic position, which in turn reinforced or created new differences of status (Curtin 1970 :
19).

Higher status slaves were often given better living quarters
and enjoyed polygynous marriage (Patterson 1967 : 54, 67).
Something of the same sort of respect was accorded to elders,
who were addressed with an honorific prefix such as Ta or Ma,
Uncle, Aunty, Tatta, Mama, Sister, Boda (ibid., p. 169–70)
while children were welcomed as security for old age (p. 168).
However, it should be noted that Patterson records the ambivalent feelings of women about having children, finding them
and pregnancy a great burden under slavery (ibid.). The special
power that could be gained by women by virtue of their sexual
services for whites, especially by the mothers of prostitutes,
further emphasizes the conditions of separation of the sexes so
evident in the Caribbean (ibid., p. 167).

Whereas in the Leewards hucksters, who were usually white,
encouraged Negroes to steal from their masters' plantations
(Goveia 1965 : 210), in Jamaica pilfering by slaves from their
masters was done for its own sake (Smith 1965a : 105) and
was not seen by them as being wrong (Patterson 1967 : 222).
Stealing from each other, however, was not condoned.

The strong attachment of slaves to place and community is
reported by Smith, who notes also that there was a high degree
of community solidarity (1965a : 106). Such a strong sense of
identification is a critical feature of contemporary life in Providencia. Tensions occurring within the slave community focused
on positions in the ranking system and mating, which reminds
us of the behavior identified as "crab antics." Mating was un-
stable, and since marriage brought no jural or social advantages,
legitimacy coming via the mother, the institution was derided
(Patterson 1967 : 164) and seen only as a mark of high status,
with the result, especially after missionary influence became extensive, that only the "better-off" and the respected elderly got
married (ibid.). Yet even though their legal rights were minimal, some fathers showed great pride in their children (Smith
1965a : 108), and one could link this up with the importance
of names and the existence of an ancestor cult among sections

of the slave population (ibid., p. 107, Curtin 1970 : 31, Patterson 1967 : 198–202).

Kinship was individualized but may well have devolved primarily upon the mother, since she was in fact the sole permanent element in the slave family and thence in any kinship proliferation (Smith 1965a : 109, Patterson 1967 : 168). The exclusion of the male from any authority in the role of husband-father is pointed to as a major reason for his demoralization by Patterson (1967 : 167), in line with many other writers' observations on the "castration" of the Negro male. Yet one wonders how complete this was, since Patterson indicates that there was some sort of rebellion or revolt by slaves almost every year from 1655 to 1832, including successful ones such as the Maroon Wars (pp. 266–73).

In the light of some of the arguments presented previously one is tempted to see in other forms of slave behavior a certain assertion of self which is part of the contemporary pattern. I am referring in particular to Patterson's excellent discussion of "quashee"—a particular form of evasion and dissembling said to characterize West Indian Negroes (known as "Samboism" in North America). Through satire (pp. 240, 248, 254), dissembling, playing the stereotype (p. 180), evasive arguing off the point (p. 176), and by general lying and deception (p. 173), slaves appear to have made an art of the practices that enable them to defeat, or one up, or put down their white masters. And not unexpectedly, the chief vehicle for such arts is language, and the most expert practitioners, the self-appointed "lawyers" who argued the cases of slaves before overseers and masters as well as before slave headmen (p. 231). Such men were "usually shrewd and loquacious and had a great deal of *congo-saw* and *sweet-mouth* and knew how to flatter and play upon the vanity of the whites" (ibid.). Such behavior is not only a form of self-assertion but may be a feature of differentiation within the community of slaves, who, being each other's equals, were free to compete against each other in order to differentiate themselves. To some extent this is confirmed by the fact that many of the recreations allowed to the slaves were put on a competitive basis (p. 248).

Such references to historical conditions suggest quite clearly that a number of values and characteristics of the organization of Negro slave society that may be found in contemporary society as well had their genesis in the past; that they are part of a larger system, not incidental oddities. It seems unlikely that such resemblances between the past and present are fortuitous; and just as reference to the past suggests a possible basis, among others, for understanding the present, so does the present argument suggest a wider scope for interpretation of the past. But the argument is based principally on one small society, and to claim to generalize from this instance, one must seek some supporting evidence by comparing contemporary societies as well as those of the past.

JAMAICA

Certainly the disparity in size and diversity between Jamaica and Providencia makes them unsuitable for certain levels of comparison. On the other hand, studies by social scientists, and by anthropologists in particular, have concentrated upon communities in the rural districts which are inhabited mainly by the lower class blacks of the total society. These community studies are representative of a common approach taken by anthropologists, and they deal with samples of the majority of the population. For present purposes then, the findings of these investigators may be considered quite comparable to my study of Providencia.

In Jamaica the ownership of land from slavery times onward became an important, if not the most important, indication of improved social status (Clarke 1957 : 20), and it is Clarke's main thesis that land is of cardinal importance in the social life of rural Jamaicans today (ibid., pp. 62–69). The basic importance of land in both the social and the economic senses is noted, indirectly, by other authors (Cumper 1958 : 87–88, Cohen 1954 : 106), while the sentimental significance of land may be gauged from the importance of the category of family land, indeed from the very term itself. Land appears to be the mainspring for the achievement of economic security and improved social status (Cumper 1958 : 87, Cohen 1954 : 106, Davenport 1961 : 441–47), and although no author traces the process of this situation, statements such as those by Davenport that land and wealth are synonymous to the lower class countryman (ibid., p. 450) are explicit enough to warrant the suggestion that the fundamentals resemble those described for Providencia.

The separation of the sexes, a basic premise of my analysis, is pointed to explicitly by Davenport, from whom we also learn that the house, yard, and kitchen (suggesting the domestic domain) are dominated by the adult woman, and that women are often confined to the household while men are free to move (ibid., pp. 436–38, Cumper 1958 : 91, Clarke 1957 : 145–49). Socializing patterns emphasize the separation of the sexes. First, men work away from the house, either in the gardens or for wages. This economic division of labor is carried through to a social division in the pursuit of leisure (Davenport 1961 : 436, Cohen 1954 : 118).

Men usually go to the rum shop in the evening and on Saturdays. Here they drink, play guitar, cards, or dominoes, and they gamble and chat in small groups. Women never attend but visit each other in their homes, a pattern which coincides exactly with that detailed for Providencia (cf. Kerr 1952 : 16, 20, 22). In the rather unusual community of Rocky Roads, Cohen mentions that prior to marriage a most important relationship for a man is that with a special male friend, a best friend. Similar associations are found among women, but these tend to be limited to gossiping groups of married women (Cohen, 1954 : 126–27). But since this suggests a pattern we have noticed as being general, perhaps Rocky Roads is not as exceptional as might at first appear. In generalizing about Jamaica, Davenport observes that there is a strong tendency for young men to associate with each other in groups (1961 : 432).

As for kinship, Henriques claims that a strong sense of kin is a distinctive feature of lower-class family life, and he goes on to stress that "there appears to be both an unconscious and a conscious bias towards the maternal" (Henriques 1968 : 139). It is the mother-child relationship that is all-important as far as the Jamaican household is concerned (Davenport 1961 : 423), and the equality and solidarity between siblings is the second major parameter of kinship (ibid., p. 425).

The separation of the sexes is further reflected in the observations made by various writers about crucial values of the society. Women are described as the carriers of respectability (ibid., p. 430), and this is closely related to the idea that marriage confers respectability and becomes a hallmark of status (Clarke 1957 : 75, 82). After marriage, which often occurs at around middle age, a man is caught up in this concern with respectability (ibid., Kerr 1952 : 86), whereas before marriage he is not subject to these ideals. Even though women are expected to bear children continuously, and childbearing confers adult status on a woman (Blake 1961 : 95–96), she is still subject to severe chastisement upon her first pregnancy. This disgraces the mother in particular and the family in general (Kerr 1952 : 11, 62).

Men expect proper decorum from their wives and the possession of a good family name is recognized as an important feature of social status (Clarke 1957 : 91, Henriques 1968 : 59). In general, though, information about what I have identified here as the concern for reputation on the part of males is rather lacking, and there is little available for comparison. But the general emphasis on female life and dominance leads one to wonder just what happens to the male in this social system. The present study indicates one likely answer.

There seems to be a clear awareness among all those who have studied rural Jamaicans that they participate in a "peasant sub-system" (Cumper 1958 : 104). But at the same time there is some hesitancy and confusion about the internal structure of this subsystem, particularly with respect to social differentiation. In Edith Clarke's study of three villages, the populations are described as being lower, middle, and upper class. But it is not clear whether this ranking is confined to the Jamaican lower class (i.e. the peasant sub-system) or whether the classification belongs to the island-wide, total social system. It is clear, however, that the criteria of social status incorporate the observance of European style, habits, and standards—having a good house, a servant, marriage, proper manners, and so forth. It is also clear that, within the communities, there is scope for mobility among these classes, though there is nowhere a satisfactory account of how this can be achieved. The only existing analyses of inter- and intra-status behavior are focused on sexual mores (Blake 1961 : 95–96, Kerr 1952 : 11, 62). The ideals of proper behavior which help to define status differences are borrowed and alien, but in a sense they are also transformed, becoming authentic within Jamaican culture. Nevertheless they still carry with them strong associations with alien, white Euro-American standards, with the result that many Jamaicans evidence considerable ambivalence over status behavior (Clarke 1957 : 157, Blake 1961 : 93).

BARBADOS

Barbados is a small (166 square miles), incredibly densely populated island (250,000 people), mostly flat and given over almost exclusively to the commercial cultivation of sugar cane. It also has the reputation of being one of the most British of the Caribbean islands.

Among the black population of the island, who are the great majority, even a small plot of land has been of inestimable value since emancipation. It has meant that vital margin of freedom allowing a man to seek a better paying job than laboring on a plantation, for the land will greatly aid in supporting the household while its men are away (Greenfield 1966 : 147). Men tend to grow sugar cane, which they sell, while the women grow provisions (ibid., p. 79). Because it is so scarce, land is a constant source of friction between siblings especially: "land causes more humbug and murderation than anything" (pp. 98–99). Apparently communities are not sociologically cohesive, although we are told that people have a strong sense of identification with place, which is extended into a very strong idea of island independence and of being *Bajan*.

Owning land provides a man with the opportunity to seek a better paying and more prestigious occupation than agriculture, which has little prestige. But his subsequent improvement in status is founded on the ownership of land, while the status itself becomes directly contingent on his occupation (pp. 70, 117–18).

Socioeconomic status is buttressed and signified by taking on the demeanor of respectability, most notably by getting married (p. 118). Marriage implies that a man will have built or bought a house, preferably on his own land (p. 100), and any man who does this exhibits a "pride that is almost visible." Once again the model for these standards of respectability is white European culture, and they reflect what contemporary white planters still refer to as "good character" and "good behavior" (p. 54). On the basis of the present study, however, one would suspect that there is a set of values that exists independently of white-associated values and which is possibly more instrumental in the definition of status.

Thus since occupation, for males, bestows varying degrees of prestige, one might also infer that the achievement of certain skills and the attainment of a job are attributes of a man's reputation, which he can convert to community status. It is noted that high among the valued skills and acquisitions is education.

Though never explicitly elaborated, the separation of the sexes in Barbados is evidently a major feature of social life: "Since men are away working for most of the day, and away from home in the evenings socializing with other men, their contacts with women and children are restricted to Sundays and holidays, and even these days are often spent at the shop with other men" (ibid., p. 85). And another writer notes of Barbados that "on highway 4, about 7 miles from Bridgetown, the visitor after 5 P.M. gets the feeling that he is entering an area where men are paramount and women non-existent" (Remy 1970 : 8).

Women, on the other hand, appear to be confined to the household, especially when they are living permanently in a marital union with a man: "A wife has very few friends, and visits other women only on rare occasions. The more limited her contacts are with people outside her house and yard, the better her husband likes it. And most of the marital disputes that occurred during the course of the study were traced to arguments over whether or not the wife was spending too much time away from her house (Greenfield 1966 : 106). One might observe that since men are away from the house most of the time, the wives are away more frequently too but are found out infrequently.

A woman aspires to be "mistress" of a household which has been provided for her by her husband. In this house she should be able to employ servants, as this would complete the public confirmation of her respectability (p. 100). Mothers try hard to keep their daughters at home under control so that they can preserve their own and their household's respectability. At the first sign of pregnancy, the same violent reaction occurs in the mother as that noted for Providencia and Jamaica (p. 109).

A man's authority in the household is a direct function of his ability to support it, but "over the years a man normally performs very few duties within the house" (p. 103), and we may assume a pattern resembling the one analyzed in detail above, though suitably modified to meet certain different environmental conditions.

Married couples do not socialize together, and in this there is a difference from the case I have put forward: on Providencia high-class couples are expected to attend events as a married couple or even as a family. In Barbados married men are expected to have extramarital affairs but women are not permitted to do so. Women are primarily responsible for raising children and the "first major responsibility of a father to his children is to see that they receive a school education" (p. 104).

It would seem not too exaggerated to claim that evidence from Barbados suggests a social system corresponding to the one proposed in this book. On most matters, of course, the data are sketchy—it is difficult, for instance, to know whether kinship is a more significant factor in the social life of women than men. And since Barbados appears to have a higher percentage of nuclear family households than is often reported from other Caribbean societies, there may be other variations to the model I am proposing (cf. Greenfield 1966 : 139, Cumper 1961 : 386–419).

GUYANA (FORMERLY BRITISH GUIANA)

Raymond Smith's book *The Negro Family in British Guiana* (1956) is a milestone in Caribbean social anthropology. It has set the tone and direction of research in the area ever since it was published. Throughout the present work I have had constant occasion to refer to it, so the present summary is little more than cursory.

Ownership of land is interpreted by Smith to be the basis of

social equality within the village, and this social value is enhanced by a generalized extension of sentiments of solidarity
that are expressed in a kinship idiom. The people of a village,
for example, speak of themselves as being "all one family"
(Smith 1956 : 51). All three communities on which Smith based
his study are "well defined," having an explicit sense of unity
and difference from other communities. Such a feeling of identification is partly related to an idea of territorial autonomy (ibid.,
p. 203).

Though he insists on the absence of internal social differentiation among the village population, Smith nevertheless describes
village stratification which includes non-Negroes and at the same
time offers a number of hints that among "black people" there
may indeed be categorical distinctions, though these may not
be transformable into a social hierarchy (p. 216). I tend to
doubt this on the basis of evidence from the Caribbean in general as well as some slight hints from Smith himself. Thus sugar
boilers enjoy high prestige, as do carpenters (pp. 37, 41–42),
and prestige in general is acquired by a rigid adherence to the
norms of what Smith terms the "total society" (pp. 216–17),
which in fact are white and church-based. Marriage confers
status on women, who may then use the title "mistress," and
marriage itself implies the achievement of respectability, that is,
conformity with the norms of the total society (pp. 180–81).
Smith mentions the fact that men wish to prove their virility (p.
141) and that young men like to boast of their ability to earn
money (p. 72), which is then converted into symbols of prestige
and reputation (pp. 41, 137). It is also extremely important
to everyone that he should not get a "bad name"—which implies the loss of esteem of one's peers. This can occur if a man
tries to "play great" or if he places too great an emphasis on
conspicuous spending in trying to raise his prestige in the village (p. 218). The situation seems to suggest not that all are
equal, as Smith would have it, but that some become more equal
than others. When they do, however, they become more exposed
and more liable to being pulled down. In fact, these few hints
strongly suggest the likelihood that Negroes in Guianese villages
conform to the pattern that I have described as "crab antics."

The separation of the sexes in social life is well attested. Men eat alone (pp. 57–58, 76) and women are described as being autonomous (p. 152) and as the nucleus of affective ties within the household, a situation projected into the wider kinship system. Women rather than men are concerned with kinship (p. 152). The sibling group is said to be solidary in a jural sense because of their equal inheritance rights but, for the same reason, not so solidary in an affective sense (p. 156).

Males spend little time in the house, rarely play with the children, and spend a considerable portion of their time outside the house in the company of other men (p. 113). Extramarital infidelity is frequent among men but rare among women (p. 114). The claim and recognition of fatherhood is most important to a man (p. 130) because (might we infer?) it is vital to his reputation and good name.

From Smith's account we can glean just enough to argue that since they appear to behave in rather the same way, the Guianese Negroes may also have a similar basic social structure to that we are proposing.

TRINIDAD

Herskovits's fieldwork was carried out over thirty years ago, but his findings and their presentation remain strikingly contemporary—that is, if we make due allowances for his preoccupation with Africanisms. The social condition of the village of Toco, where he worked, is very similar to that of present day Providencia. Both are characterized by their isolation and technological backwardness. Herskovits's account provides strong support for present suggestions for the interpretation of Caribbean ethnography (Herskovits, *Trinidad Village,* 1947).

Villages are controlled from the outside, both politically and economically, and Herskovits goes as far as to say that the withholding of political power and responsibility from the men of Toco is a form of emasculation (ibid., p. 13). A consequence of this is that moral sanctions and standards operative within the village may, in many senses, run counter to the "total system"—a situation he emphasizes in his account of the Shouters (pp. 190–223). The same sense of resentment against the outside, essentially white authority structure and moral system is noted by Braithwaite, writing twelve years and one war later

(1953 : 21). If this is so, one may ask whether a corollary of
this is not a social system adapted to circumstances and gathering its authenticity from the conditions of opposition and a rural
existence.

Owning land appears to be a prerequisite for improving economic status and becoming well-to-do (Herskovits 1947 : 32–
35), while in the matter of inheritance, land is more important
for men because "land allotted to a daughter is for life only"
(ibid., p. 133). Some of the pressure to own land is, however,
alleviated by the system of "contract," whereby a man is paid
to clear land which he then may cultivate (pp. 54–55).

Herskovits contends that there is a marked separation of the
sexes, though he does not make too clear exactly how this is
so. He claims that women are the principal exponents of the
culture and that they are paramount in the domestic field (pp.
8–9). The woman is the central figure in the household and
the family, and in the case of separation the children usually,
though not inevitably, go with the mother or her kin (pp. 130–
31). Men, although they have economic responsibilities toward
the household, do not have much control over its affairs. Female dominance in the domestic sphere is confirmed, for both
working- and middle-class Trinidad, by Braithwaite (1953 :
103), who notes that this is in part an outcome of the relative
economic independence of women (cf. Rodman 1971 : 59, 62).

Marriage, an expression of conformity to outside "white"
ideals represented by the church, is important because of the
prestige which it confers and the respectability it brings to a
woman in the eyes of her community (Herskovits 1947 : 81,
Rodman 1971 : 62–63, 69). Married women insist on being addressed as "mistress" or "madam" and, since marriage is expensive to celebrate, it also serves as a marker of economic
status (Herskovits 1947 : 84, 92–93). A household founded on
legal marriage represents an achievement of those aspirations to
respectability approved by the society at large and marked by
norms of "proper" behavior (Braithwaite 1953 : 100). But marriage often does not occur until middle age, so respectability may
come rather late. Although many children are born out of wed-
lock, recognition of the father is socially mandatory, otherwise
the girl and her family will be shamed. Rodman also points

out that pressure for marriage is a matter of ensuring the legal responsibility of the male for the wife and children (1971 : 142). This is, then, a good reason for men to resist marriage. Presumably fatherhood contributes to a man's reputation.

Herskovits gives an account of how people strive hard to earn and keep the respect of their fellow citizens, and such things as hard work, honesty, keeping a house clean, and having well-mannered children are rewarded by social prestige and go far to compensate for a low economic position. Some of this respect is garnered by spending freely, and one who is stingy is despised. Participation in religious celebrations is also attributed, in part, to the desire for prestige (Herskovits 1947 : 32, 34, 44, 121). Braithwaite speaks of the importance of "propriety of behavior" in the ordering of the social structure, which is especially contrasted to the crudeness and volatility of nearby Venezuelans—a characterization similar to that of Colombians by Providencians (Braithwaite 1953 : 80).

Herskovits's observations about prestige are supported by Braithwaite, who describes the preoccupation of the middle class with status and the external marks of prestige. He notes a tendency for conspicuous consumption and for accumulating as many as possible of the signs that will win recognition from other people (ibid., p. 115). One of the major dividing lines among the lower-class families is that between those families which are oriented toward observing middle-class standards of respectability and those to whom these standards are in large part a tedious necessity to which, at times, they are forced to adjust (ibid., p. 142). Rodman, however, points out that lower-class people may try to gain prestige in the eyes of middle-class people by only appearing to accept certain values and practices (1971 : 116). If we had more details about how this works out we might be able to say with more confidence that herein lies a major basis for "crab antics" in Trinidadian communities. As it is, the court cases cited by Herskovits give us some grounds for supposing this to be the case (1947 : 266–68).

One of the main differences between Providencia and Trinidad is the profusion, in the latter, of churches and secular clubs. In this feature, Trinidad resembles most other Caribbean

societies. It is noticeable that these organizations offer scope
and opportunity for community-wide, quasi-political activity
which in certain circumstances might become truly political.
Herskovits noted early in his book the political emasculation
of the community, but it is possible that church and club activity provide a compensation for this or even prove to be a
"counterpolitical" sphere. Thus in his description of the Shouters, and in Simpson's account of the Shango Cult (1965), one
is struck by the profusion of offices in these cults. Many of
these offices have titles satirizing the outside white political apparatus, and, as Goveia's study of the eighteenth-century Leeward Islands shows, such organizations and tendencies to satire
are of long standing. What is more, Herskovits reveals that
many of these organizations think of themselves as alternatives
to secular political structures such as the courts and police.
Furthermore the social standing of religious officials and various practitioners of magic such as lookmen and obeahmen is
surely a matter of some importance, though Herskovits does
not touch on the subject. He does note that such persons are
quite numerous, are of great importance in the daily lives of
people, and that some become quite prosperous (1947 : 227).

The possibility for a social structure based on differentiation
and for moral significance with its terms of reference *within*
the community are indeed quite likely and consonant with
Herskovits's general account. There is a definite respect for old
age and great reverence for learning, with the consequent admiration of the educated. What is more, the possibilities of
such intrinsic social standards are emphasized in Braithwaite's
observation of the admiration "by large sections of the lower
class population for the 'big bad' who violates the legal norms
and gets away with it" (1953 : 144).

Veneration for education, European style, is described by
Herskovits for Toco (1947 : 124) and is singled out by
Braithwaite as a major factor in defining prestige and social
standing, as well as creating a basis for the decline of colonialism (1953 : 56). A recent work elaborates even further on
the role of education and the expectations and hopes engendered by it (Rubin and Zavalloni 1969).

What one is led to wonder about Trinidadian villages such as Toco is how far manliness, reputation, and the development of skills special to the particular environment improve a person's social standing and sense of worth. Although note is taken of the marginality of the male to the family and household, we learn little of the process of the man's assimilation into the community, or of the ways and means by which he seeks and earns his identity. Here and there one finds a hint: Braithwaite, for example, says that a reputation for being a good stick fighter brings about high standing among one's peers in the lower class. Presently there is a vogue for building a reputation on courage and leadership in gang warfare—steel band or otherwise (Braithwaite 1953 : 144, Rodman 1971 : 180) and I have noted in the previous chapter that male peer groups called "limeys" are common.

In Trinidad as elsewhere the signs are present; one simply wishes for more solid evidence of the system of which they are a part.

CARRIACOU (GRENADINES) AND ANDROS ISLAND (BAHAMAS)

These two comparatively small island societies have been reported on at some length, but they appear to be dissimilar in some respects to the other societies of the British Caribbean. They are characterized by a high incidence of "legal" marriage, and people marry at a comparatively young age. Consequently there is a predominance of nuclear family households. In both societies men spend a lot of time away from the islands because they have to work abroad to subsist. As a result, extraresidential matings are frequent on Andros, while in Carriacou there is institutionalized lesbianism. Carriacou is also distinguished among Caribbean societies for possessing patrilineal descent groups known as "bloods." Quite understandably the anthropologists who studied these societies concentrated their attention on the explanation of these Caribbean peculiarities. This detracts somewhat from the fullness of their accounts; but nevertheless, in both societies we may catch tantalizing glimpses of a value system resembling the one I am trying to suggest (M. G. Smith 1962b, K. Otterbein 1966b).

There is indirect indication that in Carriacou land has a position of some importance as a focus of social cohesion and differentiation (M. G. Smith 1962*b* : 19, 30–33, 239–40). Large landholders and owners of cattle are envied locally (ibid., p. 49). On Andros, land is plentiful and not very valuable, though there does exist a category of ancestral land to which some families feel closely bound (Otterbein 1966*b* : 129).

Although M. G. Smith claims there is a lack of economic and social stratification on Carriacou, there are scattered references to persons who are more prosperous and important than others and who, for instance, can enjoy certain sexual privileges (Smith 1962*b* : 190, 201). People admire those who husband their resources and use them in worthwhile investment, and presumably those with such resources enjoy a somewhat more prestigious reputation among their fellows. Again, fishing and sailing are vitally important activities in Carriacou, so that being a boatowner or a skilled fisherman earns a man prestige (ibid., pp. 54–56). While we have no basis for questioning Smith's assertion of the absence of social stratification, it seems likely that there is some sort of system of ranked social differentiation.

On Andros Island, Otterbein notes that there are well-to-do families (1966*b* : 46) who improve their social standing by generosity and conspicuous consumption (ibid., p. 56). At one stage in his account the author constructs an elaborate economic index showing that female-headed households are worse off than male-headed households (pp. 113–15), but unfortunately he gives no indication as to whether these economic differences might imply any form of status differentiation. I suspect they do. The same question arises for Carriacou, though Smith writes that the elite comprise mainly professionals and storekeepers, who are almost exclusively immigrants (Smith 1962*b* : 99).

The idea of a double sexual standard is very explicit on Andros (Otterbein 1966*b* : 67). Men and women both achieve adult status by the birth of their children, but men gain even more prestige by proving themselves especially virile. They must produce many children and be able to have frequent sexual intercourse. Although women must have children to claim adulthood, Otterbein says they do not believe in having as many children as they must—and in this they differ from others in the Caribbean. There clearly exists an idea of respectability for which women are responsible, and some families are mentioned as having poorer reputations than others (ibid., p. 36), girls are chaperoned (p. 35), and there is an elaborate maintenance of the fiction of a girl's virginity at marriage (pp. 41–42).

Presumably there is a similar double standard in Carriacou since men, through membership in "bloods," exercise strict control over a woman's sexual life. In both societies "to be important a man must marry and have children" (Smith 1962b : 189), and on both islands, as elsewhere in the Caribbean, it is mandatory that a man build a house before marriage, thereby indicating his economic and social maturity.

Some of the assertions of these authors do indeed question the applicability of the model we are proposing. Otterbein writes of the Andros Islanders that the men control the domestic sphere, mainly because they earn the cash that supports the household, and that the division of labor is by no means hard and fast; but these are merely assertions. He presents no evidence, in the form of descriptions of interpersonal behavior, to back them up. We do learn that fathers are rarely at home, spending their leisure time in bars (Otterbein 1966b : 118) where their favorite topic of conversation is travel and adventure abroad (ibid., p. 37). It is also the custom to spend freely and get drunk frequently. In other words, here are a number of critical traits which I would suggest are indexes of a viable system of social values and relations, but which have not been recognized as such by the author. I suspect that Andros conforms more closely to the model I am suggesting than to the assertions of the investigator.

It is not clear from Smith's account of Carriacou how far there is a focus for male social life distinct from the household, and whether the domestic domain is the center of female social life. It is clear that, unlike other Caribbean societies, agnatic kinship in which males play the main role is "more extensive and clearly defined" (M. G. Smith 1962b : 267).

In both societies there are well-developed rules of kinship

exogamy: in Andros bilaterally related kin should not marry each other (Otterbein 1966b : 35) and in Carriacou kin may not marry each other if they can trace a relationship through the fourth ascending generation (Smith 1962b : 273). In both societies consensual cohabitation is discouraged and early marriage encouraged.

There are many features of these two societies which differentiate them from other Caribbean societies, particularly insofar as mating patterns are concerned. But in spite of these differences and the emphasis of each author on these differences, there are still hints that the total social value system of the majority of the population may be close to that outlined in this book. I cannot, of course, insist on this, but only point to the signs.

BLACK CARIB OF HONDURAS

Though a mainland society, like the Guyanese Negroes, the Black Carib seem to form a homogeneous entity within the total population and appear to be comparable in all respects to the island Negro populations of the Caribbean. Furthermore, they have been studied by Nancie Solien Gonzalez, who, through her work there has made a number of important contributions to Caribbean social anthropology.

Her chief work, *Black Carib Household Structure* (1969), which provides the basis of this summary, seeks to expound the hypothesis that the "conjugal" household dominated by the woman, as a structural form, is correlated with the imposed necessity for migration on the part of males, who must work abroad to subsist since economic opportunity within the community is so limited. This is undoubtedly so. But as our summaries of Carriacou and Andros make clear, the conjugal household does not necessarily follow from the need for migration. Both societies have a predominantly "affinal" pattern of household structure, though emigration, as in Honduras, is most pronounced. I am arguing, of course, that a system of values exists by which moral, ethical, and behavioral priorities are determined in adaptation to an environment, and that it has been a mistake to make the fulcrum of analysis the household and its structure.

Gonzalez, like most other writers, is conscious of a "dualism" in the social system of the Black Carib. She recognizes a "local" or "ethnic" social system and an "outside" or "western" system (ibid., pp. 8–10). Although the ethnic household structure is sanctioned, a household based on western marriage has prestige. The western system is more closely approximated by the local upper class and the class division itself is based on wealth, education, and the moral character of individuals (p. 81). Class status must be acquired and maintained by each individual in his adulthood (p. 77). There is, no doubt, a clear pattern of socioeconomic differentiation within the community, though there is no information on its meaning and conduct. Some inferences, however, can be made.

A man's reputation may in part derive from his fathering of children (p. 76) and his successful economic support of a household. He gains prestige through his knowledge and experience of the outside world (p. 106), and, thanks to a double standard of sexual conduct, a man is expected to achieve a reputation through demonstrable virility. Women, on the other hand, are limited in their sexual freedom and achieve adult status through childbearing.

Characteristically, the woman is most concerned with the domestic realm; her respectability is partly a function of her success there and the propriety of her sexual conduct (pp. 74–76). The traditionally strict division of labor between the sexes has in fact expanded in recent times. The male has only formal, jural responsibility to the household, his obligations being primarily economic. He is described as being marginal (p. 64). This is hardly surprising in view of the fact that a man spends so much of his time away from the household working. But even when he is at home he looks far more to the world of men for his social existence (Kaplan 1966), while the social world of women is concentrated in the home or in the compound yard. While women and children gossip and play there, men generally convene "on the beach or in local taverns" (Gonzalez 1969 : 70).

Although kinship ties are of some importance to men, it is quite clear from Gonzalez's account that the major emphasis of kinship concerns females, and that kinship for men is far more formal than affective, particularly in the brother and son roles (ibid., pp. 59–60, 85–86). The brother–sister relationship, on the other hand, is notable for becoming a particularly affective one during adulthood, especially when a woman has children but does not live with her husband (pp. 60–61).

Gonzalez, like Herskovits, argues that societies such as those described here, which she terms *neoteric,* lack structural self-sufficiency, if only because the greater part of their institutional authority is located in the dominant external system, and power within that system is inaccessible to neoterics. Undoubtedly this is a major source of ambivalence and frustration, but it does not preclude the formation of a local adaptive system through which satisfaction can be obtained and which, in certain respects, negates the dominant but exclusive alien institutional structure.

What has been lacking in the social anthropology of the Caribbean has been a full recognition, description, and analysis of such locally adaptive systems, and a consideration of their common basis. Hence one object of the present study has been to provide, as an example, such a description and analysis, while a second aim has been to establish grounds for the generalization of this analysis to other parts of the Caribbean. Exactly how Caribbean social systems operate in these other societies is for future research to determine. I have tried to offer both an analytical and a comparative framework for future research, through which not only the basic similarities of social systems can be noted, but through which their differences can be evaluated.

9 A Polemic by Way of Conclusion

The point of departure for this book is where other anthropological studies of the Caribbean leave off. I have based my analysis on the findings of my own fieldwork, carried out on the small and admittedly obscure island of Providencia. But I have tried to demonstrate by comparison that what can be discerned there may be generalized to other, better-known Caribbean societies. I hope that by this combination of intensive study and comparison I have made some contribution toward a synthesis of the anthropology of the region and thence opened up a line of thought that might promote its political, social, and cultural integration. Of course the identification and articulation of features of the social system of Providencia are not likely to be duplicated exactly in these other societies; but at least I think I have shown that there are good grounds for arguing that the model presented by the analysis of Providencia is applicable, in general, to these other societies. If not, then I can reasonably claim to have shed some light on the central problems of Caribbean anthropology. The onus is on others to prove otherwise or to offer alternatives.

The need is imperative to understand and articulate the nature of Caribbean societies (cf. R. T. Smith 1963 : 46) in order that the cultural and political integration of the region may be accomplished. As one of the outstanding students of Caribbean politics has written, the greatest need of West Indian society is for "new concepts of national and even personal identity rooted in the West Indian experience itself" (G. Lewis 1968 : 392). Though perhaps somewhat presumptuous, it is my purpose in this chapter to identify those concepts and to suggest, in sketchy terms, a course of action that might lead to their realization. By so doing I am also trying to point up the zone of transition between academic anthropology and political action. For by crystallizing into self-consciousness the assumptions and premises of social life, the anthropologist can contribute to the pragmatics of existence and can reveal the potentialities that political policies can either develop or crush. The

215

anthropologist then does not predict but rather reveals the existing state of things, such that possible courses of action may be recognized. If this is true, then the anthropologist has an almost frightening responsibility, which in turn has considerable bearing on anthropological theory and practice.

There is a tendency, which among some anthropologists has already become an actuality, to lose sight of the very purpose of their discipline. This is nowhere better illustrated than in Caribbean anthropology, where refinement of method and confinement of subject matter have become ends in themselves. Family, mating, and stratification patterns have been studied; concepts, models, and hypotheses proposed, criticized, revised, reviewed, and elaborated—but for no other apparent reason than that such activities are what anthropologists *do* if they are interested in the Caribbean. No attempt has been made to understand the social systems of the Caribbean as totalities or as things in themselves. The purpose of studying the family seems to have been forgotten, and the very existence of other dimensions of social systems seems to have been almost totally overlooked. There is no better illustration of this than the incredible fact that there has been no systematic account of the social life of males and no explicit recognition, let alone analysis, of the structure and function of male peer groups.

Paradoxically then, my study constitutes a new departure because it returns to some of the basic questions in the study of society. These were enunciated a long time ago, by Marx and Durkheim in particular.

As I understand it the anthropologist, or more broadly the social scientist, is a member of society who specializes in making society more aware of itself. He is concerned that his society and its members do not take themselves for granted (cf. Schutz 1964, 2 : 230–33). Within this broad mandate his specific task is to determine by empirical investigation, *a posteriori,* the limits and the conditions of existence of the moral life of man in society. Ralf Dahrendorf points out that it was Rousseau who broke open the cast of mind that took society for granted, by arguing that inequalities among men were not natural and that therefore they must be sociological (1968 : 155–57). It was Marx who once and for all ripped away the curtain of holiness that protected inequities in the name of society, who observed that whereas "the standpoint of the old type of materialism is civil society, the standpoint of the new materialism is human society or social humanity" (1938 : X).

Is not the obsession of Caribbeanists with the family the outcome of their concern for "civil" society rather than "human" society? Their stance is governed by the idea that the form of the Caribbean family is a departure from the civilly sanctioned norm of the nuclear family in their own society. Caribbean society, in other words, has been implicitly viewed by most anthropologists who have worked there as a rather pathetic or exotic imitation of their own society, not as a society evolving in its own terms.

Durkheim at the very beginning of his study *The Division of Labor in Society* says that his aim is to "treat the facts of the moral life according to the method of the positive sciences" (1964 : 32). But typically, anthropologists have seen fit to recognize, remember, and criticize only the latter part of this sentence, being more concerned that they be thought of as scientists than as moralists (cf. Barnes 1966 for a recent example of this attitude). Thus in Caribbean anthropology the family has become an object for the exercise of more and more ingenuity, in order to make more and more complex logical or statistical models to bolster the scientific claims of the anthropologist. We have come to understand less and less about less and less.

Neither Marx nor Durkheim was content to stop at a simple prescription, and both urged that the purpose in studying human society, or the moral life, was to facilitate its change for the better, to come to terms with change rather than to remain helpless before it, and in the end to accept responsibility for both society and social change. Marx, in what is probably the most widely quoted of his aphoristic *Theses on Feuerbach,* suggested that: "The philosophers [read anthropologists] have only *interpreted* the world differently, the point is to *change* it." And Durkheim, in a passage that could almost have been written by Marx (though not quite), observes that by his study of the facts of the moral life he hopes to be able to find "if it is not entirely in agreement with itself, if it contains contradictions, which is to say imperfections, and seek to eliminate them, or correct them" (1964 : 34). Sociology must itself become a moral force in society (cf. Dahrendorf 1968 : 87).

I have endeavored in this book to provide an analysis of the "moral life" of a society by pushing the description and analysis from its material conditions right through to its ethical core. I have sought to identify and analyze the criteria and standards by which people judge each others' worth, to explain how values of social differentiation provide a basis of social order. Some of the constituents of these values are more closely bound to and sprung from the ecological and material environment, while others appear more autonomously social, derived directly from the rationalizing ability and imagination of people, or from the perception of social relations between people viewing themselves as emotional commodities. In certain instances the origin of values, as well as their sanctions, lies in the conditions of existence of the *total* society: confinement to an island or deriving from a colonial situation, for example. Yet other aspects of social value have their origin and validation outside of the society proper, in a mainland or metropolitan culture.

Nevertheless, when we put everything together (having separated them only for the sake of analysis after all) and consider these values at a certain point in time, they exhibit a coherence, a systematic interrelationship. One can speak of the social system of a Caribbean society, and I can only agree with Gonzalez when she writes that previous studies which have viewed such societies as "disorganized," "broken," or "disrupted" have "tended to obscure the fact that these societies are functioning, thriving units" (1969 : 10). This is so, but only at a certain period of time, as colonies within a colonial structure. For whatever may be our opinions about the justice of colonialism, we cannot contest that colonial society has proved to be a realistic form of structure based on unambiguous boundaries. And yet, though these are functioning, thriving societies, there seems to have been a singular lack of understanding of the nature of a Caribbean social system. Naturally, failure to understand a system can only result in failure to appreciate the potentialities for change within that system.

This problem of understanding the nature of a Caribbean social system is more than just academic. Today many of the societies of the Caribbean are independent in name and are seeking to become so in fact. That totality of values and structure which formed an integral whole as a colonial phenomenon is no longer valid, and yet whatever is to be must grow out of or take root in what has been. I wish to argue on the basis of the foregoing analysis that a Caribbean social system provides us with what is possibly the clearest instance in history of a dialectical social system. What I have been describing is, in effect, a precariously tensile structure of relations *between* antithetical systems. On the one hand there is the imposed, alien structure of domination premised on inequality and stratification, while facing this is the autochthonous structure premised on differentiation and equality, a structure of subordination and reaction. Neither structure is independent of the other and *what is uniquely the Caribbean social system is the dynamic dialectic between them.*

That this has not been understood is evident from the theses of two recent publications which offer diametrically opposed interpretations of Caribbean social systems. One maintains that a Caribbean society is based on a single value system which is "stretched." The other argues that a Caribbean society contains two value systems which are quite distinct from each other. Both may be said to be half right and half wrong.

The single value system thesis is put forward by Hyman Rodman, who writes:

> By value stretch I mean that the lower class person, without abandoning the general values of the society, develops an alternative set of values. Without abandoning the values of marriage and legitimate childbirth he stretches these values so that non-legal union and illegitimate children within that union are desirable. The result is that members of the lower class, in many areas, have a wider range of values than others within the society. They share the general values of the society with members of other classes, but in addition they have stretched these values, or developed alternative values, which help them adjust to their deprived circumstances. [1971 : 195]

Twice Rodman mentions the "general values of the society"—
but they are not that at all. They are the values of a mainland
or metropolitan society espoused locally by a middle and upper
class whose ambitions and pretensions are directed away from
their own society and culture to that of the metropolis. Marriage
and legitimacy are prerequisites to respectability, though not
guarantees of it. Their recognition by the lower class is as much
a part of the tension between the two systems as their far more
frequent rejection of these values. It is also clear from this
passage that Rodman cannot make up his mind between a value
stretch (which implies that there is a single value system
throughout the society) and an *alternative* set of values (which
implies at least two value systems). As my study makes clear,
there is an alternative value system founded on reputation; and
this being so, the concept of value stretch serves no purpose
except to distort the situation.

   M. G. Smith's study *Stratification in Grenada* sets out to test
Talcott Parsons's action-theory postulate that a society must
have a common value system against J. S. Furnivall's concept of
a plural society, in which multiple value systems operate within
a single society. Smith's conclusion is that in Grenada there are
two distinct value systems within the single society. I have
expressed some of my criticisms of Professor Smith's study elsewhere (1966 : 62–64), but here the question goes beyond those
criticisms. On the surface it is clear that the present study confirms Smith's idea of plural value systems. But this is so only
if we ignore the historical dimension and fail to admit into
our consideration the ongoing sociological structure. These historically separable value systems are, in the Caribbean, constituents of a single, sociologically dynamic system whose crux is
the relations between the constituents. Smith himself seems
dimly to perceive the problem when he writes: "These Gre-
nadian data suggest that, besides political domination or a
common value system, symbiotic relations between people whose
values differ may also provide a viable basis for social order"
(1965 : 255).

   Symbiotic or dialectic? Either way such relations must themselves rest on some degree of common interest and value. That
the symbiosis is more likely dialectic, that is, tensing implicitly

toward change, is hinted at in the paragraph immediately following the passage from Smith quoted above: "As this symbiotic relation decayed progressively after 1930, discord increased to the point of violence. Differences of values and goals that had long been muted by this symbiotic accommodation then emerged in opposition." Both Rodman's and Smith's arguments, and they are typical, only partially account for the situation because they ignore the dialectic nature of Caribbean society—that it is a society of historically *changing* relationships.

First there is the viewpoint of the dominant sector, a viewpoint implicitly, though not deliberately, adopted by the anthropologist. From this vantage point Caribbean society is class-based and its structure is a consequence of the premise of inequality. The vast majority of the society constitute the lower class, whose values are defined as distortions (stretches) or deviations from the values of the upper class. If the white, respectable upper class marries and has legitimate children, then the black lower class lives in common-law union with illegitimate children. If a lower class couple marries it is taken as a sign that they wish to better themselves. Such betterment, of course, reinforces the upper class point of view. But this cannot be allowed to go too far, as it will eventually negate class differentiation. Hence the upper class, which values respectability, is forever shifting the grounds of its recognition in order to preserve its dominance: "They argued in effect that cultural whiteness rather than ethnic whiteness should be the criterion of high status, but even this proved to be an unattainable goal; while all were, indeed, members of the British Empire, none could be truly *English*" (R. T. Smith 1970 : 62). Such is the view from on top.

The view from underneath, from the lower class or subordinate sector of the society, sees a value system that seeks to relieve or circumvent domination, with a view, ultimately, to undermining it or overthrowing it. These are values which emphasize a sense of equality but which gain their meaning and vitality from their opposition status. Seen from the perspective of history and beginning with slavery, the entire value system, the total social system of both slaveowner and slave, was centered on freedom. The one sought desperately to withhold it,

the other tried equally desperately to secure it. The frequency
and intensity of slave rebellions and revolutions and the harsh-
ness of repression and prevention are dramatic witness to this.
After emancipation and freedom came the growth of colonial
administration, but at this point the momentum gathered for
political and economic independence, and the dialectic assumed
a primarily political form. Now, with independence having
been achieved for many, the dialectic turns on social and cultural opposition, on the relation between the *respectability* of
European white stratification and the *reputation* of indigenous
black differentiation.

Thus whichever way we look at it, the Caribbean social system is a dialectic one predicated on change, even though it is
conceptually possible to take out parts of this system and
analyze them statically. As I see it, it is a major part of the
anthropological responsibility to bring into consciousness the
potentialities of this change. I do *not* mean that we should try to
predict change, but that we should *project* change so that it can
be realized, modified, or frustrated.

What evidence, then, does the present study provide that
might make possible such a projection? What conclusions can
be drawn? In the remainder of this chapter I shall attempt to
make such projections as I consider challenging and useful.
As a social anthropologist I submit that the development of
systems of social values is as necessary to Caribbean integration as the removal of fragmented political and economic decision-making processes, and it is integration that is the desired
goal at present in the Caribbean.

> Once there is true integration among all the units of the
> Caribbean . . . and once all the vestiges of political, eco-
> nomic, cultural and psychological dependence and of
> racism have been removed, then and only then can the
> Caribbean take its true place in Latin America and the
> New World. [Williams 1970 : 515]

For the sake of convenience I will use the terms "respectability" and "reputation" to stand for the complexes of value,
behavior, and relationships which I have described above in
detail. The relationship between these complexes is expressed

in a continuous dialectic of action and reaction, of imposition and evasion, of boasting and gossiping, of climbing up and pulling down. And this interrelationship, evident at all levels, I have called *crab antics*. While all three terms refer specifically to Providencia, where they originated, I now wish to give them a general Caribbean significance. Having documented their concrete meanings, I will now make use of them as highly abstract concepts in an effort to recapitulate the argument and make projections from it.

Given a relatively short time span and only imperceptibly changing external conditions, crab antics appears to be a state of balance between reputation and respectability. But now these imperceptible changes have climaxed in many societies of the Caribbean as political independence has been achieved and as the backing for respectability has been drastically reduced with the removal of the white metropolitan power. Crab antics may now cease to be a balancing mechanism and become the process of change working from within. This is the location of my attempted projection.

The origin of reputation is *within,* and in a sense it is a reaction to respectability. It provides the majority of the population with the basis for self-recognition, since otherwise they would exist only as an "inferior" and anonymous "mass" in the class-structured society. Respectability is premised on inequality, which in turn is thought to have a racial, that is, a "natural" basis, not only by the high class but also by the lower class whose position, to them, appears as the consequence of "fate." But, though founded on moral absolutes, respectability is in fact a flexible and elusive complex deriving from an interpretation of moral values promulgated by the respectable. For them, change appears adequate so long as it is based on the conferral of civil liberties upon the lower class—insofar as they show evidence of having bettered themselves: they may be given voting rights, universal compulsory education, legal representation, welfare, and free medical treatment. Respectability, however, remains unchanged through all this, and the mass is simply wrapped more and more tightly into the bureaucracy and institutions of respectability.

Reputation tends to stress the equality of human inequalities, whereas respectability seeks to rank them. Reputation recognizes personal attainment and differentiation and it sanctions personal competition. It prizes in particular those talents and skills which bolster a self-image by putting down, undermining, and ridiculing respectability. As a system of rewards, reputation sustains a community whose measures of personal worth are an intrinsic and self-adjusting part of the community itself rather than coming from the outside.

Stated in the baldest terms, if change is to come from within it might emerge as the increasing dominance of reputation over respectability, as the crab finally succeeds in climbing out over the top of the barrel. In achieving such dominance, reputation will also acquire political power and authority and so, no doubt, will itself change. But since such a change goes beyond our present reach, the projection that interests me most is the possible rise of reputation over respectability.

I have argued that land is not only the basis of subsistence, or economic values, but that it is also of vital sentimental and philosophic value. Given the conditions imposed on them throughout their history, the people of the Caribbean have only each other and their land with which to identify. In belonging to a place and in regarding a place as belonging to him, the individual gains a sense of identity that gives him social validity, a sense of belonging *with* rather than *to* others. Slaves carried in the Middle Passage have probably come as near as any human beings to having their sense of place denied. Only the Jews have been put through a similar mass experience, and one need only mention the magnetic power of Israel to appreciate the importance of this sentiment of belonging associated with land. In a certain sense the philosophic value of land may be even greater to the people of the Caribbean than to the Jews, for they have little culture or tradition that they can call their own. Even the most primitive of tribesmen or the poorest of peasants who has been subdued by the white conqueror has at least remained on his own land and has been able to retain a sense of his own culture originating in a past without Europeans. And many are part of a tradition that began before and may outlast westernization. From all this the peasant or primitive, confused though he may often be, can still recognize a place of his own in both time and space. In a sense he can stand outside colonial structure even while he is caught up with it and by it.

But this cannot be said of the people of the Caribbean. Their culture, language, and history simply do not belong to them alone. For centuries the Caribbean islander has only known who he is, what he is, and where he is from the droppings of European or, latterly, American civilization. Perhaps if the history of the Caribbean is rewritten, and if it can provide new heroes and new precedents unique and authentic to the region, there might come to be a Caribbean culture that defines Caribbean people. The people of Providencia did this to some extent, and it is possible that other populations have their own "history." Only future research can tell. Eric Williams's recent history *From Columbus to Castro* provides some recognition of the need for new history, but the heroes remain the same. Until such time as a Caribbean culture is recognized with pride by the people themselves, much of the burden of their identity must be placed on land.

It is for this reason, more than any other, that any alienation of Caribbean land from Caribbean people must be regarded as fundamentally destructive. Even though there are more tangible economic reservations about the alienation of land, something of what Clifford Geertz has called a primordial sentiment is threatened when a person has no place to go to or go back to. It would seem to be a political imperative that the rights of the people of the Caribbean to belong to their land must be ensured by guaranteeing that their land shall belong to them. Unhappily there is ample evidence that in many if not all Caribbean societies no such thing is happening. In fact, it is quite likely that a close study of the question might reveal that land is increasingly passing into non-Caribbean hands.

I have shown that in a small and relatively uncapitalized society like Providencia, land not only sustains the poorest but is the foundation of wealth and, indirectly, of respectability. In the larger, more diverse societies of the region wealth can be accumulated independently of land ownership, but in the matter of class and respectability the end result is the same. Wealth is converted into a life-style and a life chance by which respectability establishes itself and through which it claims validity (being well-dressed for example, means dressing in European or American styles). Respectability at its material level, at its level of signification, is a show of luxury. It is a grand, well furnished home, well equipped with modern appliances, fine furniture, china and linens, good stylish clothes, an expensive education, manners, and deportment. These signifiers are also the foci of ambition for the population as a whole, because they are the most obvious and omnipresent aspects of respectability, even though for most they may be forever beyond reach. In fact, the more elusive and indefinable respectability is morally speaking, the more these indexes can become things in themselves, objects which become life ambitions. This has led many observers, including anthropologists, to observe, often a little sarcastically, the wasteful spending patterns of the Caribbean poor.

But it is no good criticizing habits or arguing against the importation of luxury goods without coming to grips with the values that direct these habits and create the demands for these goods. These values are summed up in respectability, and it is here that change must go to work. In one basic sense respectability is a frame of mind, an outlook on existence, a set of moral beliefs. Changing minds, however, is no easy matter, since the whole concept is so intangible and elusive. It is easy to pass a law against the import of certain goods, or to whack duties and taxes on various items. But how does one come to grips with frames of mind, let alone try to change them? Analogies drawn from individual psychology are no help here. It is one thing to explain social phenomena by reference to "dependency" or "inferiority" complexes, and it sounds well so long as we only talk or write about it. But dependent or inferior, paranoid or psychotic individuals can be given therapy. How do we put a population on a couch or inject it with drugs, or even organize it into a T group to change its collective mind? The matter is not psychological, however appealing it may be to be able to sum up the "character" of total societies with concepts that make them appear like individuals and imply that they may be as tractable, manipulable, and curable. The question is a social one, and we must attempt to get at this frame of mind, this value system, with sociological means and concepts and work toward a social "treatment."

Respectability is a constellation of values by which a population may be stratified into social classes. Social classes are in effect expressions of belief in absolute inequalities on the basis of which privilege may accrue. Reputation, on the other hand, is a constellation of values which emphasizes social differentiation but does not recognize the claim of absolute difference to order the society. Between orders of difference there is equality. This feature seems to have been completely misunderstood by or has simply eluded sociological theorists such as Dahrendorf, who accuses anthropologists of fantasizing "tribes without rulers," who finds it "hard to imagine a society whose system of norms and sanctions functions without an authority structure to sustain it" (1968 : 173). In systems of reputation worth, sanction, and authority is intrinsic to the system of relations and beliefs which it orders and simply does not have to be removed from it to form a separate authority structure. Unless a theorist is prepared to *demonstrate* the inadequacy of empirical analysis if he chooses not to accept them as their authors offer them, he can hardly claim the right to dismiss them as fantastic in order to argue in defense of his own imagination! So for reasons of theory as well as for pragmatic purposes, some further elaboration of reputation is in order.

Reputation is a standard of value, of moral measurement of a person's worth derived from his conduct with other people. The sanctions are intrinsic to these relations in that positive sanctions are expressed by according superior status and negative sanctions by rejection. Reputation is a standard of value that comes out of involvement with the world of relationships rather than the individualistic standards of respectability. A person is judged and given worth or recognition for each and all of his attainments, but separately, or at best, in clusters. He may be a good singer, a poor fisherman, a mediocre stud, a kind father, and a silly drunkard. In each field he enjoys a degree of reputation for which there is no absolute standard, and as a whole person he is neither condemned nor elevated by any one status. There is no such thing as a perfect singer, the ultimate fisherman, the supreme stud, the ideal father, or the complete drunkard. Such

status scales are relative to the given time and the actual performances of people in that time and place. There may certainly be some overlapping, or it may happen that one person
stands out in many roles and thence comes to enjoy esteem
and authority. But this always remains personal authority, not
transferable and not attached to a position in the structure. In
respectability authority attaches to positions rather than persons and judgments are made of the whole person. A person
is either respectable or not respectable, high class or low class,
or middle class. But no matter what, the individual is a
prisoner of such judgments—and even more so in the Caribbean, since respectability is tied so closely to race.

Reputation extends in concentric circles which in certain
circumstances may permit the crossing of spheres of influence.
Thus a nationally famous singer (i.e. one with a reputation ex-
tending to the widest circle) is of the same type as a locally
renowned bard; or, in the political arena, a national leader who
conducts himself in the culturally specific and prized style is
viewed as the same type of man as the local "boss." In this
way an entire population can see itself as being composed of
equal persons. From Archie Singham's account of Eric Gairy's
rise to power I have the impression that much of Gairy's success rested on his style, which conveyed to the people a sense
of reputation, an idea that he was one of them, but that in
political matters he was "better" than they. A basis of *continuity* was established between Gairy, local leaders, and the
masses. As "Uncle" Gairy he appeared as a man of the people,
not as a different class of man (like his eminently respectable
opponent). He was a leader sprung from the people, not superimposed on them (Singham 1968). Unfortunately, recent events
in Grenada suggest that Gairy, now that he is in power, is
using his achievement and position to fulfill old colonial-style
standards and ambitions rather than new values of independence
(see the *New York Times,* May 16, 1971).

Power and authority in reputation arise, therefore, not from
the imposition of external standards, but from the bestowal
and withholding of social recognition in a matrix of relationships. There are many examples of this in the foregoing chap-

ters, but the most obvious is the case of the alcalde, whose authority derived not from his office so much as from his reputation among the islanders for being, in every true sense, one of them. Certainly with his office came power, since he commanded the police force—but this is simply not sufficient.

In no society at the present moment does reputation dominate. It is a counter-value-structure because a real or shadow colonial situation prevails and respectability is dominant. With independence, however, this dominance is less secure and solid than in the past.

Respectability holds a society together around a stratified class structure with standards of moral worth and judgment emanating from the upper class or from overseas and imposed on the lower strata. Respectability is rationalized and even institutionalized into a set of ideals and moral absolutes enshrined in codes hedged about with a divinity. These codes are to be found notably in the teachings and commandments of the church and school, which are prefatory to the norms of bureaucracy and the numerous associations and institutions that make up the overall structure. The interpreters and arbiters of these codes include among their number the office-holders in these institutions. The closer to independence, the more colonial standards are left to an indigenous upper class. But since such a class has never, either in its own eyes or in those of Euro-Americans, been authentically respectable, then with independence the elite, the educated, those who have been straining ambivalently toward respectability, become more sharply aware that these standards are not their own. But neither are the standards of reputation. The ambivalence of this class, abetted by the absence of the Euro-American forces of respectability, makes their newfound authority shaky, so that it becomes more than likely that they must resort to forms of suppression and oppression or to democratic deception to maintain their own positions and the apparent continuity of the society. This, however, only serves to delay the solution to the problems of independence, which is to recognize that independence must be total—not just political, but social and cultural, psychological and sociological. Only then can the society become authentic and adaptable to its own circumstances. From total independence will grow, among other things, a new legitimation of authority.

How far repression and suppression come to be the dominant modes of authority in a society depends on a great many factors, chiefly on the economic and social policies pursued by the government. Although it is certainly true that nowadays economic policies in particular cannot be nationally or even regionally autonomous but must be tied to worldwide conditions, this need not preclude the achievement of an autonomous system of social values from which independence can grow, from which authority springs naturally, so that it has no need for repression. This means that Caribbean societies must cease to look to faraway alien cultures as their social and cultural references and recognize instead the validity of their own standards. For example, in Providencia, in Jamaica, and in probably all English-speaking Caribbean societies, it is said that correct English is only spoken in England, never in the Caribbean. I am saying that this outlook must go—that there must come a recognition that Jamaican English may be properly or improperly, correctly or incorrectly spoken.

For such changes to come from within it seems clear, at least in terms of the present argument, that respectability must be either redefined or removed. Either social values that define respectability and social class must be shifted to a base that is intrinsic to the Caribbean and referrable to it alone, or all criteria of respectability must be discredited and thence social class abolished. The latter is obviously the more drastic and radical option. It is also the more utopian. Either way, Euro-American values and standards of morality, of life style, or status symbolism, of institutions, of education, and of goals will have to be deemphasized. At the very least they must be subjected to searching selection and ruthless discrimination so that they may be transformed into compatibility with the true nature of Caribbean society. It will be obvious that I regard reputation as being of the true nature of Caribbean society, and that I judge it to have the evolutionary potential to transform itself into a dominant system. The question then is: where and how can this transformation, this process of change, begin?

Euro-American ideas and ideals enter the society most pervasively and influentially through the educational system. Here they are instilled, often obliquely, as the standards of right and wrong. It is here that youthful hopes and ambitions are engendered and directed—but are all too often left unfulfilled, (cf. Kerr 1952, Rubin and Zavalloni 1969, Williams 1970, chap. 26). The colonial society simply does not have the capacity to fulfill the ambitions nurtured in its schools because the goals are realizable only in the metropolis. What is more, the Euro-American educational system, reproduced in the Caribbean, is intended to *perpetuate* a society, to induct new generations into it. As educational theorists put it, it is a system of socialization or enculturation. But in passing from the metropolis to the colony it actually becomes a means of transferring generations from one moral system to another, an institution of *acculturation*. It becomes an institution of social change. But since the rest of the colonial structure is unwilling or unable to back up this education for change by providing full and fair opportunity for realizing ambitions, the change that actually occurs is one that is unlooked for, namely rejection or even revolution. Throughout the colonial world, as Philip Mason and others have pointed out, the leaders responsible for securing independence have been the best educated of men (Mason 1971 : 36). Their lieutenants and grassroots leaders have been schoolteachers and local professionals, the people who were led farthest along the path of expectancy and whose rejection comes all the harder. Thus in the colonial society the educational system becomes, in spite of itself, the forum for alternatives, the breeding ground of change—but not, strangely enough, of change within itself. Now that independence has been accomplished, the role of education must come to define new standards of morality and new values so that a new society can grow; and for the time being education must become the instrument of stabilization, perpetuation, and realization. I suggest that it might look for its new foundations in reputation, that it might develop a philosophy, a curriculum, and an educational environment that is integrated into the society, and that could assist in integrating the society.

Why not? If the values of a society based on respectability

and class can be promulgated and perpetuated through an educational system, then a society founded on an alternative and more authentic value system can be conveyed and supported in the same way. It cannot, of course, remain the same educational structure; it must change itself. It must identify new priorities that, for example, sanctify interpersonal loyalty in contrast to the institutional loyalty that respectability demands; it must overcome the separation of school from the community, of children from adults, of teachers from parents. And while literacy is a primary demand of contemporary life, a Caribbean education should also seek to give some pride of place to the riches of its oral culture and to the verbal talents of its peoples. It must shift its moral assumptions from a white Christianity to a black Christianity, or perhaps away from Christianity. In short, an education for reputation must seek not only to give authenticity and rationality to the society but also to guide education itself back into the totality of social life, thereby reducing the alienation of education from society that has come about through the specializing tendencies of the class system.

The fact is that education lies at the heart of real change, of long-range plans, of self-conscious and responsible social transformation. It is sad that so much planning has been piecemeal and framed in an economic mold, that is, that plans have called for statistical education, improving the literacy rate, counting the numbers of schools, producing commodities. They have barely called for educational reform, and they have not begun to recognize the fact that it is through education that the very nature of the society itself can come to be defined. It has been argued that there is no time to wait for education to effect change—in this fast-changing world a generation is too long to tarry. This was being said more than a generation ago!

The second major institution which validates respectability in the Caribbean is the Christian church in all its denominations. To hasten change from within, the social values supported by the church must be brought into line with the situation of the society as it is and as it is hoped for. As the church was once a reliable vehicle for propagating the moral standards of a class-based colonial society, so we may ask if it cannot be redefined to uphold the standards of an independent, autonomous egalitarian society? Clearly a Euro-American church with a doctrine of Euro-American respectability is an anachronism in an independent Caribbean society. Perhaps a first step to reform would be to give political recognition and even economic support to the various indigenous sects and cults that exist throughout the Caribbean and which have so clearly expressed for their followers an alternative ideology to that imposed on them from the outside. Given a legitimate societal position they would enjoy more power and authority and would, in turn, provide the kind of religion that Edmund Burke considered the basis of civil society. This would lead these cults to change themselves, of course, but such change is likely to be better synchronized with the total situation as it really is. Unlike the Euro-American church these cults have only their own interests to serve, and those interests are already closely integrated with the community. Or so it seems—for unfortunately these cults have been studied by Euro-American anthropologists largely for their exotic appeal, and we really know next to nothing about the relations between them and the community or about their sociopolitical functions. One can only urge the necessary research.

If change is to come from within, then, it must begin with the undermining of respectability and the removal of its foreign referents and its racial base. Respectability is the moral force behind the coercive power of colonialism and neocolonialism. This is evident, for example, in the professional standards and moral expectations that Euro-American institutions, firms, hotels, and employers impose on their employees, beginning with standards of dress and address and going deeper by nurturing ambitions and setting the terms by which those ambitions might be realized, including a "respectable" outlook on life and business. To the extent that companies and employers do this, they invade the value system of the Caribbean, and the more powerful they are, the more successful their invasion. The same may be said of the bureaucracy and government services, in that so long as they perpetuate the standards of respectability in the demands they make, they thwart the integrity of a truly Caribbean society.

I have argued in this book that, at the local level and among

the majority of the population, women are one of the strongest
forces for respectability. In large measure their conservative influence stems from the pronounced separation of the sexes in
their pursuit of social goals and social recognition. In affirming
that women have this influence I am speaking in general terms.
It is undoubtedly true that many if not most women never become "respectable" or members of the upper class and that,
furthermore, they don't care. For some it is just fate, God's
will; and in any case, as members of the lower class they are
prevented from ever thinking realistically of respectability, even
though most have a notion that "that's how one ought to be
because that's how middle and upper class people are" (cf.
Rodman 1971 : 62). In other circumstances, as when women
are engaged in trading, they must organize their lives and their
standards around their occupation, which demands a sense of
competition, often with men. By and large, however, it is
women who think and act in terms of respectability, it is
women, far more than men, who conceive of the future as respectability. If they themselves cannot become respectable, then
perhaps their children will. There is a constant tacit approval
of respectability and a deliberate working on its behalf. One can
see this, for instance, in the ultimate preference of women for
marriage, and their desire to gain support for their children
from the fathers of those children. Such tendencies indirectly
support and confirm the legality and correctness of respectability. Perhaps all this has its origins in the preferred status of
women in the colonial structure, a status they have enjoyed since
slavery times.

But if the situation is to change from within, then the social
separation of men and women must be narrowed and double
standards dropped, so that both sexes may come to participate
simultaneously and reciprocally in a single value system. It is
the existence of the two opposing value systems (reputation and
respectability) that leads to the existence of double sexual
standards, not some innate perversion of the lower class, as
some would have it. It may well be that the norms of sexual
union and socialization found at present in reputation are more
suitable and adaptable to the situation of Caribbean society
than the respectable Euro-American institution of marriage. If

this is recognized, sanctioned, and provided for, it may well assume a form different from that which exists at present, but it will be a form that has evolved out of and with the total society.

In sum, what I am saying is this: There exists in Caribbean societies an egalitarian value system which has hitherto remained subordinate to a class system but which has come into existence and has maintained itself by opposition to that class system. With the demise of colonial society, the primary support of the class system has been removed and the egalitarian system now has the opportunity to emerge into social self-consciousness and social dominance. I urge that it seize the moment. And even if the cynic argues that it will only turn into another stratification structure, I would answer that at least it would be a Caribbean structure.

Is it feasible? One can speculate and argue till the ink runs dry. Only actions can answer, and unless he is called upon to act, the anthropologist runs out his responsibilities at this point. He is, as Octavio Paz so neatly puts it, the "critic of progress." As such I would point out that the sort of value system I have here characterized as reputation exists in various parts of the world in different forms. It is most typical of small, nontribal societies or so-called part societies. These usually turn out to be colonial or quasi-colonial societies. This is exactly the category into which most Caribbean societies fall. Some of them, in fact, are among the smallest of such societies to achieve political sovereignty and independence in a worldwide political system.

It is this political autonomy that today marks off these societies from most other such societies whose social order rests on the egalitarianism of reputation or honor. Caribbean societies are thus among the first ever to be faced with the challenge of formalizing such a system of values to back up a newly acquired independent national sovereignty. As a "critic of progress" I urge that Caribbean societies become conscious of their true, their own social nature, for it is surely this that they must develop. This is their progress.

Is is advisable? Without full consideration of all the interests at stake in change, and without the responsibility for making decisions and taking their consequences, the anthropologist who

offers advice appears all too easily as the romantic conservative masquerading as the realistic liberal cavalier. So I offer no
advice; I make no challenge. From the snug security of my
study I criticize and provoke.

But, of course, I have reservations, of which I will mention
only one. Any so-called egalitarian social system must, in the
political domain, impose extensive restraints on individual freedom. At present in Caribbean societies these restraints are personal, informal, intrinsic, and self-imposed—crab antics in its
original meaning. But if such a system achieves dominance and
institutional status, its sanctions are likely to become extrinsic
and specialized, the monopoly of a new elite. This does not
have to be, but it can be and so must give pause for thought. I
admit quite freely that in this polemic I have played down
economic issues. They too must give pause for thought, and
they pose many problems about the advisability of change. But
economics has for long been uppermost in everybody's arguments about change and development. It is high time that the
equally fundamental matters of social and moral values be
given their due consideration in respect of societal problems.

Epilogue 1995

I have not returned to the Caribbean since 1961, so obviously in thirty years many changes have occurred. But not so much on Providencia itself. I have learned from Mr. Harold Bush, now studying for a Ph.D. degree at the London School of Economics, that Providencia has succeeded in achieving a "special case" status in Colombia. Its English Creole has been allowed to continue being spoken and strict immigration rules have been put in place to ensure the population is not overrun by mainlanders. Anyone from mainland Colombia requires a permit to work on the island. Tourism is strictly limited, and so too are the amenities. The consequences of this in terms of *Crab Antics* are that Providencia and its people have come to be more and more respected for what and who they are. In contrast, at the times of my visits (1958-1961), great pressure was being put on Providencians to become like other Colombians and, until they did so, they were considered inferior. Thus, within the population the standards of reputation and respectability have tended to merge rather than diverge. This is especially so in that many islanders have been given the chance of a university education and/or made more responsible for the administration of their own affairs. Recognition by an enlightened government has given Providencians an opportunity to be proud rather than ashamed of their difference from mainland Colombians, while the restrictions placed on mainland Colombians visiting the island have helped to defuse any exaggeration of feeling by Providencians toward the "pais."

The overall population remains at roughly 2,500 to 3,000 — little changed since the time of my study. As I have already mentioned, tourist visits are strictly regulated, unlike those on nearby San Andres. Although amenities have been developed to some extent — the clinic and the water supply, for example — motor traffic, casinos, hotels and bars are not a feature of life. A heartening thing to report is that many of the younger people mentioned in *Crab Antics* have, since I made my last visit, assumed positions of responsibility and have not been afraid to confront the authorities in Bogota and push for the recognition of their island. Some, rather than seek their careers abroad, have chosen to bring their skills (medical, for example) back to the island. In turn, the regularity of sailings from San Andres to Providencia has improved so that drugs and other medical supplies are not in such short supply. Needless to say, I am very grateful to Mr. Bush for this information. But whether the tempo, the feel, the ethos that I have described in the previous pages has changed, only I can judge by a return visit. New Zealand is a long way away, but the possibility exists.

In the Caribbean, in general, the obsession with family structure has abated, though not disappeared, while interest in forms of religion and the nature of politics and Caribbean history has increased. So, too, has the interest in Caribbean health and illness considered within the context of Caribbean life. However, these are general comments made from a great distance by one who has not kept up on developments in the region.

The questions as to whether the model of "crab antics" (the dialectic between reputation and respectability) has run its course is probably not for me to judge. However, I have seen it applied or criticized in recent studies not only of the Caribbean but also of communities in the Pacific. My correspondence indicates it still has interest and relevance. Some of that interest and relevance can be transferred from island and colonial settings to conditions in metropolitan centers in the U.S. and Europe. Arriving as poor immigrants, in both cases mostly from the Caribbean, people have only their own resources from which to build their self-esteem. To do so, they exaggerate their former indigenous ways of life — importing West Indian food, forming gangs, developing their sartorial and musical style and creating, or recreating, for themselves a home culture. But now it is in a foreign land where fish cannot be hauled at liberty from a sea of concrete, or coconuts and plantain plucked from city streets.

Reputation has to be supported by menial work, which is hard to come by. Gangs and their prowess in protecting their territory become the focus of reputation. This leads to a double confrontation: among gangs and between gangs and the values of metropolitan capitalism itself, the values of respectability. Probably every survivor of a gang looks forward to either his or her life, or at least the lives of their children, becoming reputable — by making it through school and university into a profession or a corporation, by moving from an inner city tenement to a suburban house. This is not necessarily to say they desire to become absorbed into the white population, but rather they seek to become reputable among their own folk, whose opinion counts for more because they know what it takes to make it. Perhaps this explains a phenomenon such as Marion Barry, newly re-elected mayor of Washington, D.C., after a spell in prison. The man had achieved respectability — he had been elected mayor — and the revelation that he was a man with as good a reputation among his folk as any other doubled his popularity (and confounded his critics).

The struggle between reputation and respectability — crab antics — is obviously not a feature confined to the Caribbean or to poverty-stricken immigrants in the U.S. and Europe. Every time we read about a politician being attacked and pulled down by opponents for sexual misdoings, or taking bribes, or fudging documents, for example, we see crab antics at work. So, perhaps new readers of this book can take it as a case study of a wider human process at work.

Appendix: Food and Social Status

It has become a commonplace in anthropology that food—its quality, preparation, and consumption—is invested with many social and symbolic values. At the same time particular social occasions are marked out as being more significant than others by the foods used, their manner of preparation, serving, and distribution. Less fully emphasized, though clearly implicit, is the fact that food may be an index of secular as well as ritual status, for in broad terms it reflects not only taste but the relation of taste to means. Thus a comparison of menus from three of our sample households summarizes the social and economic differences that exist among these people.

There is not only an increase in the variety and quantity of foods as we go from the poor to the well-off but also a change in the ratio of local to imported foods and from staples to delicacies. Such variation is usually accompanied by a certain amount of rationalization: poor people extol the good hearty values of manioc or yucca, and well-off people affect to despise it and in turn praise rice. But almost everyone holds canned foods, especially meat (Spam) and fish (pilchards in tomato sauce and salmon) in great esteem—sweetmeats of a canned civilization.

MENUS

(Asterisks indicate imported items or dishes made with imported items. Breakfast or "tea" took place at about 7 A.M., dinner at 12 noon, and supper at 6 P.M.)

Isaac and Lena

Day 1	*Day 2*	*Day 3*
Breakfast	*Breakfast*	*Breakfast*
bush tea	bush tea	bush tea
cassava bread	cassava bread	cassava bread
cornmeal	fried egg	

Dinner	*Dinner*	*Dinner*
yucca	plantain (fried)	yucca (boiled)
plantain	Bosco (boiled)	plantain (fried)
fish	fish (fried)	fish (fried and boiled)
cassava cake	mango	mango
tamarind juice	rice *	
watermelon		

Supper	*Supper*	*Supper*
roast corn	rice * (leftover)	fried egg
plantain (leftover)	cassava bread	cassava bread
bush tea with	fish (leftover)	bush tea with
powdered milk *	bush tea with	powdered milk *
	powdered milk *	

Salt and sugar are also purchased and used regularly by Isaac and Lena. Frying is done in coconut lard, which is sometimes bought from the store, and sometimes, as oil, bought from a neighbor. Charcoal, which Isaac burns, and wood are the fuels. Locally grown spices including chili, ginger, and certain herbs are used in the cooking. Bush tea is made from one of many grasses suitable for infusion, the most popular being one known as fever grass.

Cayetano and Rosalia

Day 1	*Day 2*	*Day 3*
Breakfast	*Breakfast*	*Breakfast*
homemade bread *	homemade bread *	cornmeal porridge
fresh milk	boiled corn	homemade bread *
cocoa *	fresh milk	powdered milk *
banana	Nescafé *	bush tea
molasses		

Dinner	*Dinner*	*Dinner*
canned soup *	rice *	rice *
cassava cake	crab soup	plantain (fried)
plantain (boiled)	canned sardines *	breadfruit (fried)
yucca (boiled)	Bosco (boiled)	lima beans and kidney
fried fish	homemade bread *	beans with tomato sauce *
rice *	cocoa *	boiled fish

Dinner	*Dinner*	*Dinner*
fried egg		bush tea
cocoa *		

This household eats a few more imported items and eats rice regularly as part of the main meal, unlike Isaac and Lena. Otherwise there are only slight differences between the two households. The homemade bread is made with imported wheat flour.

Mr. John and Miss Ray

Day 1	*Day 2*	*Day 3*
Breakfast	*Breakfast*	*Breakfast*
fresh milk	fresh milk	fresh milk
Quaker oats *	Quaker oats *	Quaker oats *
fried egg	fried pork	fried egg
homemade bread *	homemade bread *	homemade bread *
butter *	butter *	butter *
preserves *	preserves *	preserves *
Nescafé *	Nescafé *	Nescafé *
Dinner	*Dinner*	*Dinner*
canned soup *	homemade soup	homemade soup
rice *	rice *	rice *
fried plantain	boiled plantain	fried plantain
Irish potato *	fried plantain	boiled pumpkin
canned peas *	fried breadfruit	canned beets *
Spam *	Irish potato *	stewed beef with
onion *	coleslaw *	tomato paste *
fried egg	salami *	fried liver
bread * and milk	stewed fish	homemade bread *
pudding with raisins *	homemade bread *	pumpkin pie
tamarind drink	canned fruit salad *	Nescafé * or cocoa *
Nescafé * or cocoa *	Nescafé * or cocoa *	iced water
iced water	iced water	
Supper	*Supper*	*Supper*
canned soup *	homemade soup	homemade soup
rice *	rice * (leftover)	rice *
corned beef *	boiled yucca	spaghetti * with

Supper	*Supper*	*Supper*
red kidney beans *	Bosco (boiled)	tomato paste *
onion *	fried chicken	fried beef
fried plantain	in tomato paste *	canned corn *
homemade cake *	scrambled egg	boiled yucca
homemade bread *	canned pears *	homemade bread *
fresh milk	Nescafé * or cocoa *	fresh milk
Nescafé * or cocoa *	iced water	Nescafé * or cocoa *
iced water		iced water

There was always imported mustard, pepper, salt, vinegar, tomato ketchup, tabasco, and pickles on the table in this household. Special treats came occasionally with Mr. John's supplies. By any standard this was a well-fed household—to which one must add in tribute that Miss Ray was truly a magnificent cook.

Notes

1. All the major monographs published since 1950 by anthropologists deal with the family, the household, and domestic organization. M. G. Smith's study *Stratification in Grenada* is something of an exception. The numerous theoretical essays that stem from these studies take up the same subject, with the exception of M. G. Smith's discussions of pluralism, now collected in book form (1965*a*). Those monographs referring to English-speaking Caribbean societies are noted at various points throughout the present work. The following appear to me to be the most important syntheses and works of theory: Davenport 1961 : 420–54, Goode 1960 : 21–30, Henriques 1949 : 30–37, Gerber, ed., 1968, Horowitz 1967 : 445–53, Kunstadter 1963 : 56–66, Otterbein 1965 : 66–79, 1966*a* : 493–97, M. G. Smith 1962*a*, R. T. Smith 1957, 1963 : 24–46, and Solien 1960 : 101–06. In addition I must single out R. T. Smith's fine article on *Social Stratification in the Caribbean* in Plotnicov and Tuden 1970. A singular exception to my strictures against Caribbean anthropologists' obsession with family and mating is the work of Sidney Mintz, whose numerous and widely scattered papers illuminate a broad spectrum of Caribbean affairs.

2. I do not wish to say that one must establish what each and every individual is actually thinking of when he acts in a certain way. That would be silly given the level of analysis of studies such as the present one. I am implying something like this. For the purposes of sociological investigation I assume, as, for example, Winch puts it, that social relations occur in a setting (1958). Social relations, including people's conduct, may be treated as an investigational isolate which only makes sense when replaced in relation to its setting. The setting, the environment, is what "gives" meaning to the conduct. This may be said to be so for both the observed and the observer. For the former, the criteria of recognition of himself and his acts, that which gives them meaning, are located in the environment. For the observer the meaning of the observed's behavior is only apparent when considered in relation to the totality of which it is a part. But the "meaning" of an act or an observation is not observable or really testable, since meaning is capable of reflection. It is a matter of the mind and of thought.

   So I may describe this study as being the organization of my thoughts about what the people of Providencia are, or might be thinking about when they act; my hypotheses about their hypotheses.

3. I do not hold, with Durkheim, that social groupings are either the fundamental facts of society or of social study. Neither do I hold, with Marx, that the phenomena of social life, such as groupings,

245

are the products of materialist concerns. Groups seem to me best understood as strategies of organization mediating the self-consciousness of persons in their interaction with the physical environment, which comes to include other persons. Since groups are strategies rather than independent objective facts, they are products of ways of thinking about certain matters.

4. Thus Collingwood, for example, defines four criteria of history: that it be scientific, humanistic, rational, and self-revelatory. This could also describe most sciences! But history being so defined, the historian is only he who performs according to such criteria. On this basis Collingwood is able to designate Herodotus as the first historian—quite categorically.

5. The account of Morgan's capture of the island makes interesting and amusing reading, though Esquemeling's veracity is not beyond question. After an initial landing, Morgan's troops were beaten off by the Spanish garrison with considerable losses. Nothing daunted, Morgan sent the Spanish commander an ultimatum to the effect that "if within a few hours he delivered not himself and all his men into his hands, he did by that messenger swear to him and all those in his company, he would most certainly put them to the sword, without granting quarter to any."

The garrison commander, perhaps incredulous at his success against the legendary Morgan, was duly intimidated and agreed to surrender. However, he asked that Captain Morgan "would be pleased to use a certain stratagem of war for the better saving of his own credit, and the reputation of his officers both abroad and at home, which should be as follows: That Captain Morgan would come with his troops by night, near the bridge that joined the lesser island to the great one [the bridge in question connected Santa Catalina to Providence and had been built by Edvard Mansveldt a few years before], and there attack the fort of St. Jerome: at the same time all the ships of the fleet would draw near the castle of St. Theresa, and attack it by sea, landing in the meanwhile some more troops near the battery called St. Matthew: that these troops which were newly landed should by this means intercept the Governor by the way as he endeavoured to pass to St. Jerome's fort and then take him prisoner, using the formality, as if they forced him to deliver the said castle: and that he would lead the English into it, under the fraud of being his own troops: that one side and the other there would be continuous firing at one another, but without bullets, or at least into the air, so that no side might receive any harm by this device: that having thus obtained two such considerable forts, the chief of the isle, he needed not to take care for the rest, which of necessity must fall by course into his hands" (Esquemeling 1923 : 194).

6. This probably refers to the Roncador and Serrana Cays or Banks, about ninety miles north of Providencia.

7. Quoted from the will of James Archbold, the original of which is in the possession of his descendant Alpheus Archbold of Smoothwater Bay. I am most grateful to Mr. Archbold for allowing me to see and copy all the documents in his possession. I have made much use of this material.

8. Personal communication from James J. Parsons.

9. I use the term *ethos* in the sense stressed by Gregory Bateson (1958 : 118), who defines it as "a culturally standardised system of organization of the instincts and emotions of individuals."

10. The phenomenon of the *crew* is discussed more fully in chap. 7.

11. Some indications of the scope and scale of local export trade are given in the following figures, summarized from the records kept by the captain of the port for the year 1959–60:

Cattle	236 head
Pigs	320 head
Chickens	2,540
Oranges	221,000 (very dubious)
Melons	9,000
Copra	170 tons

Other fruits and vegetables were shipped unregistered and there was no record of the sugar cane, molasses, or rum that was certainly shipped. The value of these exports was officially recorded as 392,505 pesos (about $56,072 U.S. at that time). These figures are far from accurate, but they are useful as an indicator of scale.

12. See the Appendix for a detailed comparison of menus.

13. I use the term "in-law" to designate the relation. It does not matter whether legal marriage, common-law union, or concubinage has brought the principals into the relationship. The prim artifice of English morality shows through in this terminology.

14. The identical adage is cited by Abrahams in his description of Philadelphia Negro culture (1970b : 123). In another publication, the same author discusses the importance of a "good name" (i.e. reputation) on the island of St. Vincent (1970c : 290–301). The adage clearly seems to have originated from Shakespeare's *Othello,* act 3, scene 3:

> *Iago:* Good name in man and woman, dear my lord,
>   Is the immediate jewel of their souls.
>   Who steals my purse steals trash;
>   'Tis something, nothing;
>   But he that filches from me my good name
>   Robs me of that which not enriches him
>   And makes me poor indeed.

Not all New World Negro culture is African in origin! Many other writers have made passing reference to the importance of reputation and a good name, e.g. Henriques (1968 : 59).

15. Madeline Kerr (1952 : 88) quotes an extract from a letter sent by a Jamaican boy to his girl friend. It closely resembles in style, content, and language similar letters on Providencia:

> I take great pleasure in writing you this letter and I hope it may ly fast in your heart. As I do ly fast for you, my darling. And I hope it may not for mear curessity. But relitey. And what I told you when I first met you. I meant it from my heart, and I hope you do. As I am at this moment. Heaven only knows how I love you. You are the heart of every plan. You are the heart of love divine. Its only heaven knows how I love you.

16. The cockspur (*Acacia costarricense*) is a thorny bush that shelters a large black ant with a nasty bite.

Bibliography

ABRAHAMS, ROGER
  1970a *Deep Down in the Jungle.* Chicago, Aldine Press.
  1970b *Positively Black.* Englewood Cliffs, N.J., Prentice-Hall.
  1970c A Performance Centered Approach to Gossip. *Man* (n.s.) 5 : 290–301.

BANTON, MICHAEL, editor
  1966 *The Social Anthropology of Complex Societies.* New York, Frederick A. Praeger.

BARNES, J. A.
  1966 Durkheim's Division of Labour in Society. *Man* (n.s.) 1 : 157–75.

BARRETT, LEONARD E.
  1968 *The Rastafarians: A Study in Messianic Cultism in Jamaica.* Rio Piedras, Puerto Rico, Institute of Caribbean Studies.

BASTIDE, ROGER
  1967 *Les Ameriques Noires.* Paris, Payot.

BATESON, GREGORY
  1958 *Naven,* 2d ed., Stanford, Calif., Stanford University Press.

BLAKE, JUDITH
  1961 *Family Structure in Jamaica: The Social Context of Reproduction.* Glencoe, Ill., Free Press.

BOISSEVAIN, JEREMY
  1968 The Place of Non-Groups in the Social Sciences. *Man* (n.s.) 3 : 542–56.

BOTT, ELIZABETH
  1957 *Family and Social Network.* London, Tavistock Press.

BOURDIEU, P.
  1966 The Sentiment of Honour in Kabyle Society. In *Honour and Shame: Values in Mediterranean Society,* ed. J. Peristiany. Chicago, University of Chicago Press.

BRAITHWAITE, LLOYD
  1953 Social Stratification in Trinidad. *Journal of Social and Economic Studies* 2 : 5–175.
  1960 Social Stratification and Cultural Pluralism. In *Social and Cultural Pluralism in the Caribbean,* ed. V. Rubin. *Annals of the New York Academy of Sciences* 83 : 816–31.

CAMPBELL, J. K.
  1964 *Honour, Family and Patronage.* London, Oxford University Press.

CARR, EDWARD H.
  1962 *What is History?* New York, Alfred A. Knopf.

CLARKE, EDITH
  1957   *My Mother Who Fathered Me.* London, George Allen and
         Unwin.
CLOAK, F. T.
  1966   *A Natural Order of Cultural Adoption and Loss.* Chapel Hill,
         University of North Carolina Press.
COHEN, YEHUDI
  1954   The Social Organization of a Selected Community in Jamaica.
         Journal of Social and Economic Studies 2 : 104–33.
COLLETT, C. F.
  1837   On the Island of Old Providence. *Journal of the Royal Geo-
         graphical Society,* 7 : 203–10.
COLLINGWOOD, R. G.
  1956   *The Idea of History.* London, Oxford University Press.
COMITAS, LAMBROS
  1968   *Caribbeana 1900–1965: A Topical Bibliography.* Seattle, Uni-
         versity of Washington Press.
CUMPER, GEORGE
  1958   The Jamaican Family: Village and Estate. *Journal of Social
         and Economic Studies* 7 : 76–108.
  1961   Household and Occupation in Barbados. *Journal of Social and
         Economic Studies* 10 : 386–419.
CURTIN, PHILIP
  1970   *Two Jamaicas: The Role of Ideas in a Tropical Colony.* New
         York, Atheneum.
DAHRENDORF, RALF
  1968   *Essays in the Theory of Society.* London, Routledge and Kegan
         Paul.
DAVENPORT, WILLIAM
  1956   *A Comparative Study of Two Jamaican Fishing Communities.*
         Ph.D. dissertation, Yale University.
  1961   The Family System of Jamaica. *Journal of Social and Eco-
         nomic Studies* 10 : 420–54.
DAVIS, J.
  1969   Honour and Politics in Pisticci. *Proceedings of the Royal
         Anthropological Institute,* pp. 69–82.
DUMONT, LOUIS
  1970   *Homo hierarchicus.* London, Weidenfield and Nicholson.
DURKHEIM, EMILE
  1964   *Division of Labour in Society.* Glencoe, Ill., Free Press.
EDER, PHANOR
  1913   *Colombia.* London, T. F. Unwin.
ESQUEMELING, JOHN
  1923   *The Buccaneers of America.* London, G. Routledge and
         Sons.
EVANS-PRITCHARD, E. E.
  1940   *The Nuer.* London, Oxford University Press.

FANON, FRANTZ
1967   *Black Skin, White Masks.* New York, Grove Press.
FAYE, STANLEY
1941   Commodore Aury. *Louisiana Historical Society Quarterly*
        24 : 611–97.
FORTES, MEYER
1969   *Kinship and the Social Order.* Chicago, Aldine Press.
FRANKENBERG, RONALD
1957   *Village on the Border.* London, Cohen and West.
FRAZER, IAN
1970   *Pitcairn Islanders in New Zealand.* M.A. thesis, University of
        Otago.
GEERTZ, CLIFFORD, editor
1963   *Old Societies and New States.* New York, Free Press.
GELLNER, ERNEST
1964   *Thought and Change.* London, Weidenfield and Nicholson.
GERBER, STANFORD, editor
1968   *The Family in the Caribbean.* Rio Piedras, Puerto Rico, Insti-
        tute of Caribbean Studies.
GIEDION, SIEGFRIED
1948   *Mechanization Takes Command: A Contribution to Anony-
        mous History.* New York, Norton Library Edition, n.d., orig-
        inally published 1948.
GLUCKMAN, MAX
1963   Gossip and Scandal. *Current Anthropology* 4 : 307–16.
GOFF, JAMES E.
1965   *The Persecution of Protestant Christians in Colombia, 1948–
        1958, with an Investigation of Its Background and Causes.* B.D.
        dissertation, San Francisco Theological Seminary.
GONZALEZ, NANCIE SOLIEN DE
1969   *Black Carib Household Structure.* Seattle, University of Wash-
        ington Press.
GOODE, WILLIAM J.
1960   Illegitimacy in Caribbean Social Structure. *American Sociolog-
        ical Review* 25 : 21–30.
GOVEIA, ELSA V.
1965   *Slave Society in the British Leeward Islands at the End of the
        Eighteenth Century.* New Haven, Yale University Press.
GREENFIELD, SIDNEY M.
1966   *English Rustics in Black Skin.* New Haven, College and Uni-
        versity Press.
1968   Cultural-Historical and Structural-Functional Orientations and
        the Analysis of the West Indian Family. In *The Family in the
        Caribbean,* ed. S. Gerber.
HENRIQUES, FERNANDO
1949   West Indian Family Organization. *American Journal of Soci-
        ology* 55 : 30–37.

1968   *Family and Colour in Jamaica.* London, McGibbon & Kee.
HERSKOVITS, MELVILLE and FRANCES
1947   *Trinidad Village.* New York, Alfred A. Knopf.
HOETINK, H.
1967   *The Two Variants in Caribbean Race Relations.* London, Oxford University Press.
HOROWITZ, MICHAEL M.
1967   A Decison Model of Conjugal Patterns in Martinique. *Man* (n.s.) 2 : 445–53.
JEFFREYS, THOMAS
1762   *A Description of the Spanish Islands and Settlements of the Coast of the West Indies.* London.
KAISER, R. LINCOLN
1970   *The Vice-Lords: Warriors of the Streets.* New York, Holt, Rinehart and Winston.
KAPLAN, JOANNA OVERING
1966   *Stratification and a Color/Class System: An Analysis of the Relationship between Status and Color/Class Categories with a Creole Fishing Village, Honduras.* Manuscript, Brandeis University.
KENNY, M.
1962   *A Spanish Tapestry: Town and Country in Castile.* Bloomington, University of Indiana Press.
KERR, MADELINE
1952   *Personality and Conflict in Jamaica.* Liverpool, University of Liverpool Press.
KUNSTADTER, PETER
1963   A Survey of Consanguine or Matrifocal Family. *American Anthropologist* 65 : 56–66.
LASLETT, PETER
1965   *The World We Have Lost.* New York, Charles Scribner's Sons.
LEWIS, GORDON K.
1968   *The Growth of the Modern West Indies.* New York, Monthly Review Press.
LEWIS, I. M.
1968   Introduction. *History and Social Anthropology,* ed. I. M. Lewis, London, Tavistock Press.
LEWIS, OSCAR
1966   *La Vida.* New York, Random House.
LEWIS, SYBIL, and THOMAS G. MATHEWS, editors
1967   *Caribbean Integration.* Rio Piedras, Puerto Rico, Institute of Caribbean Studies.
LOWENTHAL, DAVID
1961   Caribbean Views of Caribbean Land. *Canadian Geographer* 5 : 1–10.

MANNERS, ROBERT
  1965 Remittances and the Unit of Analysis in Anthropological Re-
        search. *Southwestern Journal of Anthropology* 21 : 179–95.
MARX, KARL
  1938 *Theses on Feuerbach.* New York, International Publishers.
MASON, PHILIP
  1971 *Patterns of Dominance.* London, Oxford University Press.
MIDGETT, DOUGLAS
  1968 *Male Role Behavior and Migration in St. Lucia.* Paper read
        before the Central States Anthropological Society.
MINTZ, SIDNEY W.
  1967 Caribbean Nationhood in Anthropological Perspective. In *Ca-
        ribbean Integration,* ed. S. Lewis and T. Mathews.
  n.d. The Caribbean. In *International Encyclopedia of the Social
        Sciences.*
MINTZ, SIDNEY W., and ERIC WOLF
  1950 An Analysis of Ritual Co-Parenthood (Compadrazgo). *South-
        western Journal of Anthropology* 6 : 341–69.
NEWTON, ARTHUR P.
  1914 *The Colonizing Activities of the English Puritans.* New Haven,
        Yale University Press.
OTTERBEIN, KEITH
  1965 Caribbean Family Organization: A Comparative Analysis.
        American Anthropologist 67 : 66–79.
  1966a Reply to Goode. *American Anthropologist* 68 : 493–97.
  1966b *The Andros Islanders.* Lawrence, University of Kansas Press.
PAINE, R.
  1967 What is Gossip About? An Alternative Hypothesis. *Man*
        (n.s.) 2 : 278–85.
PARSONS, JAMES J.
  1956 San Andrés and Providencia. *University of California Publi-
        cations in Geography* 12.
PATTERSON, ORLANDO
  1967 *The Sociology of Slavery.* London, McGibbon & Kee.
PAZ, OCTAVIO
  1971 *Claude Lévi-Strauss: An Introduction.* London, Jonathan Cape.
PERALTA, MANUEL MARIA DE
  1890 *Limites de Costa Rica y Colombia.* Madrid.
PITT-RIVERS, JULIAN
  1961 *People of the Sierra.* Chicago, University of Chicago Press.
  1966 Honour and Social Status. In *Honour and Shame,* ed. J. Peris-
        tiany. Chicago, University of Chicago Press.
PRICE, THOMAS J., JR.
  1954 Algunos Aspectos de Estabilidad y Desorganizacion Cultural
        en una Communidad Islena del Caribe, Colombiano. *Revista
        Colombiana de Antropologia* 3 : 11–54.

REINA, REUBEN
  1966   *The Law of the Saints.* New York, Bobbs-Merrill.
REISMAN, KARL
  1970   Cultural and Linguistic Ambiguity in a West Indian Village.
         In *Afro-American Anthropology*, ed. N. Whitten and J. Szwed.
REMY, ANSELME
  1970   *Men's Cliques in Barbados.* Unpublished paper, Brandeis University.
RIVIÈRE, PETER
  1967   The Honour of Sanchez. *Man* (n.s.) 2 : 569–81.
RODMAN, HYMAN
  1971   *Lower Class Families: The Culture of Poverty in Negro Trinidad.* New York, Oxford University Press.
ROWLAND, DONALD
  1935   The Spanish Occupation of the Island of Old Providence. *Hispanic American Historical Review* 15 : 297–331.
RUBIN, VERA, editor
  1960   *Caribbean Studies: A Symposium.* Seattle, University of Washington Press.
RUBIN, VERA, and M. ZAVALLONI
  1969   *We Wish to Be Looked Upon.* New York, Teacher's College Press.
SAXE, ALLEN
  1969   *Squatters in Trinidad.* M.A. thesis, Brandeis University.
SCHOLTE, BOB
  1966   Epistemic Paradigms: Some Problems in Cross-Cultural Research on Social Anthropological History and Theory. *American Anthropologist* 68 : 1192–1201.
SCHUTZ, ALFRED
  1964   *Collected Papers, Volume 2, Studies in Social Theory.* The Hague, Martinus Nijhoff.
SERRANA Y SANZ, MANUEL, editor
  1808   *Relaciones historicas y geograficas de America Central.* Madrid.
SIMPSON, GEORGE EATON
  1965   *The Shango Cult in Trinidad.* Rio Piedras, Puerto Rico, Institute of Caribbean Studies.
SINGHAM, ARCHIE
  1968   *The Hero and the Crowd in a Colonial Polity.* New Haven, Yale University Press.
SMITH, MICHAEL G.
  1962a   *West Indian Family Structure.* Seattle, University of Washington Press.
  1962b   *Kinship and Community in Carriacou.* New Haven, Yale University Press.
  1965a   *The Plural Society in the British West Indies.* Berkeley and Los Angeles, University of California Press.

1965b   *Stratification in Grenada.* Berkeley and Los Angeles, University of California Press.

1965c   Some Aspects of Social Structure in the British Caribbean about 1820. In *The Plural Society in the British West Indies.*

1966   Introduction. In Edith Clarke, *My Mother Who Fathered Me,* 2d ed.

SMITH, RAYMOND T.

1955   Land Tenure in Three Negro Villages in British Guiana. *Journal of Social and Economic Studies* 4 : 64–82.

1956   *The Negro Family in British Guiana: Family Structure and Social Status in the Villages.* London, Routledge and Kegan Paul.

1957   The Family in the Caribbean. In *Caribbean Studies: A Symposium,* ed. Vera Rubin.

1963   Culture and Social Structure in the Caribbean: Some Recent Work on Family and Kinship Studies. *Journal of Comparative Studies in Society and History* 6 : 24–46.

1970   Social Stratification in the Caribbean. In *Essays in Comparative Social Stratification,* ed. L. Plotnicov and A. Tuden. Pittsburgh, University of Pittsburgh Press.

SOLIEN, NANCIE

1960   Household and Family in the Caribbean. *Journal of Social and Economic Studies* 9 : 101–06.

STRATHERN, ANDREW

1968   Descent and Alliance in the New Guinea Highlands. *Proceedings of the Royal Anthropological Institute,* pp. 37–52.

TIGER, LIONEL

1969   *Men in Groups.* New York, Vintage Books.

TURNER, VICTOR W.

1969   *The Ritual Process.* Chicago, Aldine Press.

WAGLEY, CHARLES

1960   Plantation America: A Cultural Sphere. In *Caribbean Studies: A Symposium,* ed. Vera Rubin.

WHITTEN, NORMAN, and JOHN SZWED, editors

1970   *Afro-American Anthropology.* Glencoe, Ill., Free Press.

WILLIAMS, ERIC

1970   *From Columbus to Castro.* London, Andre Deutsch.

WILSON, PETER J.

1961   Household and Family on Providencia. *Journal of Social and Economic Studies* 10 : 511–27.

1966   Review of *Stratification in Grenada,* by M. G. Smith. *Caribbean Studies* 6 : 62–65.

1969   Reputation and Respectability: A Suggestion for Caribbean Ethnology. *Man* (n.s.) 4 : 70–84.

1971a   Caribbean Crews: Peer Groups and Male Society. *Caribbean Studies* 10 : 18–34.

1971*b* Sentimental Structure: Tsimihety Migration and Descent. *American Anthropologist* 73 : 193–208.

1974 *Oscar: An Inquiry Into the Nature of Sanity?* (reissued 1992) Prospect Heights, Ill., Waveland Press, Inc.

WINCH, PETER

1958 *The Idea of a Social Science and Its Relations to Philosophy.* London, Routledge and Kegan Paul.

WOLF, ERIC

1966*a* Kinship, Friendship, and Patron-Client Relations in Complex Societies. In *The Social Anthropology of Complex Societies,* ed. M. Banton.

1966*b* *Peasants.* Englewood Cliffs, N.J., Prentice-Hall.

YOUNG, MICHAEL, and PETER WILMOTT

1960 *Family and Kinship and East London.* London, Penguin Books.

Index

Adventist church: as closed community, 102–03; political ineffectiveness of members, 189
Age, respect for, 160, 196, 208
Andros Island, 56, 209–12
Anancy stories, 159
Anthropologists: and preoccupation with family, 1, 3, 241; as word-game players, 3, 5; as suspected spies, 41; and obsession with science, 217
Anthropology: vocabulary of, 3; and history, 28–29; purpose of, 216
Anthropology, Caribbean: involution of, 1–2; bias toward institutions, 3–5; inadequacy of, 3
Arguments: in sport, 26; as formal activity, 157–58; and reputation, 159
Aury, Luis, 33, 41-42

Barbados, 186, 201-03
"Best friend" (*primo, compadre*), 108, 141, 144, 171, 182
Betting: and arguments, 159; and games, 176
"Big men," 166
Boasting, 155
Boat ownership, 86
Brothers: economic strain between, 142; as paradigm of equality, 145, 199
Brother–sister relationship, 133
Bryan, Oscar, 16
Burial, preparations for, 110–11
"Bush doctors," 23

Carpentry, 80
Carr, E. H., 28
Carriacou, 56, 209–12; economic differentiation in, 93

Cash crops, 82
Cash income, 82
Cattle: care of, 80; as capital, 83, 86
Cayman Islands, 26, 46
Change, projections of, 230–31
Chaperones, 100, 131, 211
Children: attitude toward, 73, 74. *See also* Socialization
Church: establishment of on Providencia, 36; and women, 73, 102; general attitude toward, 88; as moral referent, 100; secular role of, 100, 104; literature and sermons, 100–01; and marriage as sign of respectability, 100; attitude of men toward, 102; distinction between white and black, 104–05; as alien institution, 194–95; ambiguous situation of, 195; as counterpolitical force, 207–08; and social change, 232–33
Civil society: as preemptor of human society, 216–17
Clothing, home sewn, 72
Coconuts, as cash crop, 77, 80
Collingwood, R. G., and rigid view of history, 242
Colombians, stereotype of, 115
Colonialism, 6; structure of, 218. *See also* Respectability
Common-law marriage, 109
Communitas, 27, 47, 153, 181
Community: division into sections, 123; analysis of sections, 124–25; brothers as legal core of, 126; female affines and seniority as bases for structure, 131–32; as political unit, 145
Compadrazgo, 144

257